NON-OFFENSIVE DEFENCE

Also by David Gates

'THE SPANISH ULCER': A History of the Peninsular War
THE BRITISH LIGHT INFANTRY ARM

Non-Offensive Defence

An Alternative Strategy for NATO?

David Gates

Ministry of Defence Lecturer in Defence Studies
University of Aberdeen

MACMILLAN

First published 1991

Published by
MACMILLAN ACADEMIC AND PROFESSIONAL LTD
Houndmills, Basingstoke, Hampshire RG21 2XS
and London
Companies and representatives
throughout the world

ISBN 0–333–48290–5

A catalogue record for this book is available from the British Library.

Printed by Antony Rowe Ltd, Chippenham, Wiltshire

In memory of my father

Contents

Preface

Throughout the 1980s, but especially since the destruction of the Berlin Wall and the onset of the East European revolutions of 1989–90, there has been considerable discussion with regard to possible changes in NATO's strategy and force-structures. One suggested alternative is that of so-called 'Defensive Defence', which has been advocated by a number of bodies and individuals, particularly in Germany, for some years now. With the end of the Cold War, they perceive that their time has come. But just how viable and relevant are their proposals? What are their advantages and drawbacks? These are some of the questions this book seeks to answer.

I am indebted to a great many people who helped me one way or another in the course of my background research for this work. It would be impossible to list each one of them here – and several would prefer not to be identified anyway – but I would like to express my thanks to them all and especially to the following: among former or serving military personnel, Field Marshal Sir Nigel Bagnall, Sir Hugh Beach, Sir Martin Farndale, Sir Edward Burgess, Sir Julian Oswald, Group-Captain Andrew Vallance, Captain Gordon Wilson, and Colonels Michael Dewar, Clendon Daukes and Gage Williams; Mr Bill Hopkinson, the Policy Studies Secretariat and the personnel of the Concepts Staff, Ministry of Defence, London; Dr Jonathan Eyal of RUSI; Dr Colin McInnes of the University College of Wales, Aberystwyth; Dr Roy Allison, Birmingham University; Professor John Erickson, Edinburgh University; Professor Adam Roberts, Oxford University; Professor C.J. Bartlett, Dundee University; Professor P.J. Parish, Institute for United States Studies, University of London; Professor Paul Wilkinson, St Andrews University; Rolf Tamnes, Arne Dalhaug and Roald Gjelsten of the IFS and Jon Bingen of NUPI, Oslo; Albrecht von Müller, Horst Afheldt and Lutz Unterseher; and, at the University of Aberdeen, Professor Paul Dukes, Jim Wyllie and Doctors Mike Sheehan and Clive Archer. Last, but not least, Lisa, Tom, Bruce and Fiona, Kathryn, Kevin Kelly, Belinda, Claudia and all my other friends who gave me encouragement, advice and assistance. Any mistakes are, of course, my own.

DAVID GATES

1 NATO and the Quest for Alternatives, 1949–89

'You can always tell when you are making progress: the problems change.'

(John Foster Dulles)

Since the late 1970s especially, there has been an increasing number of calls from a variety of quarters for NATO to alter its military strategy. 'Flexible Response' which was formally adopted by the alliance in 1967 has, in the eyes of many commentators, either always lacked credibility or has suffered a progressive loss of whatever integrity it once possessed. As a situation of American supremacy in nuclear warfare capabilities gave way to one of parity between the USSR and the USA, and as the Warsaw Pact maintained or even increased the perceived dominance of its conventional forces over those of NATO, the latter alliance found itself in a deepening dilemma to which there were only two possible remedies. The first of these was to release more resources for defence, thus injecting vitality into the existing but ailing strategy of 'Flexible Response'. Alternatively member states could agree to jettison that strategy altogether and embrace some new policy; nuclear deterrence and arsenals might still play some part in this, but their hitherto excessive – and largely impractical – role would be diminished in favour of greater emphasis on conventional forces.

To many people the second of these approaches appeared to have much to recommend it and, as we shall see, a number of models for alternative strategies has been put forward in recent years. Yet, ever since its inception in 1949, both NATO and its military policies have had their critics, many of whom also propagated suggestions as to how the alliance's strategy might be improved, either by relatively marginal change or by radical overhaul. An examination of what became of these proposals – and why – would seem worthwhile at this juncture; the periodic debate about NATO strategy has contained a number of recurring elements, and these seem destined to influence it as much in the future as they have in the past.

There are three constant themes that stand out most in this regard.

Historically, proposals for revisions to NATO's plans and force-structures have stood or fallen in the face of political acceptability, economic viability and military credibility. More often than not the second of these considerations has proved paramount, though they have frequently acted in combination with each other. In Lisbon in February 1952 for example, NATO ministers responded to calls from their military advisers to adopt a series of 'firm force goals' in order that any Warsaw Pact attack on Western Europe that did materialise might be resisted with conventional means. According to intelligence estimates, the USSR and its allies could at this time devote around 175 small divisions to such a campaign. Successfully resisting an onslaught on this scale with the few conventional forces then available was clearly impossible, so the Western powers had had to rely on 'peripheral' strategies such as *Offtackle*, in which token resistance would be offered by a 'trip-wire' of ground units that would execute a fighting withdrawal to, if necessary, the extremities of the European land mass, while the bombers of the US Strategic Air Command (SAC) waged a lengthy atomic war against the Russian homeland. After two years of this, it was calculated, the USSR would be sufficiently enfeebled for the reconquest of the lost territories to be a viable enterprise; a D-Day style invasion would then be mounted which, it was hoped, would sweep the Russians out of the occupied territories.[1]

For a variety of reasons, the adoption of a policy less reliant on nuclear firepower appealed to both the USA and Western Europe. Amassing sufficient conventional strength to match the Russian hordes seemed a daunting task however. NATO military commanders argued that strong maritime units, some 9000 aircraft and land forces totalling 96 active divisions would be needed. The politicians felt unable to sanction these figures immediately, but pledged to field, by the end of 1952, at least 50 active and 40 reserve divisions, along with 4000 aircraft and substantial naval forces. This, they recognised, would be an inadequate gesture if it were not followed by further accessions of military strength; so they agreed that these forces were to be but the first instalment in an acquisition programme that would continue for five to six years.

However, matters were to unfold rather differently. In the lean years of post-war recovery, few Western states could spare more resources for defence. The USSR's explosion of an atomic device in autumn 1949 and the outbreak of the Korean War in 1950 highlighted both some of the limitations of nuclear deterrence and the relative flexibility of conventional strength. But general-purpose units were, in comparison with atomic armaments, hugely expensive; just the equipment procurement bill for the Lisbon Force Goals, for example, was estimated at $30 000 million. Furthermore countries such as Britain and France which still had extensive possessions around the globe could barely find sufficient units to meet these 'out-of area' commitments, let alone substantially increase their military presence in the NATO area proper. In fact in late 1949 Britain, for example, only narrowly avoided having to make substantial force reductions. Moreover the situation was further complicated by the political scene in Europe immediately after the war. The Marshall Plan had funded reconstruction in a number of states, enabling the fledgling *Bundesrepublik* especially to stave off a perceived threat of communist subversion. Yet the West Germans had a strained and difficult relationship with their European neighbours. To the East lay the Russians who, after the appalling devastation their country had suffered at the hands of Hitler's armies, were justifiably paranoid about the prospect of German revanchism – a concern they shared with other Eastern Bloc states, notably Poland and Czechoslovakia. Similarly France, Britain, Denmark, Norway and the Benelux countries eyed the revival of German industrial – and potentially military – power with understandable unease. Two gory and ruinously expensive world wars had, together with the memories of Bismarck's use of brute force in 1864, 1866 and 1870, left an indelible fear of German hegemony over the continent. But it became increasingly clear that the industrial potential and manpower of West Germany would *have* to be tapped if a robust conventional defence of Western Europe was to be mounted; and this would involve not only abandoning fear of Germany's aggrandisement but would also mean treating her as an equal partner rather than as a vanquished foe.

For many this was an anathema. After the vile deeds that had been perpetrated throughout occupied Europe during the war above all in the Nazi concentration camps, it was hard to regard the Germans as human-beings, let alone potential friends and allies. The French, who had suffered invasion by Germany three times since 1870, were especially sensitive about the issue of Germany's economic, political and military revival and were reluctant to see any degree of German rearmament at all; they preferred to build up their own forces, relying on American financial and technical assistance to do so, and to secure a greater commitment from the UK and USA to base troops on the European mainland. However conciliating the

Germans not only carried with it the risk of alienating France – and indeed most of the other European countries within NATO – but also involved certain risks for the German nation too, for it was feared that rearmament would rule out all prospect of their country being reunified. Fortunately for NATO, Konrad Adenauer, the *Bundeskanzler*, preferred to see the *Bundesrepublik* integrate with the West rather than have it reunite with East Germany on terms that would lead to increased Soviet influence in Central Europe.

This approach harmonised perfectly with the Western powers' needs: the prospect of a rearmed West Germany under their influence was far more attractive than that of a united but neutral Germany which would be susceptible to Soviet leverage and manipulation. Indeed the freedom to mobilise and exploit at least some German resources for defence was seen as an imperative by many senior members of the West's military hierarchy. Since May 1949 Britain's Field Marshal Montgomery had been talking of the need 'to use Germans in our plans', while some of his colleagues had, as early as 1948, hoped to see twelve German divisions raised for the defence of Europe.[2] Indeed by August 1950 the British Chiefs of Staff were openly advocating the creation, over the next five years, of a West German force totalling 30 divisions, 2100 aircraft and some naval units.

Similarly by May 1950 the American Joint Chiefs of Staff (JCS) had begun to make the case for rearming West Germany and incorporating her into NATO; a European defence force should be created, including German units of up to divisional size. Immediately after the Second World War the Americans had not anticipated maintaining any significant military presence in Europe; on the contrary, they had planned for demobilisation and withdrawal. Even after the signing of the NATO Treaty they saw their role in terms of giving support until Western Europe was sufficiently strong to stand on its own feet. German rearmament would clearly expedite this and accordingly President Truman formally advanced the proposal, adding, in an effort to allay French anxieties, that more US troops were also to be deployed alongside the two divisions already in Europe. The French, unconvinced, responded with the plan of René Pleven, which allowed for the inclusion of German troops in the forces of a European Defence Community, providing their units were limited to battalion size. A compromise formula was eventually approved by the North Atlantic Council, whereby the US believed it had secured French endorsement of German rearmament, and France felt it had obtained both a greater American commitment to European defence – including the appointment of an American, General Eisenhower, as the first Supreme Allied Commander in Europe (SACEUR) – and a delay in German rearmament. Certainly, for the US, NATO was now becoming the 'entangling alliance'.

Throughout all of this the problem of finding and justifying resources for defence loomed large; the Western military had to compete with other drains on their treasuries at a time when fear of economic collapse was extensive and consumer expectations were steadily rising. There was, moreover, competition between the different services. By 1948 Britain, for instance, had adopted an up-to-date version of the 'ten-year rule' of the inter-war period: the UK, it was assumed, would not be involved in any major military conflict for at least five years, despite the onset of the 'Cold War' and all that might imply. 'The Defence Committee recognise the serious nature of the risk in making this asumption', the Minister of Defence told the Cabinet, 'but consider it to be one which must be accepted in the prevailing economic and financial circumstances'.[3] Likewise in the US concern about the size of the incipient budget deficit hampered military preparations. In August 1949 even the National Security Council (NSC) had to agree that defence spending should be trimmed to $13 000 million during 1951, though the Military Aid Programme to Europe should, it argued, be preserved in order to hasten an end to the Europeans' dependence on American support. Indeed, whilst the military, economic and political power of the US made it the indisputed leader of NATO and secured it a dominant voice in the formulation of strategy, the size of commitment the Americans found themselves shouldering had been neither sought nor anticipated.

The outbreak of the Korean War however prompted them to ask their European allies for the 'firmest possible statement' of the nature and extent of their planned increases 'in both forces and military production'. Aneurin Bevan, the British Health Minister, alarmed at the prospect of cuts in welfare programmes, argued that the best defence against communist expansionism was to improve the socio-economic conditions of the countries under threat. Britain might just be able to afford additional military spending without 'fatal damage to its economic and social structure', but it was questionable whether France and some of the other European states could do the same. Nevertheless, anxious to demonstrate Britain's willingness to play its full part in NATO, and her resolve to maintain her stature and influence as a great power, Sir Stafford Cripps, the Chancellor of the Exchequer, sought the Cabinet's approval for an increase in defence spending from £2590 million to £3400 million over the three financial years up to 1954.

Ernest Bevin, the Foreign Secretary, had been arguing since May 1950 that effective negotiations with the Russians could only be conducted from a position of strength. However it was conceded that an annual military budget of £950 million was the most that could be permitted 'on general economic grounds', which would leave a shortfall of some £550 million over the three years concerned. Cripps proposed to fill this gap by taking up an earlier American offer to give their allies 'further assistance to help them to make their maximum contribution to the common defence'.[4] He would ask the US to provide the £550 million that was lacking.

That the Americans would decline to do so was something that the British Cabinet did not anticipate, but this is precisely what occurred. Furthermore Britain's expenditure proposals were dismissed as 'inadequate'. The burden the US was shouldering within NATO, and how unpopular that might become with the American people if the European allies were not seen to be pulling their weight, was stressed; and a plea for a 'substantially increased defence programme' on Britain's part was lodged with Attlee, the British Prime Minister, when he visited Washington in December 1950. Moreover the US, which in the past had hesitated to push its European allies to rearm too quickly lest this sap their recovery and thus prolong their dependence on American aid, injected a sense of real urgency into the proceedings. Marshall Aid and other unilateral actions aimed at the economic and political regeneration of Western Europe, especially West Germany, had had the almost inevitable – though probably unintentional – repercussion of hastening the souring of East–West relations. The Russians had been, as Attlee himself observed, 'behaving in a perfectly bloody fashion all over Europe'. Now it appeared that regional tensions there were spilling over into other parts of the globe and, with the outbreak of the Korean War, a world-wide conflict seemed both likely and imminent.[5] Indeed an American *National Intelligence Estimate* of 11 December 1950 concluded that:

> The overall situation is such that the possibility cannot be disregarded that the USSR has already made a decision for general war and is in the process of taking steps preliminary to its inception.

British assessments of the threat of war had varied appreciably, but this American view was now supported by the War Office's judgement that conflict was 'possible' in 1951 and 'probable' in 1952. Nevertheless opinion was divided. For example a Czech defector, Karel Kaplan, was to claim in 1977 that he had seen documents dating from this period which related to a secret meeting between Stalin and the East Bloc leaders. Stalin apparently argued that by 1955 the Americans would be too firmly entrenched in Europe for the Russians and their allies to oust them in a pre-emptive war. He accordingly unveiled plans to overrun Western Europe before the US could consolidate its position, and the Eastern European leaders agreed to put their forces under Soviet command.[6]

This was probably only a contingency plan. Certainly the attack never came, and by 1952 Stalin was trying to ward off West German rearmament and the strengthening of NATO with diplomatic initiatives. Nevertheless one result of the war scare was that in early 1951, despite a precarious economic situation, Britain undertook to raise her defence expenditure to £4700 million. This, and its implications for expenditure on public health, welfare and reconstruction programmes, led to a split in the Cabinet and, ultimately, in the Labour Party; Bevan and two other ministers resigned, having been outvoted. But as Kenneth Younger, the Minister of State at the Foreign Office, observed, Bevan's view had

> quite a strong demagogic appeal in the country, since it brings under one umbrella all pacifists, all anti-Americans, and all who believe in a neutral third force between [the] USA and USSR or else don't believe that the Soviet Union is a genuine danger at all. Most of us have misgivings on some or all of these grounds.[7]

Not long after these words were written, the divided and discredited Labour Party was ousted from government in an election coloured by the economic crisis its rearmament programme had fuelled, if not ignited. The new Conservative Chancellor, R.A. Butler, had to trim the defence budget appreciably, with the result that the original plans were never fulfilled. Nor was the UK alone in experiencing these difficulties. In early 1953 Eisenhower replaced Truman as President of the USA and promptly embarked on an austerity programme which had major repercussions for defence in particular. Eisenhower, mindful of the fate that had just befallen the British, perceived that America's security ultimately rested as much on her retaining a flourishing economy that could sustain an armaments programme as it did on the armaments themselves. The heavy costs of creating and maintaining sufficient general-purpose forces to cope with America's expanding commitments had been foreseen in the Truman administration's final strategic study, NSC 141, and the Korean War and other events seemed to confirm the validity of its projections. The situation in Indo-China for instance was deteriorating, and by 1954 the US had taken over about 80 per cent of the costs of the conflict there in order that the French might focus their efforts on Europe. Moreover the 'limited' conflict in Korea had disenchanted many Americans. It had in fact cost the US some 30 000 dead, and 100 000 wounded and missing. Indeed Eisenhower's presidential victory of 1952 owed much to the popular hope that he would rapidly bring the war to a conclusion.

Although NSC 68 of April 1950 had argued that the US economy was sufficiently buoyant to support large increases in defence expenditure and that such increases – especially on general-purpose forces – were needed, Eisenhower concluded that America's security was under threat less from abroad than from inflationary spending to meet foreign commitments. Accordingly, with the 'New Look', he discarded the build-up of conventional forces in favour of the cheaper option of massive nuclear retaliation: 'a maximum deterrent at bearable cost'. Achieving 'more bang for a buck' was coupled to maintaining a qualitative edge through the use of better technology; the substitution of equipment – notably short-range nuclear weapons – for manpower, which had consumed a disproportionately large slice of the resources available for defence; and encouraging the European pillar of NATO to do more through Pleven's brain-child, the European Defence Community (EDC).

In August 1954, however, the French National Assembly rejected Pleven's proposals. Lingering fears about Germany's revival partly explain this outcome, but there were two other considerations which were equally important. Eisenhower's 'New Look', especially the deployment of tactical nuclear warheads and his presumed desire to cut the size of America's forces on European soil, not only smacked of the 'decoupling' of the two continents' security interests but also suggested that, even with German troops, mounting a robust conventional defence lay beyond the Europeans' reach. To formally approve the EDC plan in these circumstances might, the French feared, simply furnish the Americans with a pretext for changing the nature and extent of their commitment to and guarantee of Western Europe's security.

Although the damage done by this affair was to be partially rectified soon after by the Paris and London Treaties which, together with the Western European Union Accords, enabled West Germany to join NATO, the opportunity to create both a more cohesive European wing of NATO and a more resiliant conventional defence posture was lost. The sovereignty of West Germany was formally acknowledged in October 1954, and foreign troops stationed there under the Occupation Statutes were permitted to remain under a series of bilateral agreements. On the other hand, the 'peripheral' strategies that had dominated Western strategic planning now had to be discarded. There had been no treaty obligation for either the Western European Union or NATO to defend West German territory, though the natural resources, industrial capacity and population located there were assets the Western powers would have ceded with great reluctance in the event of a Soviet invasion. Indeed until this time West Germany had been seen as a military *glacis* for the defence of the Rhine; there were plans for using terrain-enhancement, field fortifications, demolition and obstruction on a vast scale in order to impede and channel any attack. As West Germany was embraced as an ally, however, the approach had to change: active, forward defence became a *sine qua non* if she was to be expected to make a military contribution to NATO.

In the meantime the Americans had continued to forge ahead with their plans to introduce both the concept of 'Massive Retaliation' and the nuclear firepower that would be needed to implement it. This entailed, among other things, the deployment of scores of tactical nuclear weapons in Europe and the securing of NATO's approval for the new doctrine. This was achieved in 1956, when the Military Committee, in keeping with a decision made by their political masters in 1954, embodied it as alliance policy in the document MC 14/2.

The fundamental hypotheses on which the new doctrine's viability was based, however, were already crumbling. Ever since they had exploded an atomic device in 1949, the Russians had been chipping away at the Americans' superior capability for delivering nuclear strikes. In August 1953 the USSR exploded a hydrogen bomb, and by the mid-1950s it was apparent that both powers would soon have a capacity for strategic retaliation. In these circumstances the notion that either of them would use atomic weapons to repulse limited if not larger attacks began to lose credibility. Basil Liddell Hart, the eminent British military thinker, had predicted as early as 1946 that the 'fear of atomic war might lead to indirect methods of aggression . . . to which nuclear retaliation would be irrelevant';[8] and, commenting on the 'New Look' in 1954, he suggested that 'To the extent that the H-Bomb reduces the likelihood of full-scale war, it *increases* the possibilities of limited war . . .'.[9]

Nor was he alone in expressing concern over NATO's policy. In the mid-1950s a series of distressing debates in the *Bundestag* and a number of military exercises, notably *Carte Blanche*, led to a wave of anxiety engulfing both the population of West Germany and the alliance's military planners. Casualties on an atomic battlefield threatened to be so severe that army staffs concluded that more rather than less manpower would be needed, while it became evident that the wretched civilian population, caught in the midst of this nuclear crossfire, would suffer horrendously. *Carte Blanche*, for example, envisaged some 300 atomic warheads falling on West Germany, killing 1.7 million and wounding a further 3.5 million people. In October 1957, in a speech to the United Nations General Assembly and subsequently, in a memorandum to the great powers, Adam Rapacki, the Polish Foreign Minister, proposed the creation of a zone, free of nuclear weapons, which would encompass the whole of Poland, Czechoslovakia and both East and West Germany. It was rejected by NATO, partly because the idea posed enormous verification problems, but primarily because it would effectively rob the West of its deterrent and defence against attack by the Warsaw Pact's massive conventional forces. Nevertheless the concept, which harmonised perfectly with a non-provocative defence posture that had been put forward by Bogislaw von Bonin, an ex-*Wehrmacht* staff officer, was to be seized upon by the West German Social Democratic Party (SPD) and formed the cornerstone of their '*Kampf dem Atomtod*' – 'Battle Against Atomic Death' – Campaign of 1958–9. *Bundeskanzler* Adenauer managed to persuade the electorate of the ineluctable need to retain nuclear weapons, particularly to deter war, and the SPD sustained some severe defeats in the *Länder* elections of 1959. Nevertheless it is in these events that today's vociferous German anti-nuclear movement has its origins.

In fact NATO's difficulties with regard to nuclear weapons were expressed in two interlocking fears: that such armaments might be employed in the defence of Western Europe; and that they might not be. As Professor Adam Roberts, among others, observed:

The present NATO strategic doctrine, which can best be characterized as one of flexible escalation, relies to a remarkable extent on nuclear weapons – especially on so-called tactical ones. It is thus based largely on a nuclear bluff which, if called, could mean the gruesome sacrifice not merely of everything being defended, but a good deal else besides. This naturally arouses anxieties in the countries concerned.[10]

The only real solution to this dilemma lay in the Western powers devoting sufficient resources to defence to be able to match the conventional strength of the Warsaw Pact. But for a variety of reasons nobody was really prepared to undertake this. None of the Western European states had sufficiently vibrant economies to sustain a swollen defence budget, and in any case these precarious democracies generally saw the 'Soviet threat' rather more in terms of communist subversion than in those of straightforward military power. Indeed as political stability rested so much on financial strength, even the Americans were reluctant to risk distorting or undermining their economy in this fashion. Yet Eisenhower realised that, in a situation of strategic parity and mutual deterrence, the US and NATO as a whole required general-purpose forces of adequate size to deal with at least limited conflicts. Accordingly he adopted the 'New New Look', which was intended to secure military sufficiency in both the conventional and nuclear arenas.

But just what could be deemed 'sufficient'? In the opinion of, for example, Admiral Arthur Radford, Chairman of the American JCS, conventional units could only buy a breathing-space before nuclear weapons would have to be employed. Was there, then, any point in pouring billions of dollars into creating substantial forces, which in the final analysis would still be nothing more than a trip-wire? In any case Eisenhower was not willing to commit the resources necessary to prepare for a large-scale and protracted conventional conflict, anymore than were his Western European counterparts. Conventional sufficiency was therefore to be achieved through marginal increases in overall defence expenditure; the enhancement of the existing 'division of labour', whereby the European allies furnished the bulk of the ground and air combat units, while the Americans themselves provided the majority of the nuclear and naval elements, together with most of NATO's strategic reinforcements and logistical support; 'good housekeeping' and a reliance on technological superiority. To Admiral Radford however, such notions were a formula for ever-rising defence costs, and in July 1956 he put forward a plan which proposed slashing some 800 000 personnel from the American armed services, with the bulk of the cuts falling on the Army. Token atomic task forces – largely reliant on battlefield nuclear weapons, which in Radford's words had 'virtually achieved conventional status within [America's] . . . Armed Forces' – were to be retained in Europe and Asia; small Allied and US conventional units would form a trip-wire and be used in any limited conflicts that occurred; while the bulk of the resources freed by the reductions in general-purpose forces would be invested in trying to prolong America's strategic superiority.

Leaked to the press, Radford's secret proposals provoked anxiety and outrage both at home and abroad, but especially in West Germany. Here the terrifying spectre of *der Atomtod* was to dominate the political scene over the next couple of years as the Eastern Bloc, delighted by NATO's embarrassment, exploited the fears and divisions within West Germany and, with the Rapacki Plan, sought to drive a wedge between the American and European wings of the Western alliance. Adenauer immediately despatched the head of the *Bundeswehr* to Washington. He convinced many Americans of the need for powerful general-purpose forces to underpin NATO's deterrence approach, and Congress sought an across-the-board expansion of the defence budget. Indeed by 1957 even John Foster Dulles, America's Secretary of State and the principal advocate of 'Massive Retaliation', was conceding that the policy was losing credibility as a possible response to localised aggression – though he suggested, like Radford, that battlefield atomic weapons might furnish a comparatively inexpensive and more effective deterrent to limited attacks than would general-purpose forces.[11] This view impressed Eisenhower who, whilst agreeing that radical cutbacks in conventional strength were imprudent, declined to add appreciably to defence costs by completely reversing the trend; more resources were devoted to trying to maintain America's strategic superiority, while efforts were made to thicken the European trip-wire. Overall however the episode only underlined the reluctance of NATO to devise and pay for a robust conventional defence. In fact, reassured at least outwardly by America's nuclear guarantee – and by the significant US ground and air units whose very presence was not only intended to give substance to that guarantee but was also expressly designed to allay French anxieties over German rearmament – the Western Europeans continued much as before.

Indeed by 1957 NATO's military procurement and planning arrangements were virtually identical to those adopted by the UK some ten years before. The need for active, forward defence now had to be taken seriously, as had perceived improvements in the Warsaw Pact's capabilities and the potential of battlefield nuclear weapons. Yet planning was based on rolling, five-year projections of the minimum forces required to fulfil the various missions. This scheme, MC 70, called for the maintenance of just 30 active divisions. According to what had been agreed by NATO ministers at Lisbon in 1952, 50 active and 40 reserve divisions should have been available by the start of 1953, with further substantial additions scheduled to occur over the next two years. But these 'firm' force goals had, like those detailed in a 1955 document, still not been attained. Nor had it ever seemed probable that they would be. Several American projections of 1949–50 had concluded that adequate security based on conventional strength would take ten or more years to achieve, while as early as mid-1950 Kenneth Younger of the British Foreign Office, for example, had observed that 'Western defence budgets are clearly inadequate if we are to reach our targets for 1954 or 1957. The deficiencies are large and increasing, and it seems clear that only a major alteration of priorities as between "guns and butter" could fill the gap'.[12]

As we have seen, in the years thereafter Britain had endeavoured to choose guns rather than butter – and did it on a scale that no other European member of NATO could even contemplate. Cherished health, welfare and reconstruction programmes were pared back in order that a socialist administration could try to fulfil its obligations to, and maintain influence over, its country's allies, particularly the USA. But the outcome fell sadly short of expectations, and Britain's fragile economy had been further enfeebled in the process, weakening her prospects both for sustaining her military power and fending off communist subversion in the future. Yet if her contribution to Western defence was, as the Americans once dismissed it, 'inadequate', that made by the rest of the European wing of NATO was still more so. Commitments abroad which, for example, swallowed more than one third of France's disposable forces in the period 1953–5; the problems relating to German rearmament and *Gleichberechtigung*; the rivalry and suspicions that existed between the various allies; popular demand for consumer goods, and other domestic political and economic constraints; uncertainties and disagreements about the true nature of Soviet intentions and capabilities; the war-weariness engendered by the struggle against the Axis powers in the 1940s; all of these factors conspired together to defeat NATO's hopes of mounting a sturdy, forward defence with conventional means. Indeed by 1956 just 25 combat-ready divisions could be mustered to pit against Warsaw Pact forces which, drawing on Soviet troops alone, could, it was believed, field between 88 and 100 divisions, backed by at least 3000 tactical aircraft. Moreover, besides this 'head count' imbalance, the Russians, because of their geostrategic position and ability to exploit interior lines of operation, were far better placed to initiate military action and to reinforce and sustain their troops as and when necessary.

Although the crushing of the Hungarian Revolution of 1956 sent further tremors of fear through the West, especially West Germany, the latter half of the 1950s saw a brief period of uneasy calm descend on Europe, with East–West relations manifesting some improvement. Stalin had died in March 1953, and since then a series of events had suggested that Soviet foreign policy was being prosecuted with greater subtlety and refinement: an armistice was concluded in Korea; a fragile truce was secured in Vietnam; the Russians, in return for her neutrality, evacuated Austria; and Nikita Khrushchev, the new Soviet leader, embarked on a spate of both nuclear and conventional arms-control initiatives which culminated in 1959 in a speech to the United Nations General Assembly calling for general and total disarmament. Clearly there was a goodly element of propaganda in all this but, given their problematical economic position and fear of an accidental nuclear exchange, the desire evinced by the Russians to escape from the burdens of the East–West confrontation – particularly the spiralling and crippling cost of the arms-race – was probably not altogether insincere. To many observers however, the change was purely one of packaging rather than substance. Sir William Hayter, for example, the British Ambassador to Moscow from 1953 to 1957, opined that they were still adhering to their 'twin policies of consolidating their own extended empire and of undermining the rest of the world. They were talking of coexistence, but they visualized it as the coexistence of the snake and the rabbit'.[13]

Nevertheless, largely because of domestic electoral considerations, the British governments of the time were especially eager to appear committed to the cause of peace and the relaxation of tension in Europe. As Prime Minister in 1954–5, Winston Churchill made the first of a chain of initiatives which his successors, Anthony Eden and Harold Macmillan, were to continue. Eden for instance regarded the French as unreliable and inconsistent, eyed the Germans with a degree of suspicion, and expected the Russians to try to split the West with some attractive proposition on the future of Germany. Above all he feared that the nuclear stalemate between the USSR and the USA might nudge the latter into isolationism within a few years. Swift action was therefore essential, and he wasted little time before opening a dialogue with the Russians. His somewhat florid attempts to bring about a thaw in the Cold War, and to act as a bridge between the White House and the Kremlin, did not however always please Britain's allies as much as they delighted the British electorate. Anxious to avoid an accidental clash of arms on the Central Front, he suggested troop reductions and disengagement measures as a way forward. Because of the asymmetry of the military balance, these were predictably dismissed by the other Western powers as favouring the Warsaw Pact more than NATO, with West Germany moreover stressing that his proposals might end in German neutrality and the loss of American protection.

After the Suez crisis toppled Eden, Macmillan prolonged Britain's endeavour to woo the USSR, which culminated in 1959 in his celebrated visit to Moscow. Again though the influence of the 'peace race' in domestic politics loomed large, and the West Germans in particular sensed that Macmillan was gambling with their security in order to acquire an advantage over the Labour Party in the forthcoming British general election. Macmillan certainly saw the benefits of exploiting East–West affairs in this fashion and admits to having had this *arrière-pensée* in his memoirs. But Britain's persistence in trying to maintain a dialogue with the USSR can have done little harm. 'To jaw-jaw is better', as Churchill had observed in 1954, 'than to war-war', and it was important to determine precisely what Stalin's successors meant by 'peaceful coexistence', especially as Khrushchev's personality appeared to shift so much and, particularly during the period 1958–61, his fluctuations between bellicosity and concilliation suggested either a calculated attempt to test NATO's resolve and unity, or irredeemable and potentially dangerous megalomania.

Whilst the British were foremost among the Western powers in the search for better relations with Russia, the Americans also made intermittent efforts at bridge-building. In the summer of 1955 for instance, Eisenhower put forward, at the Geneva Summit, his 'Open Skies' initiative, whereby both superpowers would permit unrestricted aerial surveillance and photography of their territory, especially military facilities, by the other side. This, he believed, would 'convince the world that we are providing . . . against the possibility of a great surprise attack, thus lessening danger and relaxing tension'. Nothing came of the scheme however, and the suppression of the Hungarian Revolution the following year further dissipated the 'Spirit of Geneva' while simultaneously underlining America's inability to challenge Russian control of Eastern Europe except through a general war.

Although such an event was by no means impossible, it was never really likely, for whilst they eyed one another with suspicion, jealousy and anxiety, and harried each other with rhetoric and occasional bouts of muscle-flexing, on the whole the USA and USSR were primarily interested in consolidating their respective positions on the foundations put down with the defeat of Germany and Japan in 1945. A major war might have seemed to them to be at hand from time to time, but historical analysis suggests it was never especially probable; both parties were mindful of their own weaknesses, and experienced difficulty in fathoming the intentions and capabilities of the other. As Henry Kissinger was later to observe, they frequently behaved like 'two heavily-armed blind men feeling their way around a room, each believing himself in mortal peril from the other, whom he assumes to have perfect vision'.[14] In fact, except for the odd dose of strictly limited adventurism here and there – and even that usually involved proxies – the confrontational side of their relations was conducted at a low level.

The prospects for an easy or inexpensive victory in a general war seemed so small that it was rejected as a viable instrument of policy by all except the most ignorant or fanatical, even when the US enjoyed a monopoly in atomic weapons. The growth of parity in nuclear capabilities threatened, it appeared, to turn every and any minor dispute into an occasion for a war of annihilation. But on the other hand neither superpower had reason to see matters in such stark life-or-death terms. If they were not entirely satisfied with the post-war order, they were not thoroughly dissatisfied either. As Professor Christopher Bartlett has commented: 'Each had more, if not total reason to feel that time was on its side – if not necessarily to achieve exclusive supremacy, then at least to secure a shared if uneasy and highly competitive position at the top'.[15]

Indeed the essentially limited nature of Russian aspirations was one that several influential Westerners discerned. For example Admiral L.C. Stevens, who had worked as the US Naval Attaché in the USSR from 1947 to 1950, returned with the conviction that Russian power was being overestimated. The USSR, he believed, had no precise, expansionist plans and was principally interested in consolidating and securing its position, which could be achieved by means other than armed conflict. Charles Bohlen, a diplomat, agreed. The Korean War, he suggested, illustrated the 'extraordinarily pragmatic and opportunistic nature of Soviet policy and the absence of any fidelity to a blueprint or even a design'. During his time as SACEUR, Eisenhower too formulated a somewhat subtle view of the 'threat'. In 1951 he felt what was needed above all was for a dozen US divisions to be based in Western Europe until it had acquired sufficient confidence and military and economic strength to defend itself. The Russians seemed averse to war; it would be too much of a gamble and, if they embarked on it, Eisenhower argued, they would lose in the long run. Only the chance of an immediate victory would lure them into attacking, he believed.[16]

General Alfred Gruenther, who succeeded Eisenhower as SACEUR, concurred with this opinion. Given the reluctance of the Russians to take risks, he postulated that they could not even begin to toy with the idea of using war as an instrument of policy before 1960.[17] Instead of a febrile attempt to build up NATO's defences, the emphasis should therefore be on sustaining a long-term, controlled rivalry with the USSR, during which the main problem confronting both sides would be maintaining popular support and morale. Indeed no sooner had the Korean War ended than, as we have seen, the West's hunt for savings in military spending gathered momentum, and there were some who hoped that the Warsaw Pact would be obliged to follow suit. As early as September 1953, the Planning Board of the NSC, for example, was speculating whether the USSR's revolutionary fervour might begin to cool in time. Her increasingly acquisitive population and the growth of a professional middle class and other pressure groups could, it appeared, compel her to divert resources from the armed forces to satisfying consumer demand. Indubitably, by 1955 the threat of a general war seemed to have receded and the notion of peaceful coexistence was gaining credibility.[18] Neither side had anything to gain from a total war which would, unlike previous conflicts, probably be over in days, having claimed scores of millions of lives and devastated vast areas of the planet. Indeed, given the nuclear stalemate, the threat that communist subversion rather than open attack was the real danger appeared to have been vindicated, and whilst even small gains by Moscow might prove politically damaging, some Americans believed that the only rational choice the communists had in a nuclear world was to pursue policies which jeopardised neither their vital interests nor those of the West.

Eisenhower, whilst adamant that there should be no premature concessions, did seek to make some use of this window of opportunity. Although the chance to enhance trade between the USA and USSR was allowed to pass on several occasions between 1958 and 1960, he did take the initiative in other spheres. After Dulles resigned because of ill health, in April 1959, the president himself embarked on an intense bout of 'shuttle' diplomacy, travelling 22 000 miles and visiting eleven countries in twelve months. But his search for a meaningful dialogue with Khrushchev was to be bedevilled by one major problem in particular. This was the Russians' failure to firmly anchor their half of Germany to the Warsaw Pact and the communist ideology. While West Germany was becoming a bastion of liberal democracy, a major contributor to NATO's armed strength and a power-house of the Western economy, thousands of East Germans, especially skilled workers and professionals, were voting with their feet in an exodus to the West. This not only sapped both the political confidence and economic strength of East Germany but also the Russians' efforts to consolidate their position in Eastern Europe. Indeed by jeopardising the status quo which had been emerging since the end of the Second World War, it eroded all hope of fruitful negotiations between the two blocs. It was essential that a solution be found if stability was to be maintained.

As early as the summer of 1951 an American study, NSC 114/2, had concluded that the Russians, if faced with a choice between German rearmament and unification, might prefer the latter. It was a short-lived prophecy. Only months later, on 10 March 1952, Stalin suggested that Germany be reunited but unaligned; he was prepared to sacrifice communist East Germany provided that in doing so he secured a Germany which, whilst unified, would not pose a threat to Soviet interests in Eastern Europe for the foreseeable future.

For the West however this held little appeal. The potential benefits of a strong, rearmed West Germany far outweighed those of a feeble German *Vaterland* which would be susceptible to communist influence and manipulation. Indeed the proposal was dismissed, rightly or wrongly, as the latest in a series of Russian attempts to get the West to lower its guard and to promote rifts within NATO. On the other hand intransigence threatened to raise the ante, provoking splits in Western public opinion, doubts about current policy, and calls for compromise or reappraisals. Thus, whether Moscow's efforts were directed at undermining the West or easing the problems being experienced in East Germany, the impact was much the same: despite some unease and discord, the West held its ground, pursuing policies which, whilst presented in a fashion that mollified public concern, simultaneously sought to retain the confidence of West Germany.

In September 1959 Khrushchev met with Eisenhower at Camp David for talks about Berlin and the nuclear arms-race. Although they were inconclusive, they did create a degree of euphoria, one result being the promising agreement to hold a summit conference in Paris during the May of the following year. The 'Spirit of Camp David' rapidly faded however. Khrushchev, probably sensing that the West's resolve over Berlin could not be shaken and that the search for concessions was a futile one, called off the summit eleven days before it was due to commence, ostensibly because of the U-2 incident – the shooting down by the Russians of an American spy plane over Soviet territory. The building of the Berlin Wall – a crude but effective solution to the exodus problem – in August 1961, and the breaking that same month of an informal moratorium on nuclear test-explosions which had been in effect since October 1958, were symptomatic of both a sharp deterioration in East–West relations and the acceptance by Khrushchev of defeat. His policies had failed to secure Western concessions and, with the number of people fleeing East Germany rising each day, he had to act immediately. Nevertheless, for all the muscle-flexing and the attendant souring of relations, the possibility of a major military clash consistently seemed remote. The Russians, the American State and Defence Departments agreed as early as November 1960, would not go to war over Berlin[19] – a surmise that was proved correct and which was reflected in the lack of American preparations for such an event. In fact throughout this period American defence expenditure only rose marginally, while the size of the US forces stationed in Europe actually shrank a little.

Eisenhower was succeeded as President of the US by John F. Kennedy in January 1961. The new administration took the view that the Warsaw Pact's strength in conventional forces had been exaggerated, while that of NATO had been underestimated. Improved analytical techniques and better intelligence suggested that the Russians and their allies could not amass the three-to-one numerical superiority which most experts agreed would be necessary for the mounting of a successful offensive against Western Europe. In 1963 for example, NATO could muster some 1.5 million troops there, whereas the Warsaw Pact forces opposing them totalled 2.2 million personnel. NATO had 25 combat-ready divisions on the Central Front, with a further 29 of varying quality along the Southern Flank. In comparison the Warsaw Pact could draw on between 22 and 26 combat-ready divisions in Eastern Europe. Although these mostly Russian front-line forces could be joined by 35 more divisions, many of these were of doubtful allegiance and quality, while the 60 divisions found in the Western military districts of the USSR were also of limited use, being largely understrength in both men and equipment.

Much of that equipment was moreover now seen to be of poorer quality than that found in the West. NATO's air defence, for instance, was judged to be superior, while its 3500 tactical aircraft were more than a match for the Warsaw Pact's slightly more numerous but technologically inferior planes. Similarly the Americans were winning the nuclear arms-race. By the mid-1950s the Russians had started building up a long-range bomber arm but, unable to afford anything comparable to the SAC, had been compelled to rely on large numbers of rockets instead. In the eyes of many NATO analysts however, this ultimately led to a 'missile gap' which placed the West at a disadvantage. Conversely, Russian strategists felt that their capabilities were again being overtaken by those of the Americans, who appeared bent on acquiring the wherewithal to launch a first strike which might destroy the majority of the Soviet nuclear forces before they could be turned against the USA. With bombers, which were recallable, being superseded by inter-continental missiles, which were not, there seemed to be a growing danger that one superpower might unleash its nuclear forces in the mistaken belief that it was about to be dealt a pre-emptive blow by the other. War by accident – through imperfect command and control arrangements, mechanical malfunction, or the misinterpretation of radar signals (wild geese over the North Pole were once mistaken for incoming missiles) – seemed even more of a probability than one by design.

This had a very damaging impact on international confidence, though in fact technological innovation during the late 1950s and early 1960s did much to abate the danger of either an inadvertent nuclear exchange or, by creating a framework of mutually assured destruction and thus deterrence, a premeditated one. The first generation of nuclear missiles used liquid propellants. These were unstable and had to be pumped into the rocket immediately prior to launch. This of course took time, which meant that the missiles could not be maintained in a state of readiness and were thus vulnerable to a disabling pre-emptive strike. The survivability of the bombers of the SAC was secured by some of them being kept in the air round the clock, with a reserve ready to take off at very short notice. However, the formulation of stable solid fuels, which could be stored inside rockets, significantly reduced launch-preparation periods, and this, together with the introduction of hardened silos, afforded land-based rockets adequate protection. Meanwhile the development of submarines such as the *Polaris* force, which were immensely difficult to detect and were capable of firing missiles from the ocean depths, guaranteed the US an almost indestructable retaliatory capability.

Indeed the quest for survivability dominated this stage of the arms-race. Unable to devise an active defence against intercontinental ballistic missiles and their megaton warheads, both sides gave priority to creating and protecting deterrent forces which, if need be, could ride out a pre-emptive strike. As an article in *Foreign Affairs* by Albert Wohlstetter of the Rand Corporation concluded in January 1959: 'To deter an attack means being able to strike back in spite of it. It means . . . a capability to strike second'. The American technological lead was also jealously guarded for, as the Gaither Report warned, a 'temporary technical advance (such as a high-certainty missile defence against ballistic missiles) could give either nation the ability to come near to annihilating the other'. A development of this kind could spell the end for deterrence and so, in the eyes of many commentators, maintaining a technological edge became of paramount importance. Such was the extent of American success in this regard however, that the Russians, striving to redress the balance as rapidly and cheaply as possible, embarked on an adventure that was as desperate as it was reckless: the deployment of medium-range nuclear missiles on Cuba. This promised to effectively double their capacity for a first strike against the USA and it led to the most dramatic confrontation of the Cold War. Robert McNamara, Kennedy's Defence Secretary, later claimed that he had some sympathy for the Soviet position. Whilst like most of the American administration he was not oblivious to the advantages attached to the US securing and maintaining a nuclear lead over the USSR, he appreciated the reaction that this must have engendered. His talk of 'counter-force' targeting and 'damage limitation' and his attempts to acquire the wherewithal for a second-strike, 'counter-force' strategy probably looked to the Russians like a first-strike threat, especially if taken in conjunction with a remark made by Kennedy in March 1962:

'Khrushchev must not be certain that, where its vital interests are threatened, the United States will never strike first'. Indeed, 'If I had been the Soviet secretary of defence', McNamara later conceded, 'I'd have been as worried as hell at the imbalance of forces'.[20] Yet that imbalance would, he argued, be redressed sooner or later; the Russians were unlikely to acquiesce in a position of strategic inferiority. So were the missiles on Cuba really all that important?

There appears to be more than a smattering of speaking with the benefit of hindsight here; it was not until the mid-1960s that American hopes of achieving some type of meaningful nuclear superiority subsided and McNamara began to seriously question the wisdom of elements of his own policies. In any case Kennedy felt that he had no choice but to act as he did over Cuba. He feared he would lose credibility both at home and abroad if he did not confront Krushchev, particularly as, around Cuba, the US enjoyed an overwhelming superiority in conventional forces. If America recoiled from acting to guard Western interests on her own doorstep, her guarantee to her European allies would appear worthless.

How close the world came to nuclear holocaust in the tense days of October 1962 remains debatable. Kennedy's brinkmanship however evidently paid off: the Russians, in a rather humiliating climb-down, withdrew their missiles from Cuba. The crisis had other significant repercussions too. Both Kennedy and Krushchev were made more aware of the essentially interdependent nature of their positions; a mistake by one could culminate in the destruction of both. Indeed the difficulties experienced in handling the crisis helped clear the way for the establishment of the telephone 'hot line' – a direct channel between the governments in Washington and Moscow which would permit the swift exchange of reliable information in circumstances where time and clarity were of the essence.

For our purposes however, the most interesting outcome of the crisis was the impact it had on the military planning of the two superpowers and their respective allies. Krushchev curtailed his bullying-tactics over Berlin, but hastened the build-up of Soviet conventional forces, especially in Europe. Similarly, as McNamara anticipated, Russian efforts to achieve a nuclear balance were redoubled until, by 1970, they had brought about a rough strategic parity between the superpowers. All of this, especially the development and procurement of a new generation of solid-fuelled missiles deployed in protective silos, called for a massive expansion of the defence budget at a time when Krushchev would have preferred to see it shrink; the perennial problems of the Russian agricultural sector were becoming more acute and the demand for consumer goods was also on the increase. Nevertheless, choosing guns rather than butter, he embarked on a defence spending spree which was continued by his successors. In fact, from around the time of Krushchev's fall from office during October 1964 until the end of the decade, Soviet defence expenditure swelled by some 40 per cent. But if this was impressive, the rise in the US military budget was still more so. Indeed during the Democrat administrations of 1961–9 American defence spending, measured in constant 1983 dollars, soared from $166 000 million to $226 500 million. A disproportionate amount of this funding went on building up inter-continental missile forces, for McNamara – not content with the expansion envisaged by the Eisenhower administration – presided over a twofold increase in spending on such programmes, allocating $15 000 million for nuclear forces in the financial year 1962–3 alone. The result was that between 1961 and 1965 the number of American *Polaris* and inter-continental ballistic missiles climbed from 108 to 1507. As we have seen however, the Russians, understandably sensing that this was a bid for overwhelming nuclear superiority, responded with a massive expansion of their own strategic capabilities, while, in spite of the much higher levels of spending, the US found that generally the military balance did not swing significantly in her favour, particularly once the Vietnam War, which was to devour so many American resources, had begun in earnest. For example, between 1962 and 1969 the average number of US military personnel in the all-important European theatre declined to 333 000 men, whereas in the period 1953–60 – the era of 'Massive Retaliation', when general-purpose units were seen as a mere trip-wire – force-levels averaged 395 000 troops. Only the steady expansion of the West German *Bundeswehr* to twelve divisions and some improvements to capabilities through modernisation programmes mitigated the impact of this shortfall on the size of NATO's combat-ready forces.

This was somewhat ironic, for at the start of the Kennedy administration a very different state of affairs had appeared to be in the offing. Buoyed up by studies that suggested that NATO's conventional military strength had been underestimated and that of the communists overestimated, Kennedy had believed it possible to shift away from the excessive dependence on nuclear arms favoured by Eisenhower. Encouraged by General Maxwell Taylor, an advocate of large, versatile general-purpose forces and one of the president's

most persuasive military advisers, and influenced by Professor Walt
Rostow's book *The United States In The World Arena* which appeared in 1960 and argued the case for 'facing down' communism
wherever it raised its ugly head, he concluded that, given America's
advantage in nuclear weapons, she could, with modest accessions to
her conventional forces, adopt a strategy of 'flexible responses'.
Whilst the US proposed to apply this new policy on a global basis,
and indeed acquire the military wherewithal to simultaneously wage
what was termed 'two-and-a-half wars' – the thwarting of a Warsaw
Pact invasion of Western Europe and an expansionist drive by the
communist Chinese in Asia, while synchronously dealing with some
form of 'lesser' contingency elsewhere – it was seen as being particularly apposite to the NATO theatre where, despite the friction over
Berlin in 1961, the Americans felt fairly confident they could meet
any Soviet challenge. The Russians under Krushchev did not strike
Kennedy as being implacably aggressive; rather they appeared to be
casting about for ways to strengthen and consolidate their position.

Now, as before, the Americans' hegemony within the Western
alliance made it inevitable that any significant change in their own
military planning would have far-reaching consequences for the
organisation as a whole, and when, during the Athens meeting of
NATO ministers in May 1962, the US advanced the proposal that
'Flexible Response' should become NATO's official strategy, it was
given a mixed reception. McNamara maintained that the nuclear
threshold could be raised appreciably by inexpensive, modest improvements to conventional forces and by measures to reduce
NATO's vulnerability to a surprise attack; in the event of war,
nuclear armaments, if needed at all, could be employed on a limited
scale and later rather than sooner. The European allies however were
uncomfortable with this line of thought. Britain for example feared
that a protracted war might end in her being left with the unpalatable
decision to initiate nuclear warfare. Similarly France, together with
other states which were uneasy about the potential for the 'decoupling' of America's security interests from those of Western
Europe, saw it as a vote of no confidence by Washington in its own
nuclear guarantee.

Although it applauded measures designed to bolster the West's
conventional capabilities, West Germany also objected to the American proposals, pointing out that in practice general-purpose forces
would probably prove incapable of mounting an effective forward
defence, while the element of predictability in the new strategy

contrasted unfavourably with the old one's ability to pose incalculable risks to an aggressor, including the explicit dangers that NATO might instantly respond to a substantial conventional attack with tactical nuclear weapons and that any conflict could escalate to engulf the home territory of both superpowers. In any case the European allies could not be confident that, even if they did shoulder a greater share of the conventional defence burden, the Americans would not use this as a pretext for weakening their own general-purpose forces in the NATO area. Indeed between 1967 and 1972 Senator Mike Mansfield was to introduce a series of non-binding resolutions in the US Congress aimed at unilaterally cutting America's military presence in Western Europe, and although rejected these could only have strengthened the Europeans' perception that attempts to bolster their own security through increased resource allocations might ultimately prove counter-productive.

Nor did past experience support McNamara's belief that conventional force improvements could be achieved without appreciable economic and political sacrifices. Indeed, according to the Pentagon's calculations in 1962 for example, the two-and-a-half war plan would oblige the Americans to expand their general-purpose forces to levels disturbingly similar to those put forward in the early-1950s by the JCS in response to the policy objectives of NSC 68: around 400 naval vessels, 28 divisions and 40 fighter-attack wings. This would entail expanding the US Navy by some 19 per cent, the Army by 37 per cent and the Air Force by 42 per cent[21] – an ambitious project by any reckoning. Moreover, as the French argued, any build-up of conventional war-fighting capabilities secured by the West was liable to provoke a Soviet response which might even tip the scales still further in the Russians' favour, while large ground forces and their supporting infrastructures might even invite attack by Warsaw Pact nuclear missiles.

Not surprisingly the American proposals generated a good deal of debate and not a little acrimony. In fact the disputes dragged on for nearly five years. During this time France, utterly disillusioned by the drift in strategy and its implications for the US guarantee to Europe, withdrew from the integrated military command structure of NATO; the Cuban Missile and Berlin Wall Crises came and went, with Kennedy, eager to reassure his European allies, 'facing down' communism regardless of the inherent risks in doing so; and the Vietnam War steadily escalated, sucking in an ever greater portion of America's conventional forces until, by mid-1968, there were more than

500 000 US military personnel in action there. Finally in December 1967 NATO's ministers adopted MC 14/3, which enshrined, albeit in somewhat ambiguous terms, a doctrine of 'flexibility of response'.

The relative versatility of the new strategy was afforded by the potential synergism of three broad types of military response. Besides the old policy of full-scale nuclear retaliation, NATO might now, in reacting to aggression, confine itself to 'direct defence'. This would seek to limit the fighting in both nature and scale by thwarting an attacker at the level of military conflict chosen by him – which, it was assumed, would probably be conventional warfare, but might involve the restricted use of nuclear weapons. Thirdly, there was an intermediate response, deliberate escalation, which would alter the scope of the war by extending it to other regions, or change its character through the extensive employment of nuclear armaments, or both. The danger of escalation would, it was hoped, deter the initiation of any form of hostilities. If however armed conflict did occur, 'direct defence' promised to grant NATO a conventional warfare interlude after which the use of nuclear weapons might, if it could not be averted, at least be planned and controlled.

One could be forgiven for assuming that this meant that NATO's general-purpose forces would now take on a role which was rather more substantial than that of a trip-wire for nuclear retaliation. However, giving substance to the key distinction between MC14/2 and MC14/3 posed problems for the alliance. After balancing their respective concerns and considerations, the European wing concluded that it would be sufficient if the trip-wire were to be stiffened, whereas the Americans had been anticipating the development of capabilities for conventional warfare on a far grander scale. Indeed they had hoped that NATO would acquire enough capacity to sustain a protracted conflict, ideally without any recourse to nuclear weapons. This divergence remains of crucial significance, since it is central to any consideration of NATO's willingness and ability to embrace a change in strategy, particularly one which involves reducing dependence on nuclear arms. For despite the limitations of nuclear deterrence and the perplexing practical and moral dilemmas therein, the Western Europeans and, to a lesser extent, the Americans have deliberately chosen to rely on it as their *principal* means of countering the threat of aggression.

The military alternative would have been to invest the manpower and other resources that would be necessary to build up and maintain sufficient conventional strength to match that of the Warsaw Pact, thus relegating nuclear arsenals to a secondary role in which their primary function would be to deter attack, especially an attack with nuclear armaments. This is precisely how the Americans initially visualised the concept of flexible response. Doubts about whether that is an attainable, desirable or necessary objective have however repeatedly surfaced, with the result that NATO has pursued the reverse: nuclear deterrence and the weaponry thereof has been given pre-eminence over conventional capabilities, and the alliance has generally focused on avoiding a war rather than acquiring the means to fight one – except of course for those that are absolutely necessary if deterrence is to be seen as having any backbone and credibility.

This approach has at times appeared cynical, miserly, selfish, misguided, imprudent and duplicitous. It has for example frequently led to American jibes and complaints about the Europeans 'not doing enough' for their own defence, and to concern, for an assortment of reasons and on the part of a variety of people and pressure groups, about threats and plans to employ a fearsome and growing array of indiscriminate weapons of mass destruction. Yet the nuclear 'balance of terror' is something which, the occasional twinge of anxiety aside, most people in the West have been prepared to live with and pay for. Nor is this surprising. Not only have alternative military options seemed prohibitively costly – both in financial terms and, in the case of measures like conscription for instance, in the sense of their potential impact on personal liberties and opportunities and, through the 'militarisation' of society, on a state's social cohesion and domestic stability – they have also failed to offer an adequately convincing solution to the problems in hand. It was always easy enough to find fault with nuclear deterrence but, given the past East–West imbalance in conventional forces and the inescapable fact that the nuclear genie cannot be returned to its bottle, what was to be substituted for it? Of the whole mélange of fears, considerations, imperatives and dangers, precisely what 'threat' was to be dealt with? And what level of forces *would* be enough?

In the meantime the resources saved by the West's eschewal of relatively expensive conventional defence policies have been devoted to giving its people, or at least the great majority of them, a rather better standard of living than that enjoyed in the Eastern Bloc. The West's economies have been generally stronger – in 1988 for instance the NATO states had four times the total GNP of the Warsaw Pact countries – and its citizens have benefited from a steady flow of consumer goods, together with the hospitals, universities and other

showpiece elements of their 'welfare' states. This was an understandable and ethical choice. For many however it was also a key component
of security policy. In 1950, for example, Aneurin Bevan, the British
Health Minister, objected, as we have seen, to increasing expenditure on the armed forces. British foreign policy, he reminded his
Cabinet colleagues at the time, had been based on the view that

> the best method of defence against Russian imperialism was to
> improve the social and economic conditions of the countries threat-
> ened by Communist encroachment. The United States Govern-
> ment seemed now to be abandoning this social and political
> defence in favour of a military defence.[22]

In contrast to some of his colleagues, Bevan regarded this early
attempt to change policy as misguided, and it could be that his
experience as Health Minister exerted some influence here. For
health-care and defence are two spheres of governmental activity in
which demand is potentially limitless. One can always find a justification for some facility or capability, if only the requirements of
contingency plans. Government resources, on the other hand, are
finite. Clearly peace and security are essential for prosperity. But one
has to acknowledge limits and decide on priorities accordingly. In this
regard, Bevan the socialist was not really any different to Eisenhower
the republican, for instance, under whose leadership the USA emphasised acquiring a 'maximum deterrent at a bearable cost'. Indeed,
in his farewell address as president, he was to warn against the
'acquisition of unwarranted influence, whether sought or unsought,
by the military-industrial complex'.

Whether Eisenhower pursued the best policies to bring about the
peaceful coexistence he claimed to have sought with communism is
debatable. What is certain however, is that trying to achieve security
through military means alone poses complex problems which, at
various junctures between 1949 and 1989, both NATO and the
Warsaw Pact seem to have lost sight of. For example, during the
1960s the US inaugurated a programme to acquire military forces of a
size deemed sufficient to cope with a two-and-a-half war contingency.
By the 1970s however it was apparent that amassing and sustaining
such an awesome peacetime capacity lay beyond even America's
grasp and, in the wake of the resulting 'Nixon Doctrine', the plan was
scaled down; the ability to simultaneously wage one-and-a-half wars
became the objective.[23] Nevertheless by the early 1980s, although the

US had, at enormous cost, finally acquired virtually all the forces once judged necessary for the two-and-a-half wars scenario, aspirations and potential commitments still threatened to overstretch available resources. Indeed such was the imbalance between ends and means that even the frenzied enlargement of the US defence budget undertaken by the Reagan administration failed to correct it. As early as March 1983 Senator Sam Nunn, for instance, observed that the demand imposed by America's declared military strategy 'far exceeds our present and projected resources'; while in a statement to the Senate's Armed Services Committee some twelve months before, Under Secretary of Defense Fred Iklé admitted that

Even an increase in US military investments as high as 14% per year, continued throughout the decade, would not close the gap in accumulated military assets between the US and Soviet Union until the early 1990s. That is a bleak outlook, implying either further deterioration in our security or a need for a defense increase considerably steeper than what the Administration now proposes.[24]

Similarly the USSR has, as we shall see in more detail later, been inclined in the past to search for purely military solutions to what are essentially political problems, with the result that until the early 1980s, when the concept of 'reasonable sufficiency' began to emerge in Soviet defence thinking, the USSR engaged in a competition for military superiority with 'all the other major world powers situated near or far from Soviet borders, and in the entire range of armed forces and armaments'.[25] In fact the Russians endeavoured to accumulate and maintain sufficient forces to secure a rapid victory in every possible theatre of operations and over any foreseeable coalition of opposing states. But this approach, which devoured huge quantities of scarce resources, proved somewhat counter-productive. Threatened by the proliferation of the USSR's military power, its neighbours and other potential adversaries replied with measures of the same genre. The Russians' sense of security diminished accordingly, while the spiralling cost of defence drained the life-blood out of their economy. It was an unsustainable situation which jeopardised the status and stability of the USSR more than any discernible external threat. 'The arms race', wrote one observer, 'is causing havoc to the extent that it is beginning to shake the foundation of the economy and threaten the security of our country'.[26] Indeed the military and industrial *perestroika*, which Mikhail Gorbachev embarked upon in the mid-1980s and which brought about such remarkable change in the Eastern Bloc during the closing years of that decade, represented a major departure from, if not a complete reversal of, some of the perceptions that had guided Soviet security policies for the best part of 40 years.

Although superpower recognition of the elusiveness of securing and then maintaining any meaningful kind of military supremacy in a nuclear world was slow in coming, periodic thaws in the Cold War did occur and very largely because of a desire by one or both parties to escape from the costly and vicious circle of the arms-race. After the abortive quest for a rapprochement during the early 1950s, the next such opportunity appeared in the late 1960s, when some hesitant exchanges began between the two blocs. In 1966 NATO ministers commissioned the Harmel Report – which was to suggest avenues by which a dialogue could be pursued with the Warsaw Pact that might pave the way for confidence-building measures and force reductions – while towards the end of that year the USA made overtures about the possibility of strategic arms limitation talks (SALT). The Russians slowly responded, and in July 1968 a treaty on nuclear non-proliferation was concluded. Meanwhile, in Reykjavik the previous month, the North Atlantic Council, having accepted the Harmel Report's recommendation that security be based on the 'twin pillars of defence and détente',[27] extended an invitation to the Warsaw Pact to commence 'Mutual and Balanced Force Reductions' (MBFR) in Central Europe. Similar approaches were made regularly thereafter, to which Moscow eventually replied with proposals for a pan-European conference to resolve problems over security and cooperation.

The Russians' invasion of Czechoslovakia in August 1968 brought progress to an abrupt but only temporary halt. Indeed if the sub-sequent deployment of a further five Soviet divisions along the Czech border with West Germany provoked any anxiety in the West, it was apparently insufficient to merit any appreciable increase in NATO's forces.[28] Once better relations resumed, there was mounting evidence of Russian interest in obtaining Western technology, credits and expertise for the modernisation of key sectors of Soviet industry, all of which a new West German coalition government under Willy Brandt was particularly eager to furnish when it took office in October 1969.

By the early 1970s talk of an era of détente was widespread as 'realists' and utilitarians made marked, if ultimately ephemeral, advances at the expense of the Cold War warriors and ideologues. In the USA Henry Kissinger, a Harvard professor, was brought into the heart of government decision-making as the president's special adviser on foreign affairs and embarked on a quest to give the states of the world, especially the most powerful ones, a vested interest in international stability. Shortly after in 1974, Alistair Buchan, the first director of the London International Institute For Strategic Studies, even published a book with the optimistic title *The End Of The Postwar Era* while, the following year, the Helsinki Conference seemed to herald a new dawn of international cooperation, understanding and harmony.

Yet beneath an unruffled surface, international relations were being driven by undercurrents which were as dynamic and pragmatic as ever. The Russians remained eager to drive a wedge between West Germany and the rest of NATO but, having failed to achieve that, contented themselves with other gains: in the Polish Treaty of 1970, West Germany acknowledged Poland's post-war boundaries and, within three years, had established diplomatic relations with most of the Eastern Bloc; an accord was finally struck over the future of Berlin and on relations between the two German states; agreements on industrial, technical and economic cooperation were also forged between Bonn and Moscow; and the West Germans foreswore the possession of nuclear arms.

Important though these breakthroughs were, however, they largely occurred because of the superpowers' preoccupation with problems in other spheres and with the concomitant and pressing demand for resources that these imposed. For example, disorder in Poland toppled the government in December 1970 and imparted greater impetus to the Kremlin's search for stability in Europe; the link between better external relations and domestic prosperity and contentment was given more attention, with the result that, at the Twentyfourth Party Congress in 1971, it was announced that henceforth more resources would be committed to satisfying consumer demand. Similarly the need to cope with an increasingly bellicose China compelled the Russians to seek a rapprochement with the West. By late 1968, a slackening of the internal upheaval caused by the Cultural Revolution, and the incipient American disillusionment with the war in South-East Asia had begun to nudge Peking down the road towards better relations with Washington. The Sino-Soviet rift of the early 1960s had set the two great communist states on the slippery slope to open warfare, and numerous border clashes – most notably that over Damanski Island on the River Ussuri in March 1969 – took place in the latter half of the decade.

Deploring Russia's participation in nuclear test-ban talks with the West, China conducted her own experimental detonation in October 1964, and within five years had acquired a significant capacity for nuclear warfare. Indeed 1969 was regarded by many experts as the last year in which the USSR could permit itself the hope of destroying China's mounting nuclear capabilities with any impunity. (The Soviet leadership even went so far as to ask the new Nixon administration what America's position would be if they were to launch a preventative attack on China.[29]) Thereafter the scope for a disarming first strike would dwindle to a perilous marginality. Likewise, with regard to conventional military strength, the scales began to tip against Moscow. Faced with 800 million increasingly hostile Chinese, the Russians had no choice but to divert ever more resources from the European to their Eastern frontier. In fact, between 1966 and 1970 Soviet forces here were transformed from a token presence of twelve rather feeble divisions to an awesome army of forty, most of which were supplied with the latest equipment and weaponry.

By the early 1970s the Americans too had difficulties beyond Europe which, it was perceived, might be rendered more manageable through détente with the Russians. After the assassination of President Kennedy in November 1963, his successor, Lyndon B. Johnson, mindful of America's 'loss of China', had abandoned the search for a political solution to the conundrum of Vietnam and, having resolved to apply 'graduated pressure' on the North, steadily expanded military aid to Saigon. By mid-1965 McNamara was arguing that the communists had to be convinced that they could not win – or not easily at least – and that the budgetary and military costs involved in doing so were comfortably affordable. This belief however proved woefully misguided and by late March 1968, with American public opinion deeply divided over the conflict, Johnson was casting around for some route to peace with honour.

This of course was an acknowledgement of defeat – though American involvement in the war was actually to drag on until the beginning of 1973 – and a period of public disenchantment with America's defence expenditure and overseas commitments followed in its wake. In June 1973 for example, a Gallup poll revealed that popular opinion was virtually polarised over the question of fighting to defend Western Europe. Indeed Senator Mansfield, who had often warned that Vietnam would prove a disastrous and unwinnable conflict, continued to claim that the size of the US military presence in Europe was unwarranted and argued, in a resolution of May 1971 for instance, that it should be reduced by 50 per cent. This neo-isolationism was also reflected in the steady erosion of the Pentagon's budget. Whereas under Eisenhower's austerity the US military had lacked the funds to even contemplate serious, enduring commitments in regions such as South-East Asia, the relative largesse of the Democrats in the early 1960s was, when coupled with the healing effect the passage of time had had on the scars inflicted in Korea, seen to have furnished both the will and means to get entangled in Vietnam. The upshot of all of this was that, measured in constant 1983 dollars, the US defence budget, after peaking in 1968 at $235 400 million, slumped to $161 500 million in 1975, which was barely more than had been spent on the armed forces in 1958.[30] Indeed the 'anti-military orgy' as Henry Kissinger termed it, led to the US Army being slashed by virtually 50 per cent between 1968 and 1974 while, overall, personnel dropped from 3 240 000 to 1 267 500, some 300 000 of whom continued to be deployed in Western Europe.[31]

Against this background, the demise of America's two-and-a-half war strategy was inevitable, irrespective of its military merits or shortcomings. President Nixon first hinted at its renunciation in July 1969, and the following February did so formally in his *US Foreign Policy For The 1970s: A New Strategy For Peace*. Other domestic considerations such as balance of payments difficulties, which intensified criticism of costly overseas commitments, joined with external developments, notably the Sino–Soviet rift, in persuading Nixon that a new approach was both possible and necessary. The result was the one-and-a-half war strategy, which sought to harmonise American military doctrine and capabilities. In peacetime the US would henceforth maintain 'general purpose forces adequate for simultaneously meeting a major Communist attack in either Europe or Asia . . . and contending with a contingency elsewhere'.

Although the subsequent Ford and Carter administrations retained this concept as the model for conventional force planning, after Nixon's resignation in August 1974 the ongoing budgetary and other domestic restraints increasingly focused US military power on the 'one war' protection of Europe at the expense of the 'half war' contingency elsewhere. Other means had to be relied on to try to further American policies, notably the desire to shore up anti-communist forces in South-East Asia; and this helps explain Washington's increased willingness to parley with the East Bloc in the early 1970s. Equally the use of tools other than open military confrontation appealed to the communists at this juncture. As late as the Winter of 1989, General Yazov, the Russian Minister of Defence, was still stressing that the 'ideological-political and methodological basis' of Soviet military doctrine 'has been and remains the teaching of Marxism-Leninism on war'.[32] This was derived almost exclusively from Clausewitz's masterful study *Vom Kriege*, in which he had described war as the 'continuation of policy by other means'. Lenin, in *Polnoe Sobranie Sochineniya*, had rephrased this as 'War is the continuation of the policy of peace; peace is the continuation of the policies of war'. So to his disciples, détente, trade accords, and disarmament or arms-control pacts were essentially weapons of an alternative kind, while 'peaceful coexistence' had rather different connotations to those commonly ascribed to it by the capitalist West.

One important sphere for this calculated rivalry by other means was that of nuclear arms-control. In May 1972 the SALT I agreement was concluded, accentuating the apparent improvement in East–West relations. But again this accord probably owed more to pragmatism than philanthropy. It only restrained the growth of nuclear arsenals; it did not halt it. In fact both sides somewhat sanctimoniously agreed not to pursue options they found unattractive anyway, leaving themselves at liberty to refine and enlarge their arsenals more selectively than they would otherwise have done. The cost of building anti-ballistic missile (ABM) systems, for example, outweighed their likely advantages, whereas the acquisition of invulnerable, second-strike capabilities had much to recommend it. Thus modernisation was permitted which, because of innovations such as 'MIRVing' – the fitting of several warheads to individual missiles – led to increases in accuracy and throw-weights that neither side seems to have anticipated.

This continuing ingenuity and inventiveness on the part of both the Eastern and Western scientific communities did little for the quest for stability and parity that the SALT I agreement ostensibly stood for. Indeed whilst it would appear that the US believed the accord might make the numerical and qualitative evolution of Soviet forces more predictable and thus ease the planning of counter-measures, it is questionable whether the USSR ever intended acquiescing in the concepts of deterrence on which the Americans based their own reasoning. Among other evidence for this view is the fact that one searches in vain for a distinction between 'war-fighting' and 'deterrence' amidst the mass of Marxist-Leninist literature on the theme of military doctrine and strategy, whereas Bernard Brodie, in a work published as early as 1946, charted the course American strategic thinking was to follow:

> The first and most vital step in any American security program for the age of atomic bombs is to take measures to guarantee to ourselves in case of attack the possibility of retaliation in kind. The writer in making this statement is not for the moment concerned about who will *win* the next war in which atomic bombs have been used. Thus far the chief purpose of our military establishment has been to win wars. From now on its chief purpose must be to avert them. It can have no other useful purpose.[33]

Certainly, between 1966 and 1970, while the number of US land-based missiles remained static at around 1050, the Russians increased theirs from 292 to 1299. They also deployed a further 200 submarine-launched missiles, giving a total of 304. Both sides constantly sought to reduce the vulnerability of their missile silos through hardening programmes, while the Russian SS17, SS18 and SS19 Missiles, all of which appeared in the early 1970s, underlined the awesome destructive power which MIRVing could pack into a solitary rocket.

All of this seemed to have grave implications for the framework of nuclear deterrence and 'escalation dominance' which supported NATO's strategy of 'Flexible Response'. Because of MIRVing it was now theoretically possible to destroy large numbers of an opponent's missiles in their silos with a first strike executed by just a fraction of one's own forces; formerly any such endeavour would have consumed too many of the attacker's own missiles to leave an adequate second-strike capacity, but now the exchange ratio made pre-emption seem a more worthwhile proposition. The US land-based rockets which were chiefly armed with a single warhead at this time were perceived as being especially vulnerable in this regard, while steady growth of Russian ABM systems, coupled with an ambitious civil defence programme – to which, incidentally, many Americans, whilst advocating a similar scheme for their own country, ascribed all manner of villainous, ulterior motives – threatened to enervate any retaliatory salvo from America's submarine-launched missiles; indeed, paralysed by the threat of a second Soviet attack focused this time on cities, the American president would probably elect to hold his fire and meekly capitulate to the Russians' demands.

Or so at least ran the theory. But such concepts of 'limited nuclear war' might strike one as a contradiction in terms. Often the extension of strategic extrapolations and computations reaches such an abstract level that the notion begins to appear as ridiculous as it is repellant, while the only sense in which the conflict is 'limited' lies in the counting of probable casualties – they are to be reckoned in scores, rather than hundreds of millions.[34] In any case, as Bernard Brodie once so rightly observed, 'Whether the survivors be many or few, in the midst of a land scarred and ruined beyond all present comprehension, they should not be expected to show much concern for the further pursuit of political–military objectives'.[35] On the other hand, as James Schlesinger, the US Secretary of Defense, concluded in his *Departmental Report* of 1975:

> Whether the Soviets believe that . . . they have achieved any meaningful, exploitable advantage is not clear. However, they have not been reticent in stressing to a variety of audiences their superiority over the United States in numbers of . . . [missiles] and other strategic capabilities. Their words, at least, have suggested that they see these asymmetries as giving them diplomatic if not military leverage.

Certainly, however crudely it was defined, the arrival of strategic nuclear parity between the superpowers in the early 1970s appeared to many to have serious repercussions for NATO, an alliance which, as we have seen, had persistently relied on American nuclear firepower to offset its weakness in conventional forces. The policy had always had its flaws and critics. However, as technical developments rendered the maintenance of a 'credible' deterrent an increasingly costly and intractable problem, preserving the political cogency of the American nuclear guarantee ineluctably became a thornier conundrum. The key point was – and is – that any potential aggressor could not be 100 per cent certain that the Americans would *not* respond to an attack with strategic nuclear weapons, even if some views of rational self-interest suggested otherwise. But the French in particular had habitually manifested concern about the speciousness of that 'guarantee', and Britain too, supposedly the USA's closest ally in Europe, preferred to entrust the ultimate defence of her freedom of action and national sovereignty to her own independent, nuclear deterrent – a resolve that America's behaviour during the 1956 Suez Crisis did much to strengthen.

Between the late 1940s and the late 1970s however, profound alterations to the geostrategic environment caused doubts to become more widespread among Washington's allies. Under President Truman the US had enjoyed first a monopoly and later a significant lead in the sphere of nuclear armaments, together with superior maritime and air power. The USSR had moreover been left economically devastated by the Second World War. By the time President Carter came to power though, the relative advantages the US had possessed in terms of strategic capabilities had largely disappeared. The Russians had caught up in the nuclear race, were developing a 'blue water' navy, and had raised both the quality and quantity of their ground and air forces. Similarly, at the theatre level, the deployment of a new generation of Soviet medium-range nuclear forces – the mobile, solid-fuelled SS20, SS21 and SS22 multi-warhead Missiles, and the *Backfire* Bomber – swiftly eroded NATO's ability to dominate any process of escalation; the West no longer enjoyed a position whereby it alone could raise the level of conflict, or seek to control a nuclear exchange with the threat that escalation could only end in a deteriorating Russian position. Nuclear deterrence might thus still have a major role in preventing an attack on the USA itself, but what about on Western Europe?

Unease over this point culminated in 1979 in NATO's 'dual track' decision to deploy land-based *Tomahawk* cruise and *Pershing* II missiles in Western Europe to match the Soviet SS20s. In the eyes of the West, *Pershing* was a theatre weapon. The Russians however took the view that these highly-accurate American missiles were not only destabilising because of their potential for precise, counter-force strikes but also blurred the distinction between tactical and strategic nuclear warfare, since they could pose a threat to the Soviet homeland itself, whereas the equally accurate and provocative SS20 could only menace the territory of Washington's European allies. Similarly, European anti-nuclear protest groups objected to their deployment, fearing some flagitious conspiracy on the part of the Americans to wage a nuclear conflict which could and would be confined to the Eurasian landmass, leaving the US itself unaffected. Horst Afheldt for example, a prominent advocate of 'Defensive Defence' concepts, denounced a 'strategy that takes all of Europe hostage for political purposes' and 'gives the US president the right to decide on European survival'.[36] (If he had any objections to the Russians' culpability in all of this, he omitted to mention them.) At the same time the deployment of these missiles – which the Western European governments, especially that of West Germany, wanted in order to reforge the link between their security interests and those of the USA – was seen by many as a counter-productive measure, while others dismissed it as a superfluous and expensive gesture. The fact that these weapons, like the *Poseidon* submarine-launched missiles already assigned to NATO, were under American control undermined the rationale behind their deployment: what more did they add to the guarantee? Indeed what commitment to Western Europe's defence could a few missiles demonstrate that was not already manifest in the presence of 300 000 US military personnel, together with all their costly equipment, their families and the tens of thousands of other American citizens, not to mention billions of dollars' worth of investments, to be found there?

In fact the deployment of these missiles had, as has always been the case with Western nuclear weapons, more to do with war prevention than war-fighting, and was as such something of a piece of over-insurance inspired by the military's tendency to plan for the worst-case scenario. If the Russians failed to be deterred from launching a disabling nuclear strike against Western Europe's essential military infrastructure – airfields, seaports, depots and command, control communication and intelligence nodes – by the forces already in place, then it is doubtful that *any* level of nuclear armaments could achieve that objective. The *Tomahawk* and *Pershing* missiles, far from being intended for use in some nebulous, nefarious and – I at least would maintain – utterly implausible plot to fight a 'limited' nuclear war, were intended to convince both friend and foe that there was no prospect of the US engaging in any such thing. On the contrary, the Americans sought to confront the Marxist–Leninists in the Kremlin with what their own military idol, Clausewitz, saw as the 'negative aim' of strategy: persuading one's potential adversaries of

> the improbability of victory . . . [and] its unacceptable cost. . . .
> Since war is not an act of senseless passion but is controlled by its
> political object, the value of this object must determine the sacri-
> fices to be made for it in *magnitude* and also in *duration*. Once the
> expenditure of effort exceeds the value of the political object, the
> object must be renounced.[37]

In short the Americans were striving to convince the Russians that a resort to using nuclear weapons would be irrational; they could not hope to win – that is, preserve or further the power of the USSR, which would be their ultimate, 'political object'. Whether they could be deterred in this fashion from unleashing a crushing conventional *Blitzkrieg* was less clear however. Indeed that was precisely the predicament that had motivated NATO's switch to a strategy of 'Flexible Response' and which, during the 1970s, was, together with fears of unilateral withdrawals of US troops as a result of Congressional pressure, to inspire the European wing of the alliance to make greater efforts in the realm of conventional defence.

Whilst this led to the important initiatives of the 'AD 70' Study – which nominated nine key types of conventional warfare capabilities for special attention – in a sense the adoption by NATO of MC14/3, created as many problems as it solved. If the old, crude approach of MC14/2, with its nuclear trip-wire and threats of massive retaliation, was an unsatisfactory solution, then the new strategy turned out to be scarcely better. We have already noted how US defence spending was savaged during the early 1970s in the 'anti-military orgy' that followed the Vietnam War, and although overall European expenditure on conventional forces climbed each year by an average of about three per cent in real terms throughout the decade, few new forces were planned or created. Rather, emphasis was placed on enhancing the capabilities of existing ones through an assortment of modernisation programmes. However the high inflation and low economic growth experienced in the West in the wake of the 1973 oil crisis diminished the impact of these schemes and rendered the achievement of genuine increases in defence budgets increasingly problematical, especially since the period of détente which, as we have seen, ushered in the 1970s made them as unpopular as they seemed incongruous.

In contrast to this, the Warsaw Pact's conventional forces continued to grow both in quality and quantity. Moreover if war occurred, the concept of 'direct defence' as embodied in MC14/3 appeared to offer Soviet strategists an opportunity, albeit a slim one, of dealing NATO a decisive blow by conventional means. In the fairly lengthy phase of conventional warfare that apparently would now precede nuclear release – thought to be some four to six days – might it not be possible for the Warsaw Pact's general-purpose forces, if they could advance swiftly and resolutely enough, to rout their Western counterparts in a surprise *Blitzkrieg* which would last but a few hours, thus shattering NATO's military and political cohesion before any decision to employ its nuclear firepower could be put into effect? Indeed, once the Warsaw Pact's forces were deeply intertwined with both the West's ground units and major population centres, could such a decision be taken, let alone implemented? Did the change to 'Flexible Response' not imply an unwillingness on the part of NATO, if tested, to actually 'go nuclear'?

I, at least, have always subscribed to the view that the USSR was never especially likely to actually embark on military operations against Western Europe. The Russians have appeared more interested in consolidating their position than in expansion, and it is difficult to imagine precisely what issue or crisis would have pushed or lured them over the brink. Since the Second World War neither Western nor Eastern leaders have been inhibited in their use of force when interest demanded and circumstances permitted, be it in Korea, Vietnam, Hungary, Czechoslovakia, Egypt, Grenada, Afghanistan, the Falklands, Panama or the Persian Gulf. Usually however, force has been employed well within spheres of influence or on their fringes, and direct confrontation between the superpowers has been avoided if only through the use of surrogates – though even here, Washington and Moscow have often been seen trying to restrain their proxies from going too far.

Even before the days of Gorbachev, the Soviet leadership was, I would suggest, too aware of the potential social, political, economic and military costs involved to resort to war with the West except in the most extreme circumstances. The very existence of their state would have had to have been at stake, for, by employing armed force, that is precisely what they would have been putting at risk. Any major conflict could have ripped the fabric of Soviet society and irreparably damaged the position and influence of the Communist Party. This very nearly came about during the Great Patriotic War of 1941–5, and is regarded as the ineluctable outcome of any nuclear exchange with the USA and its allies.[38] Consequently that is the one thing the Kremlin was and is most anxious to avoid. In any case, as Marxist–Leninism preaches that war and peace are both tools for achieving the same objective, the former need not necessarily be used. In certain circumstances détente – which is to be seen as an intensification, not a relaxation of the class struggle – is the better approach; it reduces the risk of war, which could prove catastrophic, and thus paves the way for the peaceful triumph of communism that, according to the faithful, might be hastened or delayed but cannot be prevented.

Military power however plays an important role in such calculations. In the past, the very presence of massive Soviet forces on their borders has had a psychological impact on the NATO states. This passive use of military might, the mere threat of aggression, was employed in an attempt to overawe and intimidate the West. The more the 'correlation of forces tilted in favour of Socialism', as the disciples of Lenin would express it, the more the world was likely to progress peacefully towards embracing that political doctrine. In line with this reasoning, the Soviet Union's armed forces developed in such a way as to restrict NATO's options in countering either the threat or active use of force. In other words, they were geared to the classical, peacetime function of military forces: to convince any would-be opponent that resorting to war as an instrument of policy, even defensive policy, would prove counter-productive, since victory would be improbable or prohibitively costly.

The 'direct defence' phase of 'Flexible Response' and the concomitant commitment to collective forward defence presented Soviet strategists with some prospect of crushing NATO militarily without getting themselves embroiled in a potentially catastrophic nuclear exchange. Refining and applying the lessons of armoured combat they had learnt in the campaigns and battles of the Great Patriotic War, the Russians forged a military machine which, grounded in a comprehensive study of operational art, was equipped both materially and doctrinally to execute a *Blitzkrieg* that would be aimed at the rapid annihilation of the bulk of NATO's forward general-purpose forces. Military and political deception would be employed to achieve as much surprise as possible, and once unleashed the virtually all-mechanised Warsaw Pact forces would endeavour to advance with the utmost celerity. While successive concentrations of troops backed by enormous firepower pinned the 'layer cake' of NATO national corps to their forward positions and wore them down, Operational Manoeuvre Groups (OMGs) – self-contained, powerful armoured divisions acting in close conjunction with air-assault brigades and fixed-and rotary-wing aviation – would be inserted along key axes and would probe deep into NATO territory, demolishing the defence from behind and within; mobilisation and reinforcement plans would be disrupted and key infrastructure elements, such as intelligence, command, control and communications centres, depots and theatre nuclear systems, destroyed.

If all went according to plan, the sheer speed and nature of the operation would catch the West off its guard. The Russians firmly believe that men, not weapons, start wars; and even if NATO's military commanders were anticipating and predicting an attack, if, through skilful propaganda and other deception techniques, their political masters were successfully restrained from issuing the necessary mobilisation directives in time, a significant degree of surprise could be attained. Ill positioned and only partially prepared for combat, NATO's general-purpose forces would be shattered within a few hours, its cohesion would disintegrate as its members' interests began to diverge, and the much-feared nuclear riposte would become a practical and political impossibility. Securing peace, on the best terms available, would be its sole realistic recourse.

And offering terms, perhaps quite charitable ones, would probably have been the Russians' next move; for it has never seemed likely to me for one that theirs would have been a war of conquest aimed at the long-term occupation, subjugation and effective annexation of Western Europe. Rather they would have been seeking to dismember its political and military power in much the way that Bismarck wanted to cripple France in 1870 – a project renewed and widened to include Britain by the Kaiser in 1914 and which Hitler, initially at least, planned to repeat in 1940. True, a degree of social change was imposed by Hitler subsequently, but only in so far as was necessary to perpetuate France's enfeeblement. The armistice terms he proffered at Réthondes in June 1940 were 'harsh but not dishonouring'; Germany's 'chief aims', as Alistair Horne concluded in his adroit study of the Battle of France,

> were to prevent any resumption of hostilities and to provide herself with the requisite conditions for pursuing the war against Britain. . . . For Hitler . . . the war was over. France, the arch-enemy, was prostrate at last; Britain no longer counted, she would fall like a plum from a tree in due course.[39]

Similar objectives would, I suspect, have been those of the USSR in any military attack planned against Western Europe, especially in the period that elapsed between the building of the Berlin Wall in 1961 and its destruction in 1989–90. If only because they derived great benefits from the trade they enjoyed with the West's vibrant economies and because the prospects for the successful indoctrination of its relatively free, prosperous peoples must by this stage have seemed utterly bleak, the Russians had little to gain by trying to subjugate Western Europe, whereas they did have a good deal to lose. They would probably have been content to see it remain much as it was, providing it no longer possessed the necessary political will and military power to interfere with the USSR's freedom of action. Such a state of affairs could of course have proved difficult to maintain and, as moving into the territory of a vanquished opponent often proves easier than relinquishing it, the Russians might have been enticed or pushed into acquiring yet more reluctant if not recalcitrant vassal states to add to the vexatious and costly gaggle they already had.

The astounding changes wrought in Eastern Europe by the revolutions of 1989–90 demonstrated that despite – or perhaps because of – their febrile and frequently ruthless efforts over the previous 45 years, the Russians had totally failed to establish communist regimes which enjoyed much in the way of popular support. In a spate of free elections the discredited communists were routed, while to all intents and purposes the Warsaw Pact ceased to exist. If prior to 1989 there was speculation and doubt about the degree of loyalty that, for example, the Czechs, Poles, Hungarians and East Germans would extend to the Kremlin in an East–West confrontation, few people can have been left in much doubt as to where their symphathies lay thereafter. Some analysts argued that this change was not irreversible; a conservative backlash in the USSR could lead to an attempt to reimpose Russian mastery over these states.

By early 1990 however, it was clear that such a development was fast becoming grossly improbable if not impossible. Since the Second World War these countries had primarily served as a military glacis and political *cordon sanitaire* for the USSR. Domestic reform both there and in the wider Eastern Bloc unravelled much of the rationale for this 'iron curtain'; *perestroika* and *glasnost* led to a growing flow of information to the ordinary people of Eastern Europe and the USSR which rendered them far less tractable than before. A capacity for open self-criticism was created, and totalitarian rule simply ceased to be viable. At the same time, subject to the provision that they did not develop into potential threats, countries whose actual occupation and control was once regarded as essential for Russian security were given an increasingly free hand: communist rule and centrally-planned economies gave way to pluralism and the free market, while Russian occupation forces commenced a series of phased withdrawals. Even German reunification was to be sanctioned.

President Gorbachev and his colleagues had evidently concluded that all this could be allowed without the USSR's security interests being unduly jeopardised. Indeed, besides the scope for savings on defence expenditure that this approach offers – and which as we shall see are essential if the Soviet industrial base is to be revitalised – the new policy seems grounded in the conviction that the one it superseded was proving counter-productive. No sooner had the Poles, for example, secured virtual autonomy than, faced with the prospect of a powerful, reunited Germany, they started looking to the once hated Russians for some form of mutual defence pact. Likewise the process of European integration and the reconstruction of the former Eastern Bloc offers the Russians a golden opportunity to enhance trade and other links, and secure Western technology, investment, credits, and scientific and managerial know-how. Indeed the USSR might now preserve if not extend its influence in Eastern Europe and beyond through means which are subtler and internationally far more acceptable than repression and brute military force – though military *power* will still have a role to play. In the meantime Moscow's growing involvement in international trade and commerce will ease many of the problems of domestic reform, while simultaneously affording the USSR the long-term potential for power of a very different but, as the Swiss and Japanese have proved conclusively, very efficacious kind.

All of this is of crucial importance, for in evaluating the merits of a given military posture and strategy, we have to begin by asking precisely what sort of threat is to be confronted and neutralised, and what options NATO might prefer to see preserved. A military strategy devised with one challenge in mind might prove wholly inapplicable and inflexible if faced with another. Should NATO, for instance, possess such formidable military might as to be palpably capable of routing any would be opponent, or would the capacity to deny an attacker the prospect of a swift and cheap victory suffice? Should the capability to escalate a conflict be retained, not only as a deterrent to calculated acts of aggression but also as a means of halting the much feared war 'by accident'? What sort of attack is NATO most likely to have to cope with? Will it be a *coup de main*, a 'standing start' offensive by relatively few in-place units, or a much larger, more thoroughly prepared operation? Assuming that arms-reduction treaties do not make it completely impractical, should the emphasis be on forward defence, or would that be playing into an attacker's hands by exposing the bulk of NATO's disposable forces to rapid destruction? Indeed, should military, political and industrial planning focus on the waging of a long or a short war?

As we have seen, the Americans initially hoped that 'Flexible Response' would raise the nuclear threshold considerably by endowing NATO with the general-purpose forces necessary to sustain a protracted conventional conflict. It soon became evident, however, that these expectations would not be fulfilled: not only were the Western allies reluctant to commit the necessary resources, but also the Russians appeared determined to match the new strategy with innovations of their own and were prepared to finance the requisite qualitative and quantitative improvements to their forces. By the mid 1970s, détente, which had once seemed to promise so much, was on the wane. Both the SALT and MBFR negotiations had stalled, while the 'Helsinki Process' was failing to deliver tangible results: Eastern Bloc violations of human-rights persisted, and Soviet intervention around the globe was seen to be on the increase. Although there was no Third World War, there were plenty of Third World wars – many of which were entirely the result of local disputes but, especially to American observers who insisted on viewing everything through an East–West prism, seemed to be part of a communist conspiracy for global domination.

Above all, the arms-race continued relentlessly, particularly after a spate of reports drew unfavourable comparisons between NATO's conventional combat capabilities and those of the Warsaw Pact. Flexibility studies undertaken by the Supreme Headquarters, Allied Powers Europe (SHAPE); Rand Corporation examinations of various conventional defence issues; the Hollingsworth Report on the US Army's readiness and potential for operations on the Central Front; the Nunn-Bartlett 1977 study *NATO And The New Soviet Threat*, which surveyed war-fighting capabilities in the light of the evolving challenge; all of these painted a picture of such gloom that by 1977 the alliance's Defence Planning Committee was recommending 'further measures . . . to reverse effectively the adverse trends in the NATO-Warsaw Pact conventional military balance'.[40]

The most significant of these measures was the Long-Term Defence Programme (LTDP), which was formally adopted by NATO in May 1978. President Carter had already persuaded the allies to endorse plans for increasing military expenditure by three per cent in real terms each year, so the financial foundations for the scheme were already in place. In fact by this time the US and most of the other NATO countries were achieving annual economic growth rates of around three per cent and could thus devote more resources to defence even though, as a proportion of GNP, the level of expenditure stayed roughly static. This however meant that as soon as the 1979 recession began to bite and economic activity as a whole declined, so too did the purchasing power of any increases in military budgets that were secured. Indeed, during the programme's first year, only five countries genuinely achieved the envisaged increase in defence outlays, while between 1980 and 1984 the European average rate of growth in real terms dwindled from 2.7 to only 1.2 per cent. Simultaneously, the decision to deploy American *Pershing* and *Tomahawk* missiles in Europe to match the Soviet SS20s diverted both resources and political attention from conventional defence. Consequently the LTDP, just like the Lisbon Force Goals and the 'AD 70' Study, failed to come up to expectations, though some modest progress was achieved in readiness, rapid reinforcement capabilities, sustainability and the rationalisation of arms production.

Nor were the deficiencies made good by a further bout of measures and initiatives which followed the Russian invasion of Afghanistan. These, endorsed by the Defence Planning Committee in December 1980, did secure minor improvements in several crucial areas, but only some two thirds of the capabilities earmarked as priorities ultimately received much in the way of attention and resources. In the meantime the collapse of the Shah's regime in Iran dealt a major blow to the Nixon Doctrine which, in return for assistance and security guarantees from the US, had where possible sought the substitution of indigenous, allied military forces for American ones. This shared approach to security problems had promised to relieve the US of the prohibitively expensive burden of having to 'conceive all the plans, design all the programs, execute all the decisions and undertake all the defense of the free nations of the world'.[41] Iran had been the jewel in the doctrine's crown, and with the Shah's fall America's ability to project military power outside the NATO area inevitably came under scrutiny once more.

The 'half war' of the one-and-a-half war strategy enjoyed renewed attention, with the establishment of a Rapid Deployment Joint Task Force (RDJTF) for use in South-West Asia being placed high on the agenda. This however was to be achieved at the expense of commitments elsewhere. No new forces were created or significant increases in funding sought. Instead existing general-purpose units, mostly earmarked for the defence of Europe and the Far East, were restructured and re-equipped for employment in the Persian Gulf region. Indeed, throughout the late 1970s and early 1980s, American efforts to tailor more forces for rapid-deployment and contingency operations in the Third World were to render ever more units of doubtful value for high-intensity operations in the First.[42]

Once again out-of-area commitments threatened to sap the strength of Western conventional forces on the Central Front, and once again some Americans attributed NATO's chronic weakness here to the unwillingness of their Western European partners to do more for their own defence. At the insistence of Congress, the 1983 Defence Authorisation Bill imposed a ceiling on the size of the US forces deployed in Europe in peacetime, while Zbigniew Brzezinski and Henry Kissinger for example advocated anew the withdrawal of 100 000 or more military personnel to prod America's European allies into greater endeavours. Too many of these however were undergoing serious social and economic difficulties. Even once the effects of the 1979 recession began to ease, high levels of public borrowing and unemployment joined with rising interest rates and adverse demographic trends to create a situation in which maintaining let alone increasing defence expenditure became ever more problematic. Moreover the alarming speed with which the cost of developing modern, sophisticated military technology expanded meant that proportionately less money was left over for actual procurement. NATO ministers did agree, in June 1983, to extend their commitment to an annual real growth rate in their defence estimates of three per cent but, as far as the European pillar of the alliance was concerned, this was seldom if ever achieved.

Nor did the US succeed in significantly altering the military balance. Under the Reagan administration military expenditure increased dramatically during the first half of the 1980s. But as we have already noted, even this growth was regarded as insufficient to close the perceived 'gap in accumulated military assets' between the US and the USSR. Indeed while the JCS called for an expansion of the US Army to 23 active divisions, the Navy to 24 carrier battle groups, the Air Force to 44 fighter wings and the long-range transport fleet to 1308 aircarft by 1989, the Department of Defense only had plans for a force of 17 divisions, 15 carrier groups, 27 fighter wings and 348 transporters.[43] Even these goals were to prove too ambitious given the available resources, while despite the administration's attempts to equilibrate US military strength and commitments, the latter remained immoderate. Just as the power and influence of America had radiated out across the globe, the cost of militarily defending her burgeoning interests against every potential threat had expanded to a point where, as Britain had increasingly found with her empire in the first half of the Twentieth Century, it jeopardised the very basis of that power. Hamstrung by a mounting budget deficit, the US was

already permitting defence spending to taper off during the last years
of the 1980s and, given the incipient, dramatic improvement in
East–West relations, this trend was – and is – projected to persist into
the 1990s, with a formal abandoning of the one-and-a-half war
strategic guideline and cuts of up to 25 per cent in manpower and
budgets in the first five years alone.[44]

Once again the peacetime costs of sustaining military preparedness
for a war which might never come had proved more than NATO
could or would shoulder. Similarly the USSR and its allies had been
brought to the verge of economic collapse by the insatiable demands
of their military machine as they sought to compete with the West;
indeed the whole Russian centralised system was geared to the rapid
satisfaction of wartime rather than peacetime needs. Nor, would it
seem, did either side feel appreciably more secure, despite all these
sacrifices. Understandably the 1980s saw increasing talk in both
camps about 'doing more with less'. Assuming that one is prepared to
overlook the distorting crudity inherent in such comparisons and to
accept, among other flaws, the 'guestimates' made about East Bloc
budgets, it appeared that NATO often spent more on defence than
the Warsaw Pact yet still seemed to be relatively weak militarily. The
explanation for this largely lay in the contrasting nature of the two
alliances. The former, consisting of democratic, sovereign states,
each of which had its own national concerns, interests, perceptions,
traditions and policies, was never likely to match the singleminded-
ness, uniformity and conformity the latter's authoritarian regimes
were able to impose, not only in the defence sphere but in virtually
every aspect of life.

But for many critics the duplication of effort within NATO –
epitomised by individual member states' attempts to preserve comprehensive military forces and capabilities – was wasteful and inefficient. It was argued that resources could be saved and force
effectiveness enhanced through measures such as closer collaboration
over weapons development and procurement, extending mission-
and burden-sharing, expanding and improving the use of reservist
personnel, introducing more automation and other labour-saving
devices which – together with the recruitment of more women into
the services – could mitigate the repercussions of manpower short-
ages, and through the exploitation of emerging technology, both in
connection with actual armaments and in such fields as command,
control, communications, surveillance and intelligence.

For many commentators however, such suggestions were at best only part of the solution to the problem. After all they were in many ways merely the continuation of existing trends. Alliances for example were just burden-sharing on a grand scale and had been around as long as man himself. Similarly we have already noted the past reliance on the new technologies of the day – notably nuclear arms – to make up for some quantitative and other weaknesses, and also how any advantage stemming from this has proved ephemeral as, in due course, the same technology was acquired – and often improved on – by the other side. Nor was it clear that these solutions would in fact prove viable, given financial and other practical constraints. For instance the 26 American and European experts who formed the Steering Group of the European Security Study (ESECS) of 1981–3 eventually produced a series of proposals designed to enhance NATO's conventional war-fighting capabilities, and thus deterrence. Among other things, their report identified four key 'mission' areas in which special efforts would have to be made: counter-air operations, interdiction, the deep attack of enemy follow-on ground forces as they advanced into the theatre, and the destruction of hostile units actually in contact at the front. For the third of these missions alone, estimated costs would have run to nearly $6 billion, while the additional expenditure needed to fulfil all four projects was put at $9.4 billion.[45] (This vast sum, incidentally, was seen by many analysts as a crass understatement of the probable price.) Given the prevailing economic and political conditions within NATO states at the time, the costs inherent in implementing the ESECS Report were not, contrary to its claims, likely to be seen as 'feasible for the Alliance'. Nor were many of its political and military calculations and assumptions accorded much credibility. Indeed, like the Lisbon Force Goals, NSC 68 and a host of other well-intentioned but unavoidably ambitious proposals for injecting life into NATO's conventional defence capabilities, it had little practical impact.

This sort of experience convinced many theorists that instead of plodding on trying to revitalise the old approach to security questions, innovative thinking was what was called for. 'Flexible Response' seemed moribund; a fresh strategy and force structure *would* solve the problems however. Although he claimed that his proposal would bolster rather than replace existing NATO strategy, as it would 'make flexible response more flexible and forward defence more forward', perhaps the most radical notion was that of Professor Samuel Huntington, who during 1982–4 argued the case for the alliance adopting a conventional retaliation strategy. He took the view that a defensive alliance did not necessarily have to have a defensive military strategy. Indeed 'Massive Retaliation' was essentially an offensive strategy using nuclear weapons. Major conventional defence improvements, Huntington argued, were unlikely to be forthcoming. Showing an admirable grasp of the basic difficulties with which NATO had wrestled since its inception, he noted that:

> Ever since the Lisbon Conference, various efforts have been made to bolster NATO's conventional capabilities so as to decrease reliance on nuclear retaliation. . . . These efforts have not been notably successful. . . . Deterrence by conventional forces remains appealing, but it also remains an unreality. For understandable reasons European governments and publics have been unwilling to appropriate the funds and make the sacrifices that would be required to make it effective. . . . Thus, while nuclear deterrence of a Soviet conventional attack on Western Europe suffers from a lack of credibility, conventional deterrence of such an attack suffers from a lack of capability.[46]

Given this state of affairs, Huntington observed, the aspirations of the LTDP, of the then SACEUR, General Bernard Rogers – who had advocated an increase in defence budgets to bolster conventional capabilities – and of the ESECS were not going to be fulfilled. Even if they could be, Huntington maintained, the assumption implicit in these plans – namely that stronger defences would deter Soviet aggression – was essentially false. The ESECS was wrong to treat conventional defence and deterrence as interchangeable concepts. True, overcoming stronger defences would require more investment and effort. But, as Glenn Snyder had sought to demonstrate in his 1961 book *Deterrence And Defence*, these two notions were not to be equated: strategies and forces designed to achieve one objective might not be suited to the realisation of another. Deterrence – the influencing of a potential adversary's course of action – could be pursued through denial or retaliation strategies. In the case of the former, the would-be attacker can calculate what costs he is likely to incur and what risks he is likely to run in trying to achieve a given aim. These can then be compared with the probable benefits. In the case of the latter however, he cannot know what overall costs might be involved, because he cannot be as certain how his opponent will respond. It is, then, this element of uncertainty and uncontrollability that determines the effectiveness of the deterrent; a strategy of seeking to deny an opponent his objective is weaker in deterrence terms than one which combines that with a threat of some form of retaliation. In recent times conventional deterrence has rested on denial strategies, which in ten out of twelve instances between 1938 and 1979 has failed, as John Mearsheimer demonstrated.[47] This failure rate of 83.3 per cent, Huntington pointed out, 'contrasts rather markedly with the zero failure rate for deterrence by nuclear retaliation for a quarter century after 1945'.

But, as we have seen, in the course of that quarter of a century the credibility of nuclear retaliation had been chipped away. During Eisenhower's administration this process inspired an interest in stronger general-purpose forces which, having failed to come about, by the early 1980s was taking on a hint of panic. As the ESECS Report's authors commented:

> The need for attention to NATO's conventional defensive capability is not new, but for several reasons it has acquired new urgency in recent years. . . . The growth of vast and varied nuclear forces on both sides has brought home to both peoples and governments the risks and consequences of nuclear war. Our present reliance on possible early use of nuclear weapons threatens to undermine the two main purposes of the Alliance – the need for credible deterrence of adversaries and effective reassurance of our own peoples. We find ourselves in strong and unanimous agreement that the Alliance should now move energetically to reduce its dependence on such early use.[48]

But how? As we have seen, the ESECS Report was to have no tangible repercussions. Even if it had, Huntington maintained, deterrence would not have been improved. In formulating his own proposals however, he was to make essentially the same miscalculation as the Steering Group of the ESECS. He advocated that in the event of a Warsaw Pact attack on NATO, the alliance should respond with a

> prompt conventional retaliatory offensive into Eastern Europe, . . . [as], politically speaking, the Soviet Union has more to lose from Allied armies invading Eastern Europe than NATO has to lose from Soviet armies invading Western Europe. The

Soviet Union should, consequently, give higher priority to preventing an Allied offensive into Eastern Europe than to pushing a
Soviet offensive into Western Europe.[49]

Current NATO strategy, he continued,

> already contemplates the possibility of a counteroffensive. It would
> occur after the enemy's offensive forces have penetrated NATO
> territory and then been slowed or brought to a halt and NATO
> forces have been reinforced. A counteroffensive follows sequen-
> tially after the enemy's offensive and is directed to retrieving the
> initiative and recovering occupied territory. A retaliatory offens-
> ive, in contrast, occurs simultaneously with the enemy's offensive.
> Its primary purpose is not to strike the enemy where he has further
> advanced, as is usually the case with a counteroffensive; rather it is
> to attack him in an entirely different sector.[50]

Whilst acknowledging the practical difficulties NATO had experienced in meeting its established conventional defence targets, Huntington maintained that these had been overemphasised. It would, he
suggested, be possible for example for NATO units to achieve local
superiority and mount a successful offensive through the exploitation
of mobility, deception, surprise and concentration of forces. 'Major
improvements' in stockpiles of fuel, ammunition and supplies would
of course be necessary to sustain an offensive movement, as would a
switch in weapons-procurement policies to favour those items most
relevant to offensive needs. Some redeployment of existing NATO
forces would also have to be undertaken, he conceded, together with
a construction of a line of fortifications along the inter-German
border.[51] Yet he regarded none of these material problems as insur-
mountable, and saw in the US Army's 1982 *Field Manual 100-5* –
which stressed manoeuvre warfare, including ripostes and strikes at
distances of up to 150 kilometres beyond the forward edge of the
main battlefield – and the Follow On Force Attack (FOFA) Sub-
Concept – which, devised by SHAPE staff between 1979 and 1981,
envisaged interdiction attacks up to 300 kilometres into Warsaw Pact
territory – the embryo of the military doctrine that might guide such
an offensive.[52] Indeed implementing a strategy that included conventional retaliation, he reasoned,

> requires more changes in the NATO military mind-set than it does
> in NATO military forces. For thirty years NATO has thought

about conventional warfare exclusively in defensive terms. . . . [It has] developed, as *The Economist* put it, 'a Maginot-line mentality without the Maginot line'.[53]

Huntington was not the first to use this sort of language. During this period the so-called 'defence reform movement' – which consisted almost exclusively of American thinkers[54] – was having a significant impact. It emphasised the need to exploit the West's advantages and the Warsaw Pact's weaknesses, and criticised what appeared to be excessive caution, if not defeatism, on NATO's part. The alliance seemed far too ready to surrender the initiative to its putative opponents. The 'Active Defence' doctrine of the US Army which, drawing on the lessons of Vietnam and the 1973 Arab–Israeli War, had been compiled in 1976, seemed to many to epitomise this lamentable attitude and was thus singled out for particular ridicule. It offered no chance of operational success, and indeed effectively portrayed stalemate as the military's objective. In seeking to fulfil its doctrinal commitment to 'winning the first battle', the US Army was accused of having forgotten all about winning the war. As one lieutenant-colonel observed: 'For an Army traumatized by ten years of tactical success culminating in operational failure, no critique could have been more devastating'.[55]

Stung and alarmed the US Army embarked on a policy of psychological regeneration which, it was hoped, would help reinvigorate the whole of NATO, doctrinally speaking. If attacked, it was argued, the alliance should be far less reactive and should compel the enemy to fight more on its own terms. Adopting dynamic manoeuvre warfare concepts which would exploit the strengths of new weapon systems – notably the AH-64 advanced attack helicopter, the M-1 tank, and the M-2 and M-3 combat vehicles – and 'carry the battle to the enemy' were regarded as the key to this new approach.

As we have seen, American thinkers had intermittently sought some means by which communism could not only be contained but also rolled back. NSC 68 for example made much of this objective, and we have noted the influence of such theorists as Professor Walt Rostow, who during the Kennedy era called for the 'facing down' of communism. Huntington's proposals and those of the 'defence reform movement' were essentially a continuation of this tradition. But, again as we have seen, such suggestions have regularly foundered on practical difficulties, and Huntington's were to be no different in this regard.

First, given that NATO was seriously doubting its ability to mount and sustain an effective forward defence, the notion that a very substantial part of what forces it had – Huntington suggested more than two entire corps[56] – could be diverted to prosecuting an offensive elsewhere seemed naive. Determining just how many resources could or should be switched from holding the front line to interdiction missions like FOFA and other 'secondary' but none the less important tasks had always been a thorny issue. However Huntington's assumptions about force requirements were exceptionally questionable. To mount such an offensive, the units would have to be in place from the very start of a conflict. This for example ruled out using American troops based in the USA; they would have to be stationed – and *stay* – in Europe, ready to react to a Warsaw Pact attack that might develop in hours and days rather than weeks and months.

Contrary to Huntington's reasoning however, the in-place forces would not have been sufficient to both hold such an attack and stage the proposed counteroffensive. The former mission alone was daunting enough, and simulations suggested that, even if NATO enjoyed a more favourable overall scenario than was probable, Huntington's offensive would call for at least ten to fifteen additional divisions.[57] Given that no new indigenous forces were likely to be created, this would entail a doubling of the US military presence in Europe. Where would all these troops be based and where, in crowded West Germany, would they train? Furthermore, to be effective offensive forces, they would have to be armoured and mechanised divisions – *not* the type of light units on which the US Army had throughout the late 1970s and early 1980s been focusing. Heavy divisions are fearsomely expensive, and require some 18 000 personnel each. According to Congressional Budget Office calculations in 1983, four would have cost some $38 000 million over five years, assuming they were based in the USA.[58] (If they were to be stationed abroad, additional balance of payment costs would be incurred.)

In view of the palpable reluctance of the Americans to maintain, let alone increase, the size of their military presence in Europe, it was clear that adopting Huntington's strategy would impose an intolerable burden. Perhaps as many as 480 000 new military personnel would have been required and this, given the financial cost of attracting volunteers, especially from a contracting manpower pool, would probably have made conscription unavoidable. Indeed had the US been prepared to make this sort of commitment to the conventional defence of Europe, NATO's lack of resources would have vanished – and with it a host of other troubles. There would have been no need for a change in strategy.

But assuming the forces were available, what would Huntington's offensive have achieved and what risks would it have involved? First, whereas for example FOFA and the 'AirLand Battle' codified by the US Army in 1982 in *Field Manual 100–5* are essentially military concepts with military objectives, his strategy was primarily a military concept with a grand political objective. The intention was to strike into the Eastern European satellites of the USSR, not just to thwart regional Soviet aggression in line with agreed NATO aims and restore the *status quo ante*, but to redraw the map of Europe. Huntington believed great things would stem from this. In peacetime the mere threat of a NATO invasion would encourage the Eastern Bloc states to restrain the USSR, and in the event of war he envisaged the collapse of the Soviet empire in Eastern Europe as, liberated by advancing NATO units, its oppressed peoples rose against their communist masters.

It is of course possible that, in these respects at least, Huntington's plan would have fulfilled his expectations. In other regards however the scheme and its potential consequences were fraught with doubts and difficulties. For instance, it rested on the assumption that the USSR would have given a 'higher priority to preventing an Allied offensive into Eastern Europe than to pushing a Soviet offensive into Western Europe'. Certainly such a counteroffensive by NATO would have caused its adversaries some irritation and a few practical problems, but nothing that could not have been dealt with relatively easily. For above all there would be a serious lack of balance in terms of risks and gains. Whilst the Warsaw Pact would have been tearing out the very geographic and political heart of the NATO Alliance, the latter, by threatening Leipzig or Prague, would have merely been assailing a military glacis. Even if one accepts the view that the Eastern Bloc states formed some kind of Soviet empire, its principal role was that of a political and military *cordon sanitaire* which was there to protect the USSR itself from the very sort of life-endangering blow Huntington's scheme sought to threaten. Indubitably the loss of Prague, or even the whole of Czechoslovakia, would have been a reverse for the USSR and its allies, but it would have been more than offset by the political leverage which would have accrued to them from the capture of, say, Bonn, Paris or Amsterdam. Indeed the return of any territorial losses they might have sustained would then be just one of the demands the Warsaw Pact could have been expected to table at any subsequent peace conference.

In short, Huntington's plan would not have been an effective use of military power when contrasted with that of the opposition. Furthermore any gains it did make would probably have proved ephemeral. Once it had lost the battle for its own heartland NATO would have had little option other than to sue for terms, even if it still had substantial units rampaging through the Eastern Bloc. Cut off without supplies and probably having lost both their political and strategic bearings, they would have faced annihilation sooner or later. In fact the military mission confronting any such group would have been challenging in the extreme, as two prominent critics observed:

> Not only would the force have to manoeuvre and fight its way into Eastern Europe, but also it would have to defend itself from the inevitable counterattack of the Soviet second strategic echelon [of some 24-36 divisions]. In addition it would have to defend a long and vulnerable supply line through hostile territory as well as a 360 degree defense perimeter. Each of these tasks is a difficult undertaking, particularly when the risk of nuclear war would be high. Trying to do all of them simultaneously is virtually impossible.[59]

Even had Huntington's counteroffensive strategy been a more practically viable proposition, its very nature would still have made it unpalatable to the European wing of NATO. Although it reflected the discontent felt by many Americans at surrendering the initiative to their communist adversaries and acquiescing in implied if not actual inferiority, it was wholly incompatible with NATO's declared goals as a defensive alliance, threatened to undermine any prospects for détente and seemed likely to aggravate instability in times of crisis. Hardly surprisingly, it found little favour with NATO's political and military hierarchy.

When taken in conjunction with similar ideas put forward by other academics, politicians and military men, Huntington's suggestions did have one very significant repercussion however. They seemed to confirm what many West German analysts especially saw as a potentially deadly trend. Misperceptions based on ignorance were common; numerous critics mistakenly confused purely national concepts like the Americans' *Air-Land Battle* with official NATO doctrine for example.[60] Similarly schemes such as FOFA and related references to the need for the capacity to stage counteroffensive operations to 'deter or respond to conventional aggression'[61] were not regarded by some as acknowledgements of military imperatives – notably the increasing importance of adding depth to the battlefield in order to compensate for the growing range and sophistication of conventional armaments and the mobility and size of attacking forces – but as a desertion of NATO's defensive mission; counterstroke concepts were taken for invasion plans. Indeed both NATO and the Warsaw Pact *appeared* bent on having force postures and strategies which, far from bringing greater security, made for instability. Their military preparations, essentially geared to worst-case assessments of the other side's capabilities, seemed offensive in character and could only exacerbate their potential opponent's fear of attack. Moreover, given the characteristics of many modern weapons, the potential for a sudden, disabling strike, which might well prove decisive in any conflict, looked greater than ever before: the attractions of preemption might, in a crisis, seem irresistible, whereas to delay and restrict oneself to reactive measures might prove literally fatal.

Thus, according to this school of thought, the two rival alliances were confronted by the common threat of war by miscalculation as much as that of war by design because of a politico–military framework which was inherently unsteady and incapable of supporting lasting peace. What was required, therefore, was thoroughgoing change in order to transform the confrontational relationship between East and West into a 'security partnership': theatre nuclear armaments should be abolished and conventional forces reduced and reformed so as to be incapable of offensive operations. If this could not be achieved through arms-control agreements then, some radicals argued, it should be done on a unilateral basis: once potential opponents no longer felt threatened, it was reasoned, they would follow suit and restructure their forces. In the meantime the new 'Just Defence' strategy and stance would allow a credible defence to be mounted should war occur, and would eventually help give birth to a new, worldwide political order under which disputes would be settled by agreed, peaceful procedures. Violent conflict would cease to be an instrument of policy.

2 Supporters and Models of 'Non-Offensive Defence'

'All opportunities should be explored, but . . . all consequent actions should take into account Soviet military capability as well as stated intentions. . . . If you live next door to an elephant, you watch his physique as well as his psyche.'
(Lord Carrington, when NATO's Secretary-General, on détente)

The notion of adopting 'Non-Offensive Defence' strategies has attracted appreciable if often fleeting support in a number of European countries especially. Its advocates are for the most part closely associated with the international 'Peace Movement' and belong to the left of the political spectrum. They include such diverse 'think-tanks' as the British–American Security Information Council (which in April 1989 published a *Comprehensive Concept of Defence and Disarmament for NATO* that recommended the embracing of 'Defensive Defence' principles), the British 'Just Defence' organisation, the Alternative Defence Commission, and the Institute for Defense and Disarmament Studies at Brookline, USA. Some university-affiliated institutions have also been to the fore in presenting the merits of these military postures, notably the School of Peace Studies at Bradford, UK, the *Institut für Friedensforschung und Sicherheitspolitik* of Hamburg University, and the Centre for Peace and Conflict Research at the University of Copenhagen, which publishes the *Non-Offensive Defence International Research Newsletter*.

Although some pressure groups and political parties in countries like Denmark, Britain and, more recently, Poland and the USSR have evinced an intermittent interest in 'Just Defence' and closely related ideas,[1] the fountainhead of the debate was West Germany and it is from there that most of the more elaborate proposals have emerged. Indeed the discussion there dates back to the early 1950s when, as we noted in Chapter 1, in preparation for the adoption of MC 14/2 as official NATO policy hundreds of short-range atomic weapons were deployed in West Germany. Alarmed by the introduction of these armaments, the use of which would entail horrendous consequences for the inhabitants of both German states, Bogislaw von Bonin sought to find some conventional military option that would furnish NATO with adequate security against a Warsaw Pact attack, and thus obviate the need for these indiscriminate and appallingly destructive weapons. Setting this imperative in a framework of broader security considerations, he proposed that West German strategic planning should be manifestly defensive.

Haunted by their dreadful experiences in the Second World War and by fears of a revanchist Germany, the Russians in particular and the East Europeans in general were understandably paranoid about the revival of German military power that the creation of the *Bundeswehr* signalled. These anxieties, Von Bonin argued, could only be heightened by the nature of the nascent German forces, the weaponry, doctrine and structure of which were 'inappropriate to their mission'. In place of the emerging *Panzer* divisions, he maintained, a 'strictly defence-orientated' border protection force should be created, made up of light infantry deployed in camouflaged bunkers amidst a dense network of minefields, natural and man-made obstacles, and anti-tank weapons. The *strukturelle Nichtangriffsfähigkeit* – structural inability to attack – of this force, Von Bonin claimed, would allay the suspicions and fears of West Germany's Eastern neighbours, whilst the 80 kilometre-deep defensive belt he envisaged would provide West Germay with sufficient safeguards against aggression.[2]

Von Bonin's proposals found little favour among the political and military hierarchies of either West Germany or NATO as a whole. Yet his ideas have been periodically resuscitated as people have sought for some robust, conventional defence that might be substituted for the current NATO strategy of 'Flexible Response' and the dilemmas therein. Acutely aware of the ruinous cost of two conventional world wars and that their country, as the dividing line between East and West, would form the main battlefield – perhaps a nuclear battlefield – in a third, the Germans especially have had an ineluctable stake in this quest and, particularly since the late 1970s, a number of German theorists have endeavoured to modernise and refine Von Bonin's model.

The first, and one of the most significant, of these contributions came from the distinguished philosopher and physicist Carl Friedrich von Weizäcker, the brother of the current *Bundespräsident*. During the 1970s he spearheaded an attack on the morality of nuclear deterrence and 'Flexible Response', suggesting that there might be better ways of preventing and, if necessary, fighting wars. A number of theorists subsequently joined the debate, the most notable being General Franz Uhle-Wettler, Horst and Eckhardt Afheldt, Norbert Hannig, Albrecht von Müller, Lutz Unterseher and the Study Group on Alternative Security (SAS) at Bonn, Jochen Löser, and the Social Democratic parliamentarians Andreas von Bülow, Egon Bahr, Karsten Voigt and Horst Ehmke.[3]

Between 1979 and 1989 the writings of these people had an increasing impact on West German domestic deliberations about defence policy: fascinated by the emerging alternative security concepts, the Social Democratic Party (SPD) began to shift to the left of the political spectrum in the wake of *Bundeskanzler* Schmidt's 'dual track' decision of 1979; support for the nascent Green Party which, again, was closely identified with the 'Peace Movement' began to flourish; while the Free Democratic Party (FDP) started an opportunistic realignment on defence issues which was ultimately to lead to the collection of stances known as 'Genscherism' after the celebrated Foreign Minister, Hans-Dietrich Genscher. Although there were substantial distinctions between the SPD and the FDP on issues such as economic affairs, during the build up to German reunification especially many members of the former party found Genscher's utterings on security and disarmament questions entirely in tune with their own. Indeed he seemed to be adopting some of their subversively unorthodox proposals to such an extent that, as one prominent SPD member complained, 'He should pay us royalties'.

So far as the SPD itself in concerned however, the real turning point over defence policy occurred at their conference in Nuremberg in August 1986. Developments at previous Party gatherings in Cologne and Essen, in 1982 and 1984 respectively, had presaged what was to transpire, and the policy document that emerged was subsequently refined by the SPD's parliamentarians in the spring of the same year. The fundamental aims of the security policy to be found in these documents can be summarised as follows.

First, the revival of the Von Bonin concept of *Nichtangriffsfähigkeit* by the redesigning of armed forces and their strategies and weapon inventories. Units would be rendered incapable of mounting substantial assaults and would thus appear unthreatening to neighbouring countries. This would, the policy's proponents argue, reduce the advantages afforded by pre-emptive strikes and therefore be an important stabilising factor in times of international tension. Moreover recent developments in military technology – notably in the fields of surveillance, target-acquisition and weapon lethality – have, they believe, endowed the defender with significant advantages over the attacker. The mobility and armoured protection of the latter's forces have only improved marginally, whereas the defender's ability to fight from prepared positions on familiar territory, allocating firepower accurately and remotely, has increased dramatically. Armed with precision-guided weapons, and concealed and dispersed to evade detection and destruction, ubiquitous penny packets of light infantry could, it is claimed, pour a deadly hail of fire on any invading force – ensnared in a web of minefields and other obstacles, the attacker would soon face a choice between annihilation or surrender. So besides any political benefits it may confer, 'Defensive Defence' is regarded by its advocates as being strategically and tactically superior.

Precise measures to bring about the restructuring of armed forces include: the renunciation of such doctrines and concepts as FOFA, 'deep strike' and other interdiction operations; the replacement of 'offensive' units, like armoured vehicles, combat aviation and long-range missiles, with immobile 'defensive' forces such as small detachments of light infantry armed with anti-tank weaponry and dispersed and ensconced throughout an 'area defence' comprising man-made and natural bastions; the removal of bridging trains and other support equipment necessary for sustained offensive operations; greater employment of militia, home guard and other reservist personnel; the removal of all nuclear weapons (at least at the theatre level); and the supplanting of NATO's strategy of 'Flexible Response' by a new *Gesamtkonzept* based on the notion of 'Common Security', *Gemeinsame Sicherheit*. Parallel with these steps, extensive arms-control is also to be pursued, aimed at the complete elimination of nuclear arsenals and the reversal of recent arms-races. Disarmament initiatives such as the Conventional Armed Forces in Europe (CFE I) Treaty are to be followed by further measures of this genre, whilst the American Strategic Defense Initiative and the related development of anti-satellite systems are to be resisted. Chemical and biological warfare capabilities are to be outlawed, and the introduction of new nuclear weapons, or the modernisation of old ones, is to be rejected. As a preliminary step towards total nuclear disarmament, such weapons are to be cleared from various zones in Central Europe, as we suggested in the Jaruzelski Plan of 1988, the Palme Commission Report of 1983 and the Rapacki Plan of 1957.

To the supporters of 'Just Defence', the reciprocal unease

provoked by the other side's offensive capabilities suggested that both NATO and the Warsaw Pact needed to alter their military policies if international stability was to be preserved. The widespread development and deployment of increasingly sophisticated missiles armed with nuclear warheads was seen as a particular cause for concern. Egon Bahr, for instance, was to caution in 1983 that 'The shorter the flight and . . . warning times become, the greater are the risks of becoming the victims of technical errors or mistakes to which human beings must respond because and as their instruments tell them they must'.[4] This smacks of 'Stop the world; I want to get off'. Yet as far as some *conventional* weaponry was concerned, the relentless, onward march of technology was seen as being potentially stabilising and beneficial; it might allow for the creation of a credible defensive shield of the type for which, as we saw in Chapter 1, NATO had perpetually been searching. Bahr, no fan of 'Flexible Response', had himself conceded that 'As long as there is no new strategy, the old one must be kept. No radical unilateral acts can bring us more security'.[5] Now some form of viable, non-provocative defence did seem to be in the offing. With it the need for interdiction plans like FOFA – which in the event of a crisis might put both alliances in a 'gunfighter scenario', desperately seeking to beat the other to the draw – would disappear and, above all, NATO could finally be weaned off its seemingly suicidal nuclear addiction.[6]

The nomenclature applied to these 'Just Defence' strategic models is already large and continues to grow. The most commonly used terms are 'Non-Offensive-' and 'Defensive Defence', but 'Inoffensive Deterrence', 'Non-Provocative Defence' and 'Defensive Deterrence' are also widespread. Some would claim that these contrasting titles reflect an array of conceptual nuances. However, as we shall see, drawing intellectually satisfying distinctions between even defence and attack can be very problematic – and is perhaps becoming more so. The various terms for 'Non-Offensive Defence' will therefore be treated as synonymous for the purposes of this book. Similarly, while some contrasts can be made between the various *Raumverteidigung* – area defence – blueprints that have been advanced, an in-depth examination of each and every model lies beyond the scope of a work of this size. They are essentially variations on a theme and it would be impractical to approach them differently. Some discussion of their more salient points is, however, as desirable as it is necessary.

Horst Afheldt – who worked alongside Carl Friedrich von Weizäcker and was strongly influenced by his thinking, as well as that of Von Bonin and the French theorist Guy Brossolet[7] – was the first German thinker to produce a *Raumverteidigung* model in the 1980s. His initial plan envisaged the *Abhaltung* – ensnaring and checking – of any invading force by some 10 000 'technocommando' teams of 20–30 men, each of which would cover several square kilometres of territory. To the front would be regular troops ready to react to sudden attacks while, to the rear, more use would be made of local reservists. Any aggressor would be assailed by fire from short-range artillery and rockets scattered throughout the countryside and linked by an integrated communications network. As we shall see in more detail later, Afheldt also advocated the retention of some armoured 'firebrigade' or 'spider' units to support this web defence as and when necessary, as well as an ultimate guarantee in the form of American strategic nuclear forces.[8]

Norbert Hannig, a retired airforce officer and aircraft industry consultant, put forward a rather fanciful scheme for a four-kilometre-wide belt of defences along the inter-German frontier. Cleared of inhabitants and constantly monitored by electrical sensors, this *Grenznahe Feuerzone* would, in the event of attack, be saturated with shells, mines and terminally-guided munitions fired by artillery, rockets and mortars deployed in echelons according to their range. Interdiction strikes would in the meantime be executed with conventionally-armed missiles. Anti-tank helicopters and mobile light units would counter any breakthroughs that did occur, while *desant* operations and other threats to the belt's rear would be dealt with by swinging parts of its batteries through 180 degrees – a suggestion which earned the scheme the sobriquet 'FOFA in reverse'. Indeed Hanning's model did rely excessively on advanced technology and an easily-disrupted, centralised command network, while its logistical demands threatened to be as insatiable as they would be costly. Johannes Gerber subsequently endeavoured to improve it, but neither plan ever overcame the doubts of their many critics.

Albrecht von Müller was influenced by Afheldt and weaved together several of his and other theorists ideas in an imaginative scheme, the 'Integrated Forward Defence'. This too would include a border 'fire barrier' that would extent for several kilometres on the friendly side of the frontier, but would also, in the event of hostilities, take in territory some 40–60 kilometres beyond it. Behind the fire belt, Von Müller envisaged a web of local light infantry teams of between 20 and 50 kilometres in depth, to the rear of which would be a 'manoeuvre zone' where dispersed, heavily armoured 'firebrigade' units would intercept any hostile forces that succeeded in penetrating the forward layers of the *Raumverteidigung*. Finally, a 'rear defence zone', comprising the rest of the hinterland, would be protected by local, semi-mobile troops designed to counter *desant* attacks and raids by special operations units. Unlike most of his colleagues in the 'Defensive Defence' lobby, Von Müller favours a degree of 'conditional punishment' in the event of aggression. He recognises the need for both sufficient counterattack capabilities to retake lost territory and close interdiction strikes to retard and diminish the flow of enemy forces and *matériel* to the front. The second of these missions, he argues, could largely be carried out with cruise and other missiles rather than the model's relatively few aircraft which, mostly of vertical-take-off designs such as the British *Harrier*, could be dispersed to help evade destruction and yet swiftly concentrated to secure air superiority over friendly territory. Such provisions do give this posture greater military viability but, as they contradict the basic tenets of 'Just Defence', are regarded as heretical by the mainstream traditionalists.

Major-General Jochen Löser's *Raumdeckende Verteidigung* of 1981 proposed a frontier defence zone of 80–100 kilometres. In common with Horst Afheldt, he suggested the large scale use of reservists to effectively double the number of brigades in the *Bundeswehr*. Again the 'shield' forces nearest the border were to be composed of regular troops, whereas the second-echelon 'sword' units would mostly consist of mobilised reserves. Instead of relying on sophisticated, high-technology armaments as favoured by Afheldt, Löser's 'shield' troops were to be moulded on traditional *Jäger* – specialist light infantry – and would fight an attritional battle to blunt any offensive, exploiting advantages offered by terrain features and generally conducting a mercurial, *petite guerre* using fast, light vehicles and light weapons. Minefields and other prepared obstacles would serve as hinges for their mobile operations which, when the opportunity presented itself, would be reinforced by the heavy armour of the 'sword' forces. After a transitional period however, Löser favoured replacing most of these latter units with light infantry and armoured cavalry; barriers would be employed to funnel invading forces into 'killing zones' where they could be destroyed by remotely-delivered, concentrated fire.

In this regard the influence of General Uhle-Wettler's *Gefechtsfeld Mitteleuropa* of 1980 also deserves mentioning. He noted that topographical change had transformed much of NATO's Central Front – afforestation, urbanisation and enclosure had rendered large tracts of West Germany unsuitable for the movement *en masse* of heavy armoured forces. Arguing that only the North German Plain and parts of lower Bavaria were sufficiently free of wooded, hilly, enclosed or built-up areas to permit such units to manoeuvre and fight efficaciously, Uhle-Wettler suggested that more attention should be given to the utilisation of light infantry in defence planning. Studies undertaken in the early 1980s at the *Akademie der Bundeswehr* in Munich seemed to support this view,[9] and by 1985 Lieutenant-General von Sandrart, then Chief-of-Staff of the *Bundeswehr*, was stressing the importance of mobile defence based on settlements, minefields and other obstacles. Such positions, he concluded, 'could be used by light infantry, giving them better protection and serving as cornerstones in a highly mobile defence battle'.[10] As we shall see, the Russians had already deduced much the same and were planning to adjust their force-structures, strategy and tactics accordingly.

Such strictly limited and specialist applications of light infantry are however greatly at odds with the blanket use advocated by the 'Defensive Defence' school. Moreover the notion of using urban areas as battle stations is one that they find repellent. In fact they put considerable emphasis on civilian defence measures. Large conurbations are deliberately omitted from most *Raumverteidigung* models and the majority of theorists attach great importance to *Heimschutz-regimenter* – home defence regiments – both as integral parts of a country-wide defence network and as forces dedicated to the protection of installations against raids by special operations forces, airborne assaults and other deep incursions. Hannig's model, for example, also calls for large-scale, civilian evacuation schemes for use in a crisis, while Löser's proposes the provision of more civil defence shelters. Ironically however, the 'nation in arms' approach favoured by the 'Defensive Defence' lobby is likely to obscure any distinctions between combatants and non-combatants, making these and other endeavours to protect the civilian population from the ravages of war appear quite incongruous.

'Damage limitation' measures and home guard units also feature prominently in the SAS model which is already one of the most detailed and continues to undergo refinement. The main defensive system, however, comprises a web defence of some 250 battalions of infantry dispersed across a frontier zone of 100–130 kilometres in depth. This zone would initially cover the Western side of the former inter-German border, but would subsequently be extended to encompass the territory of the old *Demokratische Republik*. The web infantry units would be skeletonised with only 25 per cent of them being active personnel, the balance of their strength coming from reservists who could be mobilised on a local, decentralised basis within 24 hours. As in all other models, these forces and their call-up system are depicted as 'non-provocative' so as to preserve stability in the event of a crisis; they are doctrinally and structurally incapable of attacking an opponents's territory and, by being scattered and individually insignificant, do not constitute lucrative targets that might invite pre-emptive strikes. To give them further protection, the model proposes the use of dispersed bunkers which, it is suggested, could be quickly erected from prefabricated kits.

The web units are regarded as capable of fulfilling four main functions. They are: to delay and canalise intruding ground forces, block and decimate airborne assaults, operate and protect a decentralised network of supply depots, and present, by gathering intelligence – which is to be disseminated via a vast, buried communications system – and retarding any invasion, both a clear picture of events and sufficient time for 'rational political decision-making'. As far as armaments are concerned, they would primarily utilise weapons which would allow their operators to remain under cover: multi-sensor mines; remotely-controlled, low-weight direct-fire weapons; rapid-fire mortars; shoulder-fired air-defence missiles; and combat drones such as the American Fibre-Optic Guided Missile. Other categories of equipment would also be employed, but on a much smaller scale. These would include armoured vehicles with high-velocity guns, mechanised tube and rocket artillery systems with ranges of up to 50 kilometres, and 'multi-purpose' helicopters which, among other things, would be expected to perform anti-tank missions. 'Deep strike' weapons would be avoided, partly because of their exotic, expensive high-technology nature, but principally because of their 'destabilising characteristics'. Some 300 *Harrier*-type fighters, supported by a mobile base infrastructure, would, together with numerous clusters of surface-to-air missiles, be entrusted with the provision of air-defence.

In support of the web infantry there would also be around 100 battalions formed into small 'spider' units of armour, mechanised light infantry and armoured cavalry. These would be drawn from several NATO Armies, would be tailored to suit terrain conditions in their allotted zones of the net and would contain a very high proportion (90 per cent) of regular personnel. This, it is reasoned, would furnish a substantial, mobile force to protect the web troops during the initial stages of mobilisation and to interact with them once battle is joined. Dispersed to begin with, they would be expected to concentrate in order to contain, counterattack and ultimately destroy intruding forces. Outside of the net however, the 'spider' elements would lack a capacity for offensive operations and would thus not be seen as provocative or threatening by neighbouring states.

Lastly, the SAS model is unusual in that, unlike most 'Defensive Defence' variants, it has been extended to cover maritime security. It proposes the close integration of the German Baltic defences with those of the Danish islands and Jutland. Fighter bombers and submarines would be removed from the order-of-battle, and in their place 15–20 mobile coastal-defence units would be deployed. They would have anti-ship missiles carried on light but armoured platforms which would move randomly between dispersed, hardened and well camouflaged firing positions. Twenty fast patrol boats and a similar number of medium helicopters, again armed with anti-ship missiles, would support this network from several dispersed (heli)ports, as would a flotilla of mine-laying vessels capable of sowing semi-intelligent mines in straits and vital coastal areas.

Concentrating the German Navy on a coastal defence in closer cooperation with the Danes, while Britain, the Netherlands and the USA undertake the 'blue water' missions involved in securing the North and Norwegian Seas might well be seen as a burden-sharing and role-specialisation formula which could offer some advantages. But if the emphasis is really to be on 'Non-Offensive Defence', then such proposals could lead – as they have in the past – to difficulties. For a period during the mid 1980s Denmark was infected with West Germany's 'Defensive Defence' cold. Hans Engell, Minister of Defence until September 1987, and the former Chief of the Defence Staff, Colonel G.K. Kristensen, were perhaps the most prominent participants in a debate that deeply divided Danish society. Matters came to a climax over the issue of nuclear warheads on visiting NATO warships,[11] and although a general election in May 1988 essentially resolved the dispute, it was palpable that some members of the politico–military hierarchy had concluded that a 'Defensive Defence' stance would prove inimical to membership of NATO's integrated military command if not the alliance itself.

After these distressing events, Denmark's fascination with 'Just Defence' abated considerably. In Germany however the debate continued and, as the Cold War gradually passed into history, some people sensed that alternative military postures were about to acquire greater significance. Not only did NATO's 'Flexible Response' appear increasingly anachronistic, but Eastern Bloc member states were also expressing interest in strategic reforms to parallel the revolution that was underway in their domestic social, political and economic structures.

Indeed as early as 1987 signs of *novoye myshleniye* – 'new thinking' – could be detected within the Warsaw Treaty Organisation's armed services. A summit in Berlin that May outlined measures to convince NATO that the Warsaw Pact's doctrine was 'non-offensive'. Declarations of peaceful intent carried little weight, it was conceded, if the nature and deployment of military power looked menacing. As Admiral Alexander Astafyev pointed out, this meant that arms-control would have to go beyond cutting numbers to redesigning 'armed forces as well as the character of their weapons and their military–strategic concepts'.[12] To Western eyes, it was acknowledged, the Warsaw Pact's general capacity for sudden, massive offensive operations could only look threatening, while its powerful, tank-heavy OMGs, airborne assault units and other deep-penetration forces were singled out for particular criticism.

A few weeks before this summit, Gorbachev had spoken of possible 'measures to reduce and, best of all, eliminate the possibility of suprise attack by removing the most dangerous offensive arms from the zone of contact [Central Europe]',[13] and even prior to this, at the Twentyseventh Congress of the Soviet Communist Party in 1986, had stated his willingness to 'limit military potentials to reasonable sufficiency', depending on 'the positions and actions of the US and its partners'. All of this was followed in December 1988 by his celebrated speech to the United Nations General Assembly in which he announced unilateral force reductions by the USSR totalling 500 000 personnel. Large numbers of tanks, together with bridging equipment and air assault units were also to be withdrawn from Eastern Europe.

The 'Defensive Defence' movement understandably hailed these developments as a sign that the USSR and its allies were unreservedly embracing their creed. However the details of what was occuring within the Soviet armed forces suggest, as we shall see in Chapter 4, something quite different; the Army in particular was reforming itself not so much to be more 'defensive' as the advocates of 'Just Defence' would comprehend it but, rather, better able to cope in a new technological and tactical environment. Similarly, on the level of international politics, Moscow's decision to reduce its forward-deployed forces and evacuate its *cordon sanitaire* in Eastern Europe were to be greeted as important gestures by NATO. Yet this and the various other arms-control and political initiatives that emerged during this period should not be attributed entirely to altruism, welcome though they were. In fact they were reflections of the acceptance of certain harsh realities. As we have seen, just as the USA had progressively found sustaining the armed might necessary to wage a world-wide war too much of a burden, so too had the Russians been compelled to move towards a less ambitious foreign and military policy. Furthermore, gradual changes in weapons technology and the geostrategic situation had made 'defence sufficiency' as militarily rational as it was economically desirable.

Huge conventional forces and an Eastern European glacis had been the logical way to defend a Russia confronted by military power of a predominantly conventional nature. But once the proliferation of atomic warheads began and was linked to missile technology, the protection afforded by Russia's sheer size started to wane: the main threat ceased to be an invasion by general-purpose forces and became instead that of attack by nuclear-tipped missiles. Unless this threat could be abolished through arms-control, it was best dealt with by deterrence in kind. This however brought the need for such large conventional forces still more into question. Moreover, throughout the 1980s but especially after the Chernobyl calamity, the Russians came to appreciate just how disastrous the repercussions of any nuclear exchange would be. Victory, in any meaningful sense, could not be achieved.[14]

Sooner or later Soviet defence policy had to alter to take account of these factors. Gorbachev, pushed along by economic imperatives, began the necessary changes which, although executed with a speed the services found unsettling, have evidently been accepted. It was only by persuading his military staffs that reform could be safely implemented that Gorbachev secured this. NATO, he convinced them, was not a threatening alliance. Indeed, ironically the new Soviet 'defensive' doctrine and concomitant notion of 'defence sufficiency' bear more than a passing resemblance to NATO's 'Flexible Response' and the concept of deterrence at bearable cost.

The Russians therefore seem more relaxed about NATO's current military posture than do the supporters of 'Non-Offensive Defence' who advocate radical revisions to make it appear more benign. But as we have noted, the 'Just Defence' lobby is closely identified with the 'Peace Movement' and regards its prescriptions as part of a grand crusade for a 'non-aggressive world'.[15] As such, their alternative defence concepts can be seen as new solutions to a problem that has bedevilled mankind since history began, and it is to the details of this that we will now turn.

3 War, Peace and Collective Security

'The most persistent sound which reverberates through man's history is the beating of war drums.'
(Arthur Koestler, *Janus: A Summing Up*, Prologue)

'They start bloody wars they can't afford . . . [like] that old fool Chamberlain. . . . "Peace in our time". . . . Didn't give a thought to the cost of it. Didn't enter his head to go into a few figures, get an estimate – soppy old sod.'
(Alf Garnett in *The Bird Fancier* by Johnny Speight)

In a piece that predated her own country's 1989 invasion of Panama, and its massive intervention the following year in the Persian Gulf, Randall Forsberg, Director of the Institute for Defense and Disarmament Studies in Brookline, Massachusetts, and an ardent supporter of 'Defensive Defence', spoke of 'The end of conventional warfare among the big powers'. This, she insisted,

represents a sea change in human history. . . . It signals the beginning of the end of war . . . because it involves an unprecedented constraint on the use of force as a tool of power. . . . We *have* ended war, at least . . . among some countries. [But people] . . . think we *cannot* end war; it lies too deeply embedded in human nature. . . . We must change the deeply held belief that we cannot avoid war indefinitely, except perhaps by [retaining] nuclear annihilation as the penalty. . . .

If the big powers continue to threaten to . . . intervene militarily . . . whenever their perceived 'interests' warrant it, fear of conventional war among the big powers will be sustained. . . . Leaders and citizens of countries . . . who are prepared to use force to achieve political . . . ends in the Third World can reasonably be expected to consider going to war in the northern hemisphere . . . if the penalty of nuclear annihilation is eliminated.[1]

Ms. Forsberg's primary aim in writing these words was to advocate the adoption of a policy of non-intervention by the major powers in

71

the affairs of the Third World, although one could conclude that instead, and almost unwittingly, she argued a strong case for the retention if not proliferation of nuclear weapons – 'an unprecedented constraint on the use of force as a tool of power' – which, in a deterrence framework, have been so effective in bringing about 'the end of war' among at least some of the big powers of the Northern Hemisphere. However she finds this situation disagreeable and, whilst stressing that if the risk of nuclear annihilation were greatly reduced or eliminated ordinary citizens could *not* be confident that their leaders would do everything humanely possible to avoid war, she looks forward to an age in which people will

> Learn to avoid conventional war permanently, by choice, without having to live under the risk of nuclear war. . . . A Third World nonintervention regime will help instill and reinforce internalized inhibitions against the use of force as an instrument of power. . . . As democratic institutions have grown . . . in many different arenas, the use of force to advance interests has declined as socially accepted behaviour, leaving defence against such uses by others as the only legitimate role.[2]

Whatever the merits and demerits of these views, much of Ms. Forsberg's language is typical of a school of thought which, perhaps rather ominously, has existed now for many decades. She predicts the 'end of war', criticises the tendency of states to employ force to achieve political ends and protect their perceived interest, and maintains that, with the diffusion of liberal democratic values, such practices are becoming illegitimate. Like many before her, she advocates détente and disarmament as the route to a stable peace, and cites the Scandinavians as examples of 'imperialistic warring nations' which have been transformed into peoples 'among whom war is unthinkable even *without* armed deterrence'.[3]

The philosophical roots of the 'Defensive Defence' lobby extend deep into the history of the analysis of the causes of peace and war. In the sixteenth century classical scholar Desiderius Erasmus, for instance, we find an early example of a man who, repelled essentially on humanitarian grounds by the apparent wastefulness and irrationality of war, dismissed it as foolish and unnatural. By way of contrast Sir Thomas More, a statesman, intellectual and devout catholic, was to offer a Utopian vision of how Christian 'just war' theory might be applied to render conflicts as innocuous as possible.[4] For unlike

Erasmus, More realised it was not enough to bemoan the scarcely disputable fact that war was repugnant. Given the realities of the state system, it remained the one means by which disputes could ultimately be resolved. Anyone and everyone might deplore that. The real issue however was how armed conflict, if it was ineluctable, could best be controlled whenever it occurred.

During the Seventeenth and Eighteenth Centuries, these and connected strands of thinking were weaved together by such writers as Emeric Crucé, Hugo Grotius, Thomas Hobbes, Jean Jacques Rousseau and the other *philosophes*, Jeremy Bentham, Immanuel Kant and Thomas Paine. Often views diverged. Hobbes and Kant, for example, argued that war was a natural phenomenon: man, in nature, was violent and so the threat of conflict was ever present. Montesquieu on the other hand claimed that in his presocietal state man was peace-loving and too weak to wage war. That capacity had only been endowed by the collective strength of society. Thus war was an unnatural evil which grew out of structured society. The latter was therefore to be condemned rather than war justified. Whilst Francis Bacon and John Locke suggested that states themselves were in a state of nature and war was thus an entirely natural phenomenon, Rousseau argued, like Montesquieu, that it stemmed from the development of organised society which had corrupted and restricted mankind. But how could Adam be returned to a state of innocence after this Fall?

The answer to Rousseau and many of the other great thinkers of the Enlightenment lay in regenerating society and the nature of international trade. By the second half of the Eighteenth Century, Adam Smith and his disciples in Britain and the Physiocrats in France were mounting increasingly effective assaults on the bastions of mercantalism. War, they argued, was ceasing to pay and yet was so often provoked by commercial disputes. Free trade should be adpted so as to strengthen the interdependence of individuals and nations which natural law stipulated: economic interests coincided rather than clashed, and to believe otherwise was a misperception. Similarly the *philosophes* took the view that war was caused by misunderstandings and by the social dominance enjoyed by warrior classes. Together with foreign policy, warfare was conducted according to professional protocol and remained the last exclusive privilege of the crown. It was a great game which, according to William Cowper, 'were their subjects wise, kings would not play at'.

Indeed, far from appearing as a comparatively orderly, reasoned

and civilised medium for controlling conflict and checking its ex-
cesses, the rituals of eighteenth century warfare and diplomacy struck
the *philosophes* as being a barbaric and sinister mechanism whose
sole function was to consolidate the power, prestige and other vested
interests of the establishment, both at home and abroad. If, through
the introduction of a political system in which popular interests were
genuinely represented, absolutism were to be abolished, then war
would also disappear. International disputes, like domestic ones,
would be resolved by appropriate institutions, and mankind would
return to his natural state of living in perfect harmony.

But as the *raison d'être* of the ruling elites was so bound up with
perpetuating a *status quo* which had a propensity for war at its heart,
any attempt to abolish the latter need must have also entailed the end
of the former. Kant for example saw the creation of 'republican
governments' – those in which the supreme power is invested in the
people or their elected representatives rather than in a monarch – as
an essential part of any process leading to 'the general and continuous establishment of peace'.[5] Clearly however the selfish European
monarchies would never agree to this, so, to thinkers like Rousseau,
the Marquis de Condorcet and Thomas Paine – all of whom firmly
believed that *le peuple* were essentially peace-loving and only became
involved in wars through the evil machinations of their rulers –
revolution, as had been demonstrated in the case of Britain's
American colonies where, in 1776, Paine's pamphlet *Common Sense*
had had such an impact, was the only solution. Once the *ancien
régime* had been swept away, man would be liberated, as Paine put it
in his *Rights of Man*, from the 'savage idea of considering his species
his enemy', and a new 'morning of reason' would break.

That such notions would appeal to and flow from the thinkers of
the Enlightenment is scarely surprising. Throughout the Eighteenth
Century the gospel of Newtonian science had been gaining converts
all over Europe, and by the 1730s, having enjoyed the unstinting
support of François-Marie Voltaire, the great pioneer of the *philosophes*, had firmly established itself in France especially. It was not so
much the details of Newton's physics and mathematical verities that
fascinated the bulk of the intelligentsia but rather what this triumph
of science and reason suggested; namely that there was an enduring,
rational framework within which *every* aspect of reality could be
analysed. This ideal concept of universal knowledge permeated the
numerous barriers – notably religious antipathy and disputes over
constitutional theory – which otherwise divided the *philosophes* and

united them in the belief that mankind could come to comprehend everything, including the causes of peace and war.

But as Michael Howard phrased it, whatever morning was being heralded by the French Revolution, it was scarcely that of Reason, let alone of peace.[6] Only months after Paine's *Rights of Man* appeared, the French Legislative Assembly declared war on Austria. Amid cries of 'the constitution or death', the People's deputies voted to wage total war, to win absolute victory or suffer annihilation – a decision that was later emphasised by the *levée en masse* decree of August 1793.[7] Gradually, as the fighting engulfed more and more of Europe and culminated in the great national liberation struggles of the German *Befreiungskrieg* and the Spanish *Guerra de la Independencia*, it became clear that this war was unprecedented in scale, intensity and ferocity. Yet faith in the liberal theories of international relations as espoused by the Enlightenment survived surprisingly unscathed. Nor was it to be totally destroyed by either the periodic bouts of bloodletting which, as a supposedly legitimate part of the various struggles for nationhood, blighted much of the remainder of the Nineteenth Century, or the two World Wars of the Twentieth. Despite the spread of 'government of the people, by the people, for the people', the burgeoning of commerce, trade and assorted other transnational links, the ascendancy of *les industrieux* and other prosperous *bourgeoisie* and the related, progressive removal or limitation of the power of the old, aristocratic establishments, war stubbornly defied eradication. How could this apparent contradiction be reconciled with the theories of these first-generation peace researchers?

From around the end of the French Revolutionary and Napoleonic Wars, one can discern the emergence of what was to become known as the 'Peace Movement'. In 1816 a Quaker, William Allen, established the London-based Society for the Promotion of Permanent and Universal Peace, and a similar organisation was also founded in the USA. Much like its modern day descendant, the 'Peace Movement' of the early Nineteenth Century was an international political body, largely dominated by middle-class liberals who believed war to be unnatural, obsolescent or immoral, wasteful and irrational, and the product of selfish, irresponsible, governmental systems. The American Peace Society for instance agitated for the abolition of armed conflict through the foundation of a 'Congress of Nations'. This would settle 'all national controversies by an appeal to reason, as becomes rational creatures', and its decrees would be 'enforced by public opinion that rules the world'.[8]

Such notions were not exactly new. Crucé, for example, had proposed a form of pan-European security organisation as early as 1623, while Bentham, in his *Plan for a Universal and Perpetual Peace* of 1789, had recommended the establishment of a 'Common Court of Judicature' which, like the United Nations Organisation (UNO) of the Twentieth Century, would dispose of international troop contingents should its rulings need enforcing. Similarly the Helsinki, Pugwash and other great peace conferences of our time had their precursors. From 1848 annual 'Peace Congresses' were held in different European cities until the outbreak of the Crimean War in 1854 – the first major conflict to involve the great powers for nigh on 40 years – shattered a few hopes. Among other factors, the evident apprehension of the British government could not have contrasted more starkly with the boundless enthusiasm for war evinced by so great a part of the population as a whole. Again this type of bellicose nationalism, which had first surfaced during the French Revolutionary Wars, was all too irreconcilable with the fundamental tenet of the liberal creed: that it was only the ruling classes and their entourages which had any relish for war; the people, given the choice and the right to speak for themselves, would always prefer peace.

The utilitarian reasoning of people like Bentham, Paine and James and John Stuart Mill fused with that of Free Trade activists like Jean-Baptiste Say, Richard Cobden and John Bright to give the message of the 'Peace Movement' an intellectual dignity which, often conveyed with a pursuasive oratorical flair, rendered it as enticing as it seemed worthy. But its prescription for eternal peace – free trade, disarmament, non-intervention, the shunning of colonial or continental entanglements, and the settlement of disputes by arbitration – was not universally welcomed or venerated. With the outbreak of the Crimean War, Bright and Cobden, for instance, found themselves increasingly at odds not just with public opinion in general but with that of the very manufacturing and trading classes whose views they had once believed themselves to personify. Like virtually all of the thinkers mentioned here, they were not absolute pacifists. In contrast to Jonathan Dymond, a prominent 'Peace Movement' activist from the Quaker tradition who had refused to distinguish even between 'defensive' and 'offensive' wars,[9] they accepted the need for what to day is termed 'defence sufficiency' and acknowledged national self-defence as a legitimate cause. But they were highly critical of 'costly war establishments' and regarded the Crimean conflict as just another case of unnecessary, expensive, overseas adventurism; the

British government's concern for the 'balance of power' was dismissed as iconolatry, while the public's zest for the war was to be seen in terms of their corruption by a pugnacious aristocracy. Nor did the end of hostilities bring any comfort for the two beleaguered radicals. Cobden for example, having lost the constituency he had held since 1841, was not re-elected to Parliament until 1859. He then declined Cabinet office, however, in order to remain an independent critic, ready to champion any cause which might further his ideals. By the end of his life in 1865 he was a sadly disillusioned man.[10]

Whilst the butchery at Magenta and Solferino during the 1859 war launched by the French – ostensibly to help the Italian national cause – did increase the clamour for some form of transnational medical service and thus helped establish the Red Cross, there was nothing else about the conflict that gave the 'Peace Movement' grounds for optimism. Indeed worse was to follow. The concert of great European states – which since the 1815 Vienna Congress had done much to help preserve a balance of power and avoid potentially dangerous confrontations – was gradually losing its cohesion, while beyond the Atlantic the Americans embarked on a civil war that not only claimed well over 600 000 lives and resulted in widespread devastation but also divided their society right down to the family level. Meanwhile in 1864 the Germanic states pushed aside the little Danish Army and annexed Schleswig-Holstein. This was however just the first phase of Bismarck's scheme for German unification. Only two years later the Prussians turned on their Austrian brethren and, in an especially gory confrontation at Sadowa, conclusively smashed Vienna's claims to dominance within Germany. Then, in the Franco–Prussian War of 1870–1, France in turn was defeated. The peace treaty which among other things transferred Alsace-Lorraine to the victorious German emperor in classic, eighteenth century style, might have seemed somewhat anachronistic in an age of growing national consciousness with its concomitant notion of self-determination. But as Gerhard Ritter was to conclude in 1954, it was out of the Franco–Prussian and these other nineteenth century conflicts that there arose 'that sinister problem of modern national war, from which the great catastrophes of our [own] epoch have developed, and on which we have foundered twice in succession'.[11]

Indeed, in the rock of bellicose nationalism the tide of the 'Peace Movement' found a formidable opponent. The former mocked the latter's priggish naïvety, highlighted its parochialism and insularity, and rebuffed the assumptions that underpinned so much of its reasoning: *le peuple* could be as illiberal and truculent as their aristocratic masters; the balance of power had to be taken seriously, however unpalatable the implications of that might sometimes be; international courts and the like could only have limited authority, since the utilitarians' belief that all nations, and their cultures and values, were homogeneous, or could be made so, was palpably flawed; and prescriptions such as free trade, far from being a panacea for the prevention of war, often only served to confirm and maintain the dominance of the more industrially and commercially developed countries over the weaker ones – a state of affairs which all too often spawned resentment, rivalry and conflict.

After 1815 the conviction that, as a prelude to eternal peace, 'just' wars were necessary to liberate nations and establish the legitimate, natural frontiers of their states manifested itself in a dozen sizeable conflicts which extended across the globe from the USA through France and Germany to Italy and the Balkans. With the end of the Franco–Prussian War in 1871 however, an important turning point seemed to have been reached. The great powers of Europe and North America, having achieved nationhood, appeared to be settling down to an era of growing cooperation. From the ashes of war had risen the phoenix of the promise of lasting peace – a development which, whilst in many ways embarassingly ironic for the 'Peace Movement', gave it a fresh injection of vitality.

Between 1871 and 1914, those who had campaigned for the abolition of war must have believed their goal was about to be realised. The *Alabama* claim of 1872, which was decided against Britain and in favour of the USA by an international tribunal, was upheld as a triumph of arbitration. It was followed by nearly 200 other accords containing arbitration clauses, which in 90 cases were successfully applied to settle altercations. In the interim, scores of functional links were forged between countries, while the number of peace organisations spiralled to 425 by the end of the 1800s – no fewer than 211 of them being based in Scandinavia.[12] Similarly in 1900 Andrew Carnegie founded the Endowment for International Peace, which was tasked with analysing the causes of war, educating and influencing public opinion against it and developing international law. There was a new round of great peace conferences too. Besides the Universal Peace Congresses which took place every year after 1892, the Tsar proposed one to limit armaments. This convened at the Hague the following year with delegates from 26 states. Little was achieved on disarmament, but a Permanent Court of Arbitration was established in 1901 to resolve 'disputes involving neither honour nor vital interests'. A second Hague conference in 1907 produced a series of conventions designed to mitigate the effects of war, and plans were made for a third to be held duirng 1915 in a specially dedicated 'Palace of Peace'.

Opened in 1913, only months before the Great War began tearing the civilised world apart, this building was to become a pathetic monument to the shattered dreams of the 'Peace Movement'. But long before this there had been actual clashes and war-scares enough to demonstrate the limitations of their liberal approach to international relations and the constraints imposed by *Realpolitik*. Besides the Boer War, Russia and Britain appeared on the brink of armed conflict in 1878, for instance, while in 1898 the latter and France came close to blows over the Fashoda incident. Substantial sectors of society in all three countries had seemed willing to go to war, yet the governments held back. Earlier, in the 1870s, the British especially had been dismayed by Turkish atrocities in the Balkans; they had been doing their utmost to prop up the Ottoman Empire against Russian expansionism and now this association with the heathen, uncivilised Turk left the government vulnerable to censure both at home and abroad. William Gladstone spearheaded the attack. Although in 1854 he had defended the Cabinet's decision to go to the aid of Turkey, twenty years later he was as critical of it as he had once been supportive. For to Gladstone, Russian aggression and Turkish pogroms were both violations of the 'public law of Europe'. Of course no such law had been codified and internationally accepted. Nor was there a court to administer it. It existed in the minds of Western liberals, by whose standards the Turks' behaviour was barbaric. The concert of European powers should intervene to prevent it, and if they did not, then Britain, Gladstone maintained, had a moral duty to act alone.

This reasoning eventually obliged Gladstone, in 1882, to sanction military action in Egypt to impose peace and order. In so doing he, like the UNO in Korea in 1950, Eden in Suez in 1956 and George Bush and the UNO in the Gulf in 1991, argued that the use of force was justified since it upheld his conception of the rule of law. Thus, even for a liberal, armed force could not always be ruled out. Indeed it might even be necessary to substitute a new war for an old one. But how far was this to be taken? Should, for example, a small nation's bid for independence be permitted to jeopardise world peace?

The conflicting desires to promote the rule of law on the one hand and the freedom and sovereignty of nations on the other plagued liberal thinkers during the last decades of the Nineteenth Century and the first of the Twentieth. Military imperatives, too, undermined international accords which sought to mollify the impact of conflict. The 1856 Declaration of Paris for example, a well-intentioned effort to furnish merchant shipping more legal protection in wartime, contradicted the emerging thesis of the French Navy's *Jeune École* during the 1880s. The best response to British naval supremacy was to engage in commerce raiding, it was argued. Unarmed merchantmen should be attacked without warning by torpedo boats under cover of darkness. Undefended coastal towns should also be bombarded. Similarly, at the Hague Peace Conference of 1899, one British admiral insisted it was absurd to try to humanise war, while in *Das Volk im Waffen* (1883) Colmar von der Goltz opined that the supremacy of the political arm over the military in war, as argued by Clausewitz, was anachronistic in a Europe of increasingly armed and bellicose nations. Von Moltke the elder agreed. Once war erupted and mobilisation commenced, the political adviser, Moltke felt, 'should fall silent, and take the lead again only when the strategist has informed the king, after the complete defeat of the enemy, that his task has been fulfilled'.[13] In fact several editions of *Vom Kriege* were accordingly mutilated, with Clausewitz's passages on political supremacy being changed or their meaning blurred.[14]

Although in Germany the Schlieffen Plan clearly had a major impact on foreign policy, and in most developed states there were companies that stood to make money from substantial military expenditure, notably on navies,[15] the profit motive and military calculations were not the only driving forces in international relations at this time. Social Darwinism for example was wedded to other intellectual concepts such as Georg Hegel's theories on the lessons of history. To Hegel the very possession of might implied right. Strife was nature's final arbiter, Darwin maintained, and Hegel, pointing to Prussian and German experience since the Eighteenth Century, agreed. So did Heinrich von Treitschke, the German historian and political analyst, who dismissed the notion of perpetual peace as not just impossible but immoral too. Treitschke died in 1896, so we can only speculate as to what he would have made of the carnage of the First World War. But there remained plenty of other intellectuals, especially Germans, who were similarly persuaded. In *Germany and the Next War* (1911), General Friedrich von Bernhardi, for example, devoted chapters to such themes as 'The Right to Make War', 'The Duty to Make War' and 'World Power or Downfall', while Max Weber, the celebrated economist, depicted international politics as an endless conflict between autonomous states, a battle for the survival of the fittest. He agreed with Admiral Tirpitz that naval might was essential to protect the German economy in an era of world politics. 'Power alone', he wrote, 'will have a decisive influence on the extent to which nations will share in the economic control of the world, and thus determine the economic prospects of their own peoples.'[16]

Nor was this an isolated or particularly extreme opinion at the time. Despite the endeavours of critics like Cobden and Gladstone, the British steadily expanded their maritime forces too; indeed his Cabinet colleagues' insistence on maintaining a large naval programme contributed significantly to Gladstone's decision to resign as Prime Minister in 1894. To many in the 'Peace Movement' these arms-races were not just symptomatic of competition between countries but causes of wars in themselves. Yet the need for new markets and sources of raw materials inevitably turned the great powers' attention overseas, and these imperial interests, together with the sealanes that linked them, had to be defended. Often territory was taken simply to keep out a rival. Gorchakov, the Russian Chancellor, for instance maintained that his country's Asiatic expansion was 'irresistibly forced, less by ambition than by imperious necessity'.[17] But there were all kinds of internal, external, pragmatic and ethical arguments for colonialism, with Social Darwinism especially furnishing a convenient pseudo-scientific justification for the expansion of 'civilised', advanced peoples at the expense of declining or underdeveloped countries.

Leaving aside the disasters that befell the British at Isandhlwana and the Italians at Adowa in 1879 and 1896 respectively, this process was furthermore a fairly painless one for the developed nations. Equipped with the latest death-dealing devices their industrialised societies could manufacture, comparatively tiny units of relatively disciplined European troops regularly swept away great masses of primitively-armed natives and tribesmen. In his poem *The Modern Traveller*, Hilaire Belloc's character, Captain Blood, was to encapsulate these unequal contests with the chilling, dismissive lines: 'Whatever happens we have got, the Maxim Gun, and they have not'. But slaughtering effectively defenceless opponents with rapid-fire, breech-loading rifles and cannon, and belt-fed, water-cooled machineguns was one thing; engaging similarly equipped bodies of disciplined adversaries was another. How, the general staffs of the European armies increasingly asked themselves, could positions defended by such weapons be successfully assailed? Indeed, had modern technology rendered effective attacks almost impossible?

Indubitably, numerous incidents in the American Civil and Franco–Prussian Wars illustrated the ascendancy of modern firepower over shock tactics, and the Russo–Turkish War of 1877–78, the Boer War of 1899–1901 and the Russo–Japanese War of 1904–5 all confirmed the trend. Everywhere troops ensconced in well-prepared positions and equipped with up-to-date weaponry inflicted unsustainable losses on attacking units. To the military planners, this suggested a need for more firepower and troops with which to overwhelm the defenders. To others however it seemed to herald the end of successful offensive operations, perhaps the end of war itself.

One such thinker was Jan Bloch. His six-volume study of 1898, *The War of the Future in its Technical, Economic and Political Relations*, warned that modern armaments so favoured the defensive that conflicts were likely to become attritional struggles which, if persisted in, could climax with economic collapse and social revolution.[18] Similarly Alfred Nobel, who died in 1896, had come to the view that war was ceasing to be possible; dynamite and the other high explosives he had developed had – besides making him a vast fortune, which paradoxically enough was partly used to endow the Nobel Peace Prize – furnished man with a capacity for destruction hitherto undreamt of. Sadly for Nobel however, war was not impossible, just different, and between 1914 and 1918 millions of men were to be maimed and killed by shells containing cordite and other charges, whose formulae an inventive scientific community had extrapolated from that of Nobel's dynamite.

Much of Bloch's thesis, on the other hand, was borne out by the experiences of the First World War. Its attritional nature led to the social and economic collapse of Germany, Austria-Hungary and Russia, and the ruination of Britain and France. Yet whilst the firepower of entrenched infantry and artillery so often proved overwhelming, not every offensive ended like that launched against Verdun or on the Somme in 1916. True, major breakthroughs were rare, especially once both sides had constructed adequate defensive lines. But in 1914 the Germans reached the Marne before being checked, while on their Eastern front they not only halted the Russians but, during 1915, drove them back to within a few miles of

Minsk. Two years later General Oscar von Hutier breached Russian defensive positions around Riga by employing new assault techniques rather than technology: following a short but intense cannonade that caught the opposition unawares, quickly moving units of light infantry and mobile artillery infiltrated into the enemy's lines, by-passing any strong points that defied subjugation. 'Hutier tactics' were again utilised against the Italians at Caporetto seven weeks later, where this blend of surprise, relative mobility, mass and economy of force led to the virtual destruction of the Italian Second Army.

Having perfected their new tactics, the Germans now employed them in an all-out bid to break the stalemate on the Western Front. During the spring of 1918, Ludendorff launched a series of hammer-blow assaults, each spearheaded by 'shock' units of light infantry. Again the infiltration tactics yielded rewards; Ludendorff's offensive penetrated as far as the Marne. But the leading German forces soon outran their supply trains. Nor could heavier units be brought forward with sufficient rapidity to exploit and consolidate their gains. Thus, because of a lack of strategic, tactical and logistical mobility, the assaults ultimately failed. The concept remained alluring however. If, through improved technology for instance, these deficiencies could be rectified, relatively light forces might concentrate their strengths against a seemingly stronger opponent's weaknesses with spectacular results.

Indeed the technology that would permit this was already available, albeit in a rather embryonic form. The crude tanks and aircraft of the First World War evolved into the ever more sophisticated machines which, employed in skilful combinations and controlled by radio, were to help make possible the German *Blitzkrieg* victories of 1939–41, despite unfavourable odds in terms of force sizes. On the north-east front in the Battle of France, for example, the balance of manpower was roughly equal, with 136 divisions on each side. Yet the British and French disposed of some 3400 tanks, mostly modern vehicles, whereas the Germans had only 2200. The French heavy *Mark B* tank was moreover probably the best in the field in 1940, having denser armour than any German rival, a powerful 47 millimetre cannon in its revolving turret and a 75 millimetre gun in its hull. Similarly the agile, medium *Somua* tank mounted the high-velocity 47 millimetre cannon, which had better penetrating power than virtually any other gun of the period. Likewise the French artillery was numerically – and in many instances qualitatively – superior to that of the Germans. The former totalled some 11 200 guns as opposed to the latter's 7710, but too many of the French cannon were horse-drawn and thus woefully vulnerable, especially to aerial attack – a situation that was worsened by an utterly inadequate provision of anti-aircraft weapons. Indeed the main advantage that the Germans enjoyed lay in the strength and flexibility of their air power. They could pit 3000–3500 planes against just 1800 Allied machines and were quickly able to dominate the skies beneath which the battle was fought. Coordinated by a superior command, control and communications network, German armour and aircraft were repeatedly focused on the enemy's weakspots, the latter providing close fire- and reconnaissance support for the former. The effect was to prove decisive.[19]

For the 'Peace Movement', the outbreak of the Second World War was a particularly bitter blow. After the 1914–18 'war to end all wars' it had appeared, at least for a time, as though their hopes would be fulfilled. In Europe and the USA especially there was a general and, initially, universal war-weariness that promised to make further conflict unthinkable. President Wilson's 'Fourteen Points' was a veritable liberals' charter, while, like that between 1870 and 1914, the inter-war period was dotted with the milestones of a road which many were convinced must this time lead to eternal peace. In 1920 the League of Nations was created to settle disputes by conciliation and arbitration, and this it did in a number of instances in South America and the Balkans. It had no armed forces to coerce or punish states which violated its covenant however, and its membership fluctuated: Brazil, Japan and Italy withdrew in 1926, 1933 and 1937 respectively, the USA never became a member, Germany took part only between 1926 and 1933, and Russia from 1934 to 1939. This had grave repercussions. Without the military forces, economic power and diplomatic influence of America, the world's greatest liberal democracy, it was immensely difficult for the League to impose its decrees. When, for example, Italy attacked Abyssinia in 1935, lack of American support only made the limited sanctions it imposed that much less effective; Italy continued to receive oil from the USA for instance. Nor did the League's great powers, France and Britain, relish the thought of having to police the world alone on its behalf. What if this brought them into conflict with another major power such as the USA? Just how much of their national interests could they be reasonably expected to sacrifice on behalf of others?

Because of these inherent flaws, the League could not halt Japanese aggression in China and Manchuria, Italy's attack on Abyssinia, or the Russian invasion of Finland in 1939 – even though all of these countries were member states. Indeed the great powers increasingly came to disregard the League and followed their own national self-interests. Nor did the other major treaty structures of the era yield much of enduring value, except perhaps for a few lessons. Whilst the Washington Agreements of 1921–22 did provide some relief in the cripplingly expensive naval arms-race, they were only a temporary solution and illustrated some of the practical problems involved in negotiating arms-limitation pacts. For example, because of the differing ages and configurations of the fleets, they were barely comparable, and a world power like Britain, which perceived an array of potential threats, had fundamentally dissimilar security problems to, say, Japan. Indeed this was an obstacle that was to re-emerge during the compiling of the Locarno accords of 1925. Every state sought to enhance its security, yet they all had contrasting interests: the Dutch, Swiss and Scandinavians favoured disarmament, the East European countries wanted protection either from Germany or Russia or both, while Britain and France had both converging and diverging concerns. The Locarno Treaties sought to increase international confidence and cooperation within a framework of collective security. But the harmony on which they were founded was, as subsequent events were to prove, more apparent than real.

Much the same can also be said of the Kellogg-Briand Pact of 1928, under which 65 states – including Germany, the USA and USSR – repudiated war as an instrument of policy. But as they were conceded the right to defend their interests and carry out regional undertakings such as the Monroe Doctrine, and as the pact made no provision for punishing violators, it imposed no real restrictions on its signatories' freedom. Nor did the 60-nation Geneva Disarmament Conference of 1932–34 – which endeavoured to outlaw 'offensive' weapons and secure general disarmament in accordance with the League's covenant – fare any better. Three technical commissions were unable to agree as to which armaments were 'most specifically offensive, most efficacious against national defence and most threatening to civilians'. Negotiations ultimately collapsed, partly because of demands that some type of effective, collective security system should precede disarmament and partly because of the change in the international atmosphere following Hitler's election as German Chancellor. Indeed the Germans walked out of the conference in October 1933.

Alongside the failure of these great, formal undertakings was that of individual peace advocates. Ernst Friedrich for example, the German pacifist and anti-authoritarian, established an international anti-war museum in Berlin during 1924. That same year he also published a book entitled *War Against War*, of which Kurt Tucholsky, writing in *Die Weltbühne* in 1926, was to say:

> The photographs of battlefields, these slaughterhouses of war, and the photos of those mutilated by war belong to the most horrendous documents that I have ever seen. There exists no publication that offers anything similar in monstrousness, in basic truths, and in education.[20]

Through this gruesome collection of photographs, Friedrich was to reiterate the horror and disgust voiced by Erasmus some 400 years before. But there the similarity ends. For Friedrich's work was not just an expression of personal revulsion for war but a political document. Up to one million copies of it, in various languages, were circulated by trade unions. In common with so many members of today's 'Peace Movement', he was well-meaning enough, but intolerant of any opinion which implied that peace might be preserved by means other than those which he suggested. Whereas the French socialist deputy Jean Jaurès argued in his book *L'Organisation Socialiste de la France: L'Armée Nouvelle* (1911) that, provided they were never used for threatening other states but just for defence of the homeland, military forces had a legitimate role, to Friedrich defence, attack, militarism and fascism were all synonymous. Above all however, like Jaurès – who was assassinated in July 1914 while trying to induce German socialists to strike rather than accept mobilisation – he saw war as a product of the class and capitalist systems. Embracing the views embodied in J.A. Hobson's *Imperialism* (1902), which had such a profound influence on Lenin, he concluded that 'There will always be wars as long as Capital rules and oppresses the people'. In a vitriolic address 'To Human Beings in all Lands', he called for general strikes, resistance to conscription, and other forms of peaceful, direct opposition to 'militarism'. 'It is we proletarians that make the conduct of war possible', he claimed. 'It is for us likewise to prevent wars! . . . Then we should have peace, eternal peace on this earth!'[21]

As late as 1933, Ernest Bevin was to remind the British Labour Party Conference that the UK was one of a handful of states that enjoyed a strong, well-organised trade union movement; so the international general strikes favoured by Jaurès, Friedrich and much of the European left as 'the first weapon in the war against war' was a blunt sword. In any case, international socialism, brotherhood and class unity were not the only creeds to choose from at this time. As Friedrich discovered to his cost, there were others. Besides the numerous defamation cases his writings provoked, his anarchistic and pacifistic views incurred the wrath of the Weimar authorities, and in 1930 he was jailed for a year for treason. But this was as nothing compared with the treatment meted out to him by the Nazis; they wrecked his museum, beat and imprisoned him. Released because of ill health and American Quaker pressure, he fled to Belgium where he reopened his exhibition, only to see it destroyed once again when the Germans invaded in 1940.

In *War Against War*, Friedrich had implied that socialisation – schools, the Church and even their toys – tended to prepare children psychologically for warfare. As a radical socialist however, he primarily blamed the capitalist military – industrial complexes for the manufacture of both the machinery and mentality of modern conflict; the entrepreneurs had merely supplanted the aristocrats as 'the establishment', he maintained. Although even many armament firms enjoy far greater profitability in peacetime and, as the stock exchange slumps which greet the mere rumour of war underline, most companies regard conflict as potentially ruinous, in the inter-war period, especially during the lean days of the Great Depression, there was widespread sympathy for such beliefs. The work of the 1935 Nye Commission, for instance, led many people to conclude that the US had become entangled in the First World War because of the Western European interests of American bankers and weapon manufacturers. In addition the Depression was largely attributed to the distorting effect the war had had on the global economy. But we should also note the reasoning of people like Norman Angell, who was awarded the Nobel Peace Prize in 1933. His book *The Great Illusion* (1909) pointed to growing international economic and financial interdependence, and dismissed war as unprofitable. Nobody would therefore be so rash as to commence one, Angell opined, and 'on a general realisation of this truth depends the solution of the problem of armaments and warfare'. Critical though he was of capitalism, he, like Cobden before him, felt that an international network of shared commercial interests could only help promote peace. Indeed by the

1930s when he published *The Unseen Assassins*, Angell was wondering if it was not capitalism but nationalism that threatened the tranquility of Europe.[22]

The rise of Communism and Fascism, especially National Socialism, confronted Western liberal thinkers like Angell with the antithesis of their own creeds. How should one treat people who hold such contrasting beliefs to one's own? The answer to many practitioners of the social sciences, which from the 1930s onwards steadily grew in popularity, was as interesting case studies. The likes of Stalin, Hitler and Mussolini were perfect illustrations of what Maurice Walsh once termed the 'aggressively perverted and psychiatrically abnormal men'[23] that were all too often chosen as national leaders. As we have seen, Ernst Friedrich had suggested that from childhood man was conditioned to be a warlike creature, while Hobbes, Montesquieu and Kant, among others, had all pondered whether humankind was by nature peace-loving or violent.

Such issues increasingly provided food for thought for an assortment of social and natural scientists including geneticists, psychologists, sociobiologists, ethologists and anthropologists. Ethology, for instance, operates on the premise that Homosapiens are like any other animals and are primarily motivated by instinct rather than reason. Among these instincts are aggression – which lies at the heart of the Darwinian concept of survival of the fittest in an unending process of natural conflict and selection – and a sense of territory, which furnishes security and identity. For most of his history man has been a hunter-gatherer, a predator rather than an agrarian. But in modern society, natural dangers like starvation and wild animals have receded whilst man's ability to manipulate his environment has mushroomed. Thus, although wars are inspired by primeval instincts such as that to defend territory, social organisation and technology have, according to theorists like Konrad Lorenz, distorted the natural model.

But this is one of the flaws in the ethologists' position. There are too many significant distinctions between man and animals. The former has, for example, a capacity for reflection and self-awareness, and a sense of custom, tradition and history. As Frederick the Great once commented, 'What distinguishes a man from a beast of burden is thought and the faculty of bringing ideas together. A pack mule could go on ten campaigns with Prince Eugene of Savoy and still know nothing of tactics'. Even if aggression were congenital in animals, that would not necessarily mean it was congenital in humans too; even if it were, that would not necessarily make it innate in states. And this in turn raises other important points. Ethology can explain neither the transformation in the scale and nature of conflict, nor its diversity. Why are some groups more truculent than others, and how does one explain periods of peace? How did the instinctive, territorial jousting of prehistoric man grow into enormous, organised confrontations between states? Indeed the ethologist seems incapable of accounting for the behaviour of specific groups of Homosapiens and has to limit himself to focusing on man *per se*.

The psychologists' approach contains similar pitfalls.[24] They too explain war as a product of man's aggressive instincts. These are suppressed, initially by parents and later by the state, giving rise to frustration. A process of 'transformation' then directs this resentment towards some distant target group, while 'displacement' simultaneously transfers some of the individual's more positive feelings to a grander third party such as his country. Meanwhile a third mechanism, 'projection', acts as a safety-valve for what would otherwise be destructive psychological tensions; self-hatred is converted into hatred for someone or something else.

Were these cycles truly an ineluctable feature of a universal and enduring human nature however, one would expect war to affect all societies perpetually. Yet it does not. Unlike simple violence – for war is a very specialised type of violence – it is intermittent and unevenly distributed, with some groups only experiencing it very occasionally; peace is arguably just as natural a condition as war. Psychologists have little option other than to acknowledge this, but in doing so they fail to adequately elucidate why the change from tranquil coexistence to war occurs. They can only offer explanations for war *per se* and not for any specific cases. However, as Blanning has pointed out in his scholarly, cogent but witty overview of the causes of great wars, 'war *per se* is only the aggregate of all wars, past and present'.[25] Similarly the psychologist's methodology only lends itself to addressing human nature *per se* – that of the whole of humankind, past, present and future. If enough information is available, an individual's psychological portrait can also be painted. But like the ethologists, psychologists are quite unable to throw much light on the behaviour of groups of human beings, notably ruling elites, where one encounters an assortment of personalities which interact. If human nature is constant, what makes these groups swerve from peace to war and *vice versa*? And what makes the many follow the few in their decision? For whilst popular pressure was indubitably a contributing factor in the origins of several conflicts – the Crimean and Franco-Prussian Wars for instance – one casts around in vain for an example of a war which was begun solely in response to such pressure. On the contrary, popular enthusiasm has tended to greet and follow the outbreak of hostilities rather than precede it.

Anthropologists would tend to present this last phenomenon in terms of the 'puppetmaster' view of the relationship between the governed and their governors. Thus the First World War is depicted as a family quarrel. In so doing they resort to the old device of blaming 'the establishment', which, even if it did not fly in the face of the available evidence regarding the origins of so many conflicts, would still not explain why the ruling class chose war on some occasions and peace on others. In contrast to ethologists like Richard Dawkins, for example, who in *The Selfish Gene* argues that man's nature is exclusively determined by his evolving genetic profile,[26] anthropologists maintain that Homosapiens are shaped by their environment, education and culture.[27] Aggression is therefore not an instinct, but a derived characteristic, while war is but another invention of human society which is furthermore to be distinguished from other forms of violence: it is a relatively recent phenomenon and is not ubiquitous. Indeed, like Montesquieu and Rousseau before them, the anthropologists regard war as a product of organised society. But what ultimately makes these organisations wage war has received little attention from this school of thought, and what conclusions have been arrived at seem more than a little doubtful.[28] As Geoffrey Blainey has observed: 'The explanations that stress aims are theories of rivalry and animosity and not theories of war. They help to explain increasing rivalry between nations but they do not explain why the rivalry led to war'.[29]

Indeed factors that are so frequently presented as the causes of war are at other times seemingly instrumental in preserving peace. So what actually brings about the transition from one situation to the other? Why, for example, did the Germans' invasion of Czechoslovakia in 1938 not lead to war – even though that country, possessing 32 quite respectable divisions, evidently had the capacity to fight one – whereas their invasion of Poland the following year did? The ethologists have stressed an important and often overlooked reason: as in the animal kingdom, battles over territory only occur when an occupier elects to resist an intruder. In 1938 nobody resisted the Germans; in 1939 somebody did. Thus war has a reciprocal nature

which in *Vom Kriege* Clausewitz cited as one of its two enduring
characteristics, the other being the use of force. In response to the
question 'What is war?', he wrote:

> War is nothing but a duel on a larger scale . . . an act of force to
> compel our enemy to do our will. . . . Force . . . is thus the means
> of war; to impose our will on the enemy is its object. To secure that
> object we must render the enemy powerless; and that, in theory, is
> the true aim of warfare. . . . If the enemy is to be coerced you must
> put him in a situation that is even more unpleasant than the
> sacrifices you call on him to make. . . . The worst of all conditions
> in which a belligerent can find himself is to be utterly defenseless.
> Consequently, if you are to force the enemy . . . to do your
> bidding, you must either make him literally defenseless or at least
> put him in a position that makes this danger probable. War,
> however, is not the action of a living force upon a lifeless mass
> (total nonresistance would be no war at all) but always the collision
> of two living forces. . . . There is interaction.[30]

From all of this it can be seen that war is always about power – its
consolidation, extension, preservation or enforcement. In fighting,
states are assessing and testing their respective powers, having
exhausted the potential of other forms of political intercourse. 'War',
as Clausewitz discerned, 'is merely the continuation of policy by
other means. . . . What remains peculiar to war is simply the peculiar
nature of its means.'[31] Having clarified the nature of their power
relationship through fighting, the states will return to conducting
their affairs through peaceful means, and the more decisive the
conflict has been, the more starkly their respective powers are
portrayed and the more durable the ensuing peace will be.

Statesmen and -women, and the diplomats and military personnel
who advise them, are perpetually concerned with the preservation of
their country's power and fear some future deterioration in their
relative position. This perception has often sparked off so-called
'defensive' or 'pre-emptive' wars. For example, both Japan and
Wilhelmine Germany in 1941 and 1914 respectively felt that they
were confronted with a 'window of opportunity' which would soon
shut for ever. A blend of short-term optimism and long-term pessi-
mism dictated that they had to fight immediately if they were to have
any prospect of success; to put it off would only guarantee defeat.[32]
Similarly by early 1938 Hitler was becoming obsessed with the danger

that time was running out; Germany had to secure her basic objectives in the world before the other powers became too strong. None of this was just malign thinking, but a seemingly logical response to the international alignments and technological developments of the day. As Michael Howard has observed:

> Whatever may be the underlying causes of international conflict, even if we accept the role of atavistic militarism or of military–industrial complexes or of socio–biological drives or of domestic tensions in fuelling it, wars begin with conscious and reasoned decisions based on the calculation, made by *both* parties, that they can achieve more by going to war than by remaining at peace.[33]

Indeed efforts by Hobbes and Lenin, among others, to categorise wars – those of the oppressed versus their oppressors, for gain, for security, for ideology, and so on – are quite misleading since *all* of these labels can, if desired, be applied to *any* conflict. Even Clausewitz, that great doyen of military thinkers, was troubled by this, as it seemed to jeopardise his universal theory of war. He eventually concluded that 'War is more than a true chameleon that slightly adapts its characteristics to the given case'. It is a 'remarkable trinity', he observed,

> composed of primordial violence, hatred, and emnity, which are to be regarded as a blind natural force; of the play of chance and probability within which the creative spirit is free to roam; and of its element of subordination, as an instrument of policy, which makes it subject to reason alone. . . . [It] has to be treated as part of some other whole; the name of which is policy. . . . Only if war is looked at in this way . . . can we see that all wars are things of the same nature.[34]

Above all the notion of 'war by accident' is one that has been very much in vogue of late, especially with the advocates of 'Non-Offensive Defence'. Randall Forsberg for example, working on the rather eclectic and expedient assumption that we can rule out 'deliberately initiated warfare among the big powers', opines that

> The main fear today is a war like World War I, triggered by a minor incident or lesser conflict. . . . Intervention in the Third World is becoming the *only* expected large-scale use . . . of the

military forces . . . of the big powers. Still, [they] . . . maintain enormous standing forces, both nuclear and conventional, and they plan to keep 'modernising' these forces indefinitely to deter another big power conventional war.[35]

Likewise Horst Afheldt, for instance, categorises the Great War of 1914 as a confrontation brought about by an arms-race, by the 'cult of the offensive' and other military imperatives, by mobilisation systems and, first and foremost, by miscalculation. The Second World War, by contrast, he attributes to acts of deliberate aggression and coercion, and has argued that NATO planning, at least up to 1990, was being wrongly determined by the fear of war occurring solely through this latter process – through a calculated attempt by the USSR to invade and subjugate Western Europe:

> The history of our century shows that continuing confrontation and arms races between two leading powers, combined with the perception that initiative and pre-emption have a military pay-off, can also lead to war. Which of both ways is more likely is a useless question. . . . Both roads have to be blocked if freedom and peace are to be secured. NATO [has done] . . . a lot to block the one road in the 1939 manner. It is high time now to address the second, the way of the 'guns of August 1914'.[36]

Whatever the history of the Twentieth Century might show, it is certainly not that the First World War was in some way accidental or the result of miscalculations. On the contrary, neither this nor any other war occurred by accident; and should the superpowers ever indulge in a nuclear exchange, I doubt that there will be anything 'unintentional', as Philip Sabin has syncretically suggested, about that either:

> The threat is not so much to go deliberately to nuclear war as it is to participate and persevere in an escalatory process, even though it might *result* in nuclear war. The risk of displaying resolve through such action is, of course, that events *will* get out of hand and that the superpowers will slide into an unintended conflict.[37]

Indeed it is only with the development of technology like computer-controlled weapon systems which might conceivably malfunction that an accidental war has become a possibility – and an *extremely* remote one at that – while, at the risk of appearing pedantic, one could fairly question whether such a 'war' would in fact be one by any classical definition of the term.

But both Ms Forsberg and Dr Afheldt are members of what, as we have seen, is a very long line of 'Peace Movement' theorists who have made well-intentioned proposals for either avoiding war or control-ling it and mitigating its effects. In doing so they have variously condemned war as unnatural, irrational, immoral and even imposs-ible; as the product of militarism, nationalism, imperialism, genes, capitalism, arms-races and of selfish, secretive, evil and undemocratic governmental regimes; and as a wasteful diversion of resources from welfare to destruction. Non-interventionism, free trade, disarma-ment, pluralism and democracy have all been offered as possible cures, as have new technology, military alliances, shared economic interests and international institutions coordinating collective se-curity arrangements.

The last of these has perhaps been the instrument that has most fascinated Western liberal thinkers during the Twentieth Century and which – as we approach the next, with revolutionary reforms under way in the USSR and its former satellites, and with the economic and political integration of Europe gathering speed – is currently enjoying a fresh bout of interest. After some 40 years, the ideological, political, military and economic division of Europe, like the walls and barbed-wire fences which once epitomised it, is being swept away. There is talk of a 'Common European Home' in which the ideals the liberals have promoted for over 200 years would prevail: the rule of law; freedom of speech, assembly and religion; unrestricted trade and movement; liberty, democracy, and shared economic interests and prosperity. Above all, with the Warsaw Pact having disintegrated as an effective military alliance and with NATO uncertain about its role in the future, there are blueprints for a new, collective security structure involving the participants of the Confer-ence for Security and Cooperation in Europe (CSCE).

The wider European community does indeed seem to be poised on the threshold of an era of great international cooperation. But devising a collective security system – which is subtly but significantly different from an alliance like NATO that comprises states primarily interested in their own defence – is one thing; making it effective, as even recent history shows, is an entirely different matter.

On 24 October 1945 the UNO Charter, formally endorsed by 29 states, came into force. In many senses it was the successor to the discredited League of Nations, which in April 1946 disbanded itself, transferring its assets and responsibilities to the UN. The new body was soon confronted by thorny problems. In 1948 for example the Security Council attempted to settle the Berlin Blockade crisis, but its efforts were thwarted through the use of the Soviet Union's veto. Then in June 1950 the Security Council voted by seven to one (the USSR delegate was absent) to assist South Korea in repelling North Korean aggression.

This led to the commitment of, first, US units and, later, British, Commonwealth and other forces drawn from a total of fourteen member states. Many of these countries however sent only token or noncombatant contingents, and the bulk of the fighting – and the casualties and monetary costs – fell on the Americans. In all the Korean War claimed the lives of 118 515 UNO military personnel. A further 264 591 were wounded and 92 987 taken prisoner. Of this last figure, a large proportion died because of maltreatment or starvation; only 3746 out of 10 218 Americans taken captive ever returned for example. South Korea was utterly devastated. Her battle casualties came to 70 000 killed, 150 000 wounded and 80 000 captured, while civilian losses stemming from the conflict and its repercussions have been estimated at around 3 000 000. A further 400 000 civilians perished or were injured in North Korea, while the communist forces sustained at least 1 600 000 casualties – the bulk of them Chinese.

This was quite a 'butcher's bill' for a supposedly limited war. It had moreover threatened to be still larger; the use of atomic weapons had seemed possible on occasions, and the conflict might very easily have dragged on or escalated. Efforts to contain and control it led to sharp divisions between politicians and the military – notably between President Truman and General MacArthur[38] – while public unease and disillusionment over the war made, as we noted in Chapter 1, a significant contribution to Eisenhower's election victory of 1952.

Indeed, if the protocol-regulated, surgical conflicts of the Eighteenth Century were gory and disruptive, then they have been steadily superseded by something still worse. 'Total' war involves not just a distinct military elite and any civilians unfortunate enough to get in the way, but entire societies which, increasingly organised and industrialised, possess an unprecedented capacity for waging war. A crucial factor has however been their willingness to sustain any conflict – to endure punishment and make the concomitant sacrifices. And just as war has become more destructive and more terrible for more people, so too has its attractiveness as an option abated.

Military staffs – somewhat ironically, for they are so often portrayed by their critics in the 'Peace Movement' as mindless warmongers – tend to be among those who are most aware of this. MacArthur was untypical. In fact most recent conflicts have been commenced by politicians *against* the counsel of their military advisers. In 1938 for example, even the half-hearted opposition of France and Britain led General Ludwig Beck, Hitler's chief of staff, to conclude his master was about to plunge Germany into a premature war which would end in her defeat. He resigned.[39] Similarly, the following year as Hitler prepared to turn against France, *Generaloberst* Heinrich von Brauchitsch, having read out a memorandum detailing the Army's pessimistic assessments, was berated by the *Führer* in much the way the entire general staff was to be shortly thereafter.[40] 'I hold quite different views', Hitler snapped.

> Firstly, I place a low value on the French Army's will to fight. Every army is a mirror of its people. The French people think only of peace and good living, and they are torn apart in Parliamentary strife. Accordingly, the Army, however brave and well-trained its officer corps may be, does not show the combat determination expected of it. After the first setbacks, it will swiftly crack up.[41]

Hitler's prophesy proved to be accurate. Moreover, whilst we must be careful when drawing such parallels, at least some of the agents that sapped France's strength in 1940 are clearly present in the affluent societies of the developed world. Indeed it will be interesting to see whether the UN will ever again be able to muster the necessary political will and material resources to sustain a military operation of the length, scale and intensity of that staged in Korea. Although there were Cold War overtones, in keeping with the liberal democratic tradition of the Nineteenth Century it fought to uphold its concept of the rule of law, and in doing so exchanged a new, arguably worse, war for an old one. And once again the values of Western liberal democracy came into conflict with those of a very different culture and philosophy. Since then the UN has done sterling service in many ways and in many areas of the globe. However, as far as keeping the peace is concerned, its performance has been somewhat specious. For all its good offices, it could not prevent Britain and Argentina going to war in 1982. Nor could it stop Turkey and Greece fighting over Cyprus in 1974; in fact, throughout the August of that year, the Turks expanded their occupation zone despite the cease-fire arrangements the UN had helped negotiate.

Nor did its intervention in the Congo between 1961 and 1964 put an end to the violence and instability there; indeed the UN forces here had to be steadily wound down because of a lack of funds and political will to support them. Elsewhere UN observer units were, with the consent of the belligerents, successfully employed in policing acknowledged lines of demarcation between warring factions: in Suez in late 1956, for example, and along the Golan Heights in 1974. But here, as in so many other instances, the UN was not so much imposing peace as assisting to preserve fragile cease-fires. The basic problems were not resolved, and in time exploded into military confrontation once again. Sovereign states were simply not prepared to entrust their security to the international community, and whenever they perceived that war might best preserve, extend or enforce their power, they resorted to it – regardless of the UN. If, of course, the conflict did not go the way they had hoped, then the UN might, as in the case of the Iran–Iraq War of the 1980s, help in securing an armistice. But this would essentially be an acknowledgement that the military option had failed; it had more to do with the improbability of victory and the costs to the belligerents of continuing the war than to any UN attempts to halt it. Indeed one might fairly ask whether the UN has really been any more successful as a peace-keeping organisation than were the Concert of Europe and the League of Nations.

All of this bodes ill for those who advocate the creation of a new, European collective security system. As we have seen, generations of liberal theorists and statesmen have grappled with the fundamental problems involved, many of which persist to this day. The great panaceas of free market economics and democratic government are permeating an ever larger area of the Eurasian land mass, while, in Western Europe at least, internationalism seems poised to displace nationalism. Yet elsewhere the scene is less encouraging; one sees disintegration rather than integration. In Central and Eastern Europe and the USSR, nationalism is reasserting itself as the Russian Confederation, Byelorussia, the Ukraine, Latvia, Lithuania, Estonia and the constituent republics of Yugoslavia strive to reclaim their sovereignty and individual identities. In so doing, many threaten the power of their neighbours and former rulers, if not their security; territorial and ethnic disputes are widespread for example, while the

likely implications of German reunification are causing understandable misgivings within a number of countries, both to the East and
West. Whether many of the fledgling democracies of Eastern Europe
will survive is also far from clear. Most face potentially destabilising
social, financial and ecological difficulties as they make the switch to
market economics; while embracing and sustaining Western-style
pluralism and representative government in countries which have
neither the necessary experience nor the proven political organisations and institutions would, even in the best of circumstances, be a
hazardous undertaking. The same experiment has already failed in a
dozen African states; and we should perhaps not forget the sorry tale
of the Weimar Republic, whose own people, assailed by dreadful
economic deprivation, turned their backs on one of the most liberal
constitutions ever devised and voted instead for totalitarianism.

The fact is that the very nature of democratic societies poses both
problems and advantages. Whilst there are those who believe that
liberal democracies are less likely to go to war, at least with each
other, the more democratic countries are, the more their elected
governments embody and represent the people's collective values,
interests and perceptions; and, as we have seen, *le peuple* can be very
bellicose at times, often embarrassingly so. In 1935 for example,
when the British government feared that by supporting the League
and collective security they might involve themselves in a war with
Italy, they sought to secure a peaceful settlement with Mussolini over
Abyssinia. But once the public learnt of the Hoare-Laval Pact, this
well-intentioned policy was doomed; the people would not permit
Italy to be rewarded for its aggression and Hoare had to be repudiated by his colleagues in the Cabinet. Abyssinia was not saved
however, neither was Mussolini appeased nor deterred; and less than
two years later, when Chamberlain returned from Munich having
sacrificed Czechoslovakia in a bid to maintain 'peace in our time', he
was greeted by many of the British public as a hero.[42]

In any case, a European collective security system will have to deal
with a variety of potential threats, not all of them stemming from
liberal democratic states. Within the Balkans and Eastern reaches of
Central Europe, there are potentially dangerous ethnic, religious and
territorial disputes. Likewise the USSR might be evolving into a
more democratic confederation, but there is a long way to go, and in
the meantime there are grave ideological, national and ethnic divisions which, together with a dismal economic situation, threaten the
internal cohesion and external relations of this rickety, polyglot

empire. Even if it largely stays intact, as *the* leading military power in the region, retaining, despite massive reductions, enormous conventional and nuclear forces, it will ineluctably continue to be a major security concern for neighbouring states[43] – several of whom would be aspiring members of the same security organisation. If on the other hand the USSR is excluded, then there is a danger it will perceive the new defence community as threatening. Moreover, as we noted throughout Chapter 1, there are the problems posed by the gradual breakdown of the bipolar balance of power. The Vietnam War highlighted, among other things, the growing strength of regional powers, whose interests, values and perceptions will not necessarily harmonise with those of a European commonwealth. In addition to established ones like China, India and Japan, countries like Brazil have enormous potential, as have parts of the Arab world; and, at a time when NATO and the former Eastern Bloc states are reducing their own arsenals, some of these countries are developing not only impressive conventional forces but nuclear and chemical weapon capabilities, too.

1990 witnessed a stark and depressing manifestation of these trends. When, in response to Iraq's seizure of Kuwait, the US, UK and other UN states despatched forces to the Persian Gulf, a realisation of the potential human and monetary costs of any war steadily eroded popular support for military action. The economic expense involved in the unavoidably lengthy preparations chipped away at the peace dividend that the end of the Cold War had seemed to promise and exacerbated the financial plight of the British and American governments especially. Military analysts predicted tens of thousands of casualties in the event of hostilities and, whilst taking steps to ensure that their political overlords had military options at their disposal if required, warned that strategic objectives might be difficult to identify, let alone fulfil: Iraq had a vast, battle-hardened Army that had had ample time to prepare its positions, would be fighting on its own front-doorstep and which, equipped with chemical and other sophisticated weaponry, could amass substantial firepower. Kuwait would be devastated, as would the region's oil industry. A war could all too easily escalate, perhaps embroiling Israel, and it was far from clear how – and on what terms – any conflict could be terminated without major changes to the local balance of power which themselves might lead to further bouts of instability. If on the other hand the UN did not fight, it seemed that the only way the long-term security of Saudi Arabia, for example, could be sustained was by the US in particular shouldering the burden of maintaining a significant military presence there. Above all, any peaceful solution to the crisis would appear to reward Iraq for its brutal aggression. It would be the UN's Abyssinia. If it could not effectively protect a member state even when, in stark contrast to the Cold War era, it enjoyed the backing of both the USA and the USSR, what could the UN do?

For the foreseeable future at least, it is difficult to envisage a European collective security organisation that would be immune to the sort of problems that have plagued the UN just as they plagued the League before it. War hangs like a sword of Damocles over any system of essentially sovereign nations in which each member country has its own peculiar characteristics and interests that it wishes quite legitimately to preserve, and in so doing recognises no final arbiter other than the limits of its own power. And the ultimate and most direct test of a state's power, as well as being the last prerogative of a sovereign country, is war. To be efficacious, collective security requires both a cultural homogeneity and a commonality of interests which does not yet exist in Europe, let alone the world.

So there are awesome difficulties to be surmounted if a European collective security community is to be forged. But as the *London Declaration On A Transformed North Atlantic Alliance* of July 1990 conceded,[44] now that the 'twin pillars' of the Harmel approach – the maintenance of security through both adequate military strength and the willingness to improve East–West relations – have helped bring about change among its putative adversaries, NATO will have to adapt or risk appearing increasingly anachronistic. Any change should however be cautious and gradual. Above all, any new security organisation should, for the foreseeable future, supplement NATO rather than replace it. The North Atlantic Treaty is, in the eyes of the Americans, a tried and tested basis for cooperation, 'the most successful defensive alliance in history'. It might prove quite impossible to get Congressional approval for a substitute accord and, whilst the US will obviously continue to have interests in Europe, it is essential that North American forces remain committed to maintaining peace and stability there. As we have noted, the absence of the world's pre-eminent liberal democracy proved a fatal flaw in the League of Nations; and if collective security is to be anything other than a shibboleth, if states really are to refrain from behaving in any manner 'inconsistent with the purposes and principles of the United Nations

Charter and with the CSCE Final Act', then the US will have to play an active role.

Not the least of its tasks will be to serve as a counterweight to not just the potential power of Russia but that of Germany too; for without the US, the Germans promise to dominate Europe to an extent that might cause understandable disquiet in Britain, France, Russia, Poland and many other countries. They need to be reassured. Yet at the same time the Europeans must assume more responsibility for their own defence, if only because the size of forward-based US forces seems bound to dwindle. Indeed it may well become a matter of maintaining a floor rather than a ceiling as the relaxation of East–West tension, the search for a financial peace dividend and American preoccupation with other parts of the globe strengthen the long-standing desire to 'bring the boys back' from Europe.

This might well end with the US role in NATO reverting to that of 1949 and the very early 1950s – the period before it really became the 'entangling' alliance. Just as some in a wider Europe would welcome such a development, having always attributed the Cold War exclusively to the presence and actions of the Americans, so would others view it with apprehension. What we can almost certainly be confident of however, is that it will perpetuate if not aggravate the arguments about burden-sharing which, as we saw in Chapter 1, have troubled NATO throughout its history. Who, in any future collective security regime, will perform what tasks – including the possession and accommodation of nuclear forces – and who will pay for them? Which among the major powers other than the US will take the leading role, including that of supreme commander? If, for the sake of argument, Hungary and Rumania actually come to blows over their border and ethnic minority disputes, who will actually interfere, militarily if necessary, to stop them? Will it be the Russians (again), or will the other thirty or so member states democratically decide among themselves that the Belgians can resolve this particular *contretemps* singlehandedly? What if they however decline to fight 'somebody else's war'? The Russians are the only nation in the region possessing the necessary military power to police it.

But would the Eastern European states be any more willing to tolerate the perpetuation of Soviet influence in their affairs than an increasingly self-assertive Germany would be likely to welcome the restoration of the four wartime powers' rights over her? Indeed what if, as often happened with the League, individual states come to sense that they are having to meet a disproportionately large share of the costs of 'collective' security and that they are being asked to sacrifice too many of their own national interests for the benefit of others? Do they secede? If so, will there be a 'half-way house' like that occupied by France *vis-à-vis* NATO after 1966? What if, as is probable, the state concerned is a major power like Germany? What would the rest of Europe do if, say, the German electorate were to vote for some ethnocentric policy? After all, as was highlighted by the 1991 Gulf War, Germany's current constitution expressly forbids participation in military operations outside the NATO region. Similarly, what will become of those states which have a long tradition of non-alignment? Although there might no longer be Eastern and Western blocs to be neutral between, the cornerstone of their foreign policies has been the avoidance of alliances and foreign entanglements. Would membership of a pan-European security community be consistent with their image – which has often proved advantageous – in the world?

Lastly, if, as the supporters of 'Defensive Defence' advocate, states eschew the wherewithal for strategic mobility, how will alliance obligations be discharged? France, in the inter-war period, adopted a defensive posture which, although epitomised by the Maginot Line, imposed constraints that affected far more than just the protection of her own soil. 'The conception of the defensive army which . . . [had] had priority since the Treaty of Versailles', Marshal Petain concluded by 1936, had 'had its day'. Yet not until later – and even then only on an inadequate scale – did France turn to developing air and mobile ground forces that were capable of using 'modern offensive techniques . . . [and] effectively collaborating with an ally in peril'.[45] This meant that she lacked the means to give effect to the mutual guarantee pacts she had concluded with Poland and Czechoslovakia as part of the Locarno collective security system. When Hitler moved against them, France had no option other than to watch helplessly as her allies were eliminated. The contradiction between her diplomatic and military policies not only reduced collective security to a mere slogan but also ended in disaster for all concerned. Will NATO or any successor organisation end up in the same trap? The gestation period for military capabilities is after all to be measured in years and decades, whereas political intentions can change literally overnight. It remains to be seen how far emerging models for collective security will be underpinned by practical measures and, when necessary, sacrifices.

In concluding this section, I would juxtapose the views of three people: Randall Forsberg, a representative of the modern Peace Movement and some of whose opinions opened this chapter; Sir Michael Howard, whom I have quoted at several points before and who has done so much to enlighten scholarly opinion on these matters; and Immanuel Kant. In 1795 the last of these produced what was to become one of the most celebrated monographs on man's quest for lasting peace: *Zum ewigen Frieden*. Kant dismissed the 'so-called peace treaties' of history as mere 'ceasefires'. He believed that the *Friedenszustand unter Menschen* was not a natural state, but one that had to be 'established'. Like most of the *philosophes*, he regarded democratic government and a universal public law founded on a federation of free states as prerequisites for this, and he viewed achieving the objective of eternal peace not as some 'empty notion' but as a responsibility – *Aufgabe* – incumbent on all of mankind.

Yet he doubted that it would *ever* be attained. He could only express the hope that progress towards this goal would accelerate as the time interval required to achieve each successive step would grow smaller.[46] To Randall Forsberg, if big powers were to renounce the use of force in smaller countries, it would represent just such a 'small step in a larger, longer-term historical process'.[47] The human race has taken many steps since Kant composed his paper, including the vast strides of the East European revolution of 1989. Indeed, as the Europeans embark on the 1990s, there is an atmosphere of great expectation tinged with a sense of finality, of having reached the end of the road to perpetual peace. Nobody looking back at the gory history of the continent could fail to be moved by this. Yet in a way it is as disturbing as it is exhilarating. For, as Kant implied, the *Aufgabe* of seeking eternal peace is an eternal one; and as Michael Howard has discerned, 'no formula, no organisation and no political or social revolution can ever free mankind from this inexorable duty'.[48]

4 Dimensions of 'Defensive Defence'

1. OPERATIONAL, STRATEGIC AND TACTICAL CONSIDERATIONS

'Petty geniuses attempt to hold everything; wise men hold fast to the key points. They parry great blows and scorn little accidents. There is an ancient apothegm: he who would preserve everything, preserves nothing. Therefore, always sacrifice the bagatelle and pursue the essential.'
(Frederick the Great in his *Instructions For His Generals* [1747])

In seeking to argue the case for military efficacy of a purely defensive posture, the advocates of 'Just Defence' ritually employ two principal arguments: that operationally, strategically and tactically speaking, defence is superior to attack; and that the former has gained a lasting ascendancy over the latter because of the advantages afforded by modern, advanced-technology equipment and weapons. The second of these contentions will be examined in some detail later. For the time being, we can content ourselves with the observation that whereas technological change has, it is claimed, only marginally enhanced the attacker's capabilities, recent improvements in reconnaissance, target-acquisition and weapon accuracy, particularly over longer distances, are perceived as having brought far greater benefits to the defender. Let us first examine the professed supremacy of the defensive on the operational, strategic and tactical levels of warfare.

In an effort to give their claims greater credibility, the 'Just Defence' lobby have often cited the views of Clausewitz, history's pre-eminent military theorist, on defence. But this approach is at best eclectic and at worst disingenuous and nescient. True, in *Vom Kriege* Clausewitz did write of the 'superiority of the defence over attack'.[1] He stressed however that this had 'to be rightly understood'.[2] The object of defence is preservation and, as it is easier to hold ground than take it, 'defence is easier than attack, assuming both sides have equal means'.[3] The 'chief advantage' the defender enjoyed, he suggested, was that of being able to await and then react to the enemy's actions,[4] together with a natural superiority in the use of the means – other than the absolute strength and quality of the forces – that determine tactical and strategic success. Among them are terrain, . . . advantages of the theater of operations, support of the population and the harnessing of moral forces. . . . The defender waits for the attack in position, having chosen a suitable area and prepared it; which means he has carefully reconnoitred it, erected solid defences at some of the most important points, established and opened communications, sited his batteries, fortified some villages, selected covered assembly areas, and so forth. The strength of his front . . . makes it possible for him, while the forces at the point of actual combat are destroying each other, *to inflict heavy losses on the enemy at low cost to himself* as the attack passes through the successive stages of resistance. . . . In the final [phase of] . . . the battle, when the enemy has revealed his whole plan and spent the major part of his forces, the defender . . . [should open] a minor offensive battle of his own, using every element of attack – assault, surprise and flanking movements. . . . The defender may be handicapped by his numerical weakness and his circumstances; but frequently what should be seen as the result of necessity has been interpreted as the result of defense as such. In this absurd manner it has become a basic assumption that defensive battles are meant merely to repulse the enemy, and not to destroy him. . . . Naturally, various degrees and stages are possible, running gradually from positive counterattack to local defense . . . [but] we do insist that the offensive element must never be completely absent.[5]

Indeed, Clausewitz maintained, the very concept of defence was the parrying of a blow, and its characteristic feature was awaiting that blow. 'It is this feature', he pointed out,

> that turns any action into a defensive one; it is the only test by which defense can be distinguished from attack. Pure defense, however, would be completely contrary to the idea of war. . . . We must return the enemy's blows; and these offensive acts in a defensive war come under the heading of 'defense' – in other words, our offensive takes place within our own positions or theater of operations. Even in a defensive position awaiting the enemy assault, our bullets take the offensive. So the defensive form of war is not a simple shield, but a shield made up of well-directed blows. . . . [It is] a means to win a victory that

enables one to take the offensive after superiority has been gained; that is, to proceed to the active object of the war. . . . Wherever a victory achieved by the defensive form is . . . allowed to wither away unused, a serious mistake is being made. A sudden powerful transition to the offensive – the flashing sword of vengeance – is the greatest moment for the defense. If it is not . . . an integral part of [a commander's] . . . idea of defense, he will never be persuaded of the superiority of the defensive form.[6]

There is a little support here for the tenets of 'Just Defence'. On the contrary, Clausewitz regarded defence as better only because it enabled one to 'take the offensive after superiority has been gained' – a transition which his own military idol, Napoleon, described as 'one of the most delicate operations in war'.[7] Nor would Clausewitz permit a distinction to be drawn between ripostes on the battlefield and 'a reaction that *expands into the realm of actual strategic offense*'. This would be 'basically unacceptable', as, he insisted, 'the idea of *retaliation* is fundamental to all defense'.[8]

Nevertheless, particularly in the period 1870–1914 when technological developments seemed to further strengthen the defensive and thus conflicted with the attitudes of military staffs brought up on a diet of *l'offensive à outrance*, theorists who favoured the attack speculated as to whether Clausewitz might eventually have altered his views on the matter; he had after all been revising *Vom Kriege* when he died, but had not got round to tackling its lengthy and Daedalian Book Six, 'Defence'. However this was probably just wishful thinking on their part. Clausewitz would doubtlessly have devised a more coherant presentation of his thinking, but it appears improbable that he would have radically changed his ideas on the relative merits of attack and defence. He recognised the advantages of both, but regarded the latter as a temporary state which was an ideal prelude to the former; if to him the notion of absolute defence seemed 'absurd', then the opinion of Colmar von der Goltz and others who believed that 'to make war means to attack' would scarcely have appeared more sensible. Moreover Clausewitz took great pains in explaining the value of military history in the study of the art of war. He saw the danger of applying lessons from past conflicts which changed circumstances, notably technology, had rendered obsolete: 'The further back one goes, the less useful military history becomes, growing poorer and barer at the same time'.[9] This point has to be made about *Vom Kriege* too.

Many of Clausewitz's prescriptions apply only in the context of the 'musket and horse' period in which he lived. In his time the assailant could select the time, nature and axis of attack, while the defender could pick his ground and decide on the character of his resistance while waiting for his opponent's plans to unfold. Today however, technological developments such as precision targeting devices and accurate, long-range attack systems have distorted this balance, rendering the distinctions between attack and defence less clear. The defender need no longer wait for the enemy to deploy and come into close contact before starting the engagement. Equally the attacker can strike at the defender from much greater ranges. This means that actually making contact with opposing forces through manoeuvre rather than fire is becoming more difficult and potentially costly, even if they are not fully deployed by any classical definition of the term. Yet closing with an adversary is acquiring ever greater importance, since it reduces his ability to exploit high-precision weaponry to its maximum effect.

Thus surprise and rapid initial manoeuvre leading to a mingling of friendly and hostile forces will be essential; linear battles with units echeloned in depth and massed on particular axes will be superseded by a mercurial, fragmented style of combat in which relatively small but very capable and agile forces will grapple for control of points or areas; and units well suited for the prosecution of this type of warfare – air assault brigades, various kinds of 'light' infantry and armour, reconnaissance-, attack- and transport-helicopters – will be accorded greater priority. As two Soviet theorists commented in 1988: 'Whereas in the Great Patriotic War such [independent] actions were chiefly characteristics of airborne forces and advance parties, in our day they may become universal'.[10]

Indeed by 1990 the Russian military's thinking on these matters was already well advanced. They had always appreciated that NATO would execute interdiction strikes in the event of war, but by the early 1980s technological innovations were making it theoretically possible to engage a much larger number of targets over a far greater land area: FOFA was becoming threateningly feasible. Above all it was clear to them that emerging technology such as the weapons and targeting devices of the American 'Assault Breaker' programme – which we will examine shortly – would, within a few years, severely compromise the effectiveness of their armoured *Blitzkrieg* strategy. This of course is precisely what the US hoped it would do. Long before this technology was perfected however, the Russians were already devising possible organisational, operational and technical countermeasures.

A discussion of the last of these more properly belongs in the next section of this chapter. As far as operational and organisational change is concerned however, the Russians commenced experiments with new force structures during the early 1980s. Doubts were already being expressed about their existing strategy's long-term viability because of topographical change in the likely theatre of operations. The monotonous, almost featureless steppes of the USSR had been ideally suited to the immense armoured sweeps of the Great Patriotic War. Here the Russians had been able to compensate for tactical inferiority by achieving an ascendancy at the operational level. Similarly in the campaigns in Poland, Prussia and Brandenburg during 1944–5, most of the fighting had occurred on relatively open and level countryside. But topographically the Western reaches of Germany were very different. True there were large areas of comparatively uncluttered and flat terrain, especially in the North. Generally however there was little to compare with the broad, undulating heaths of Silesia, Pomerania and Prussia. Furthermore crowded West Germany was being transformed by urbanisation, afforestation and enclosure, all of which were likely to hamper, cramp and funnel the movements of invading forces.[11]

The potential impact of topographical change on warfare in Central Europe had first become apparent as early as the second half of the eighteenth century. Then, armies were increasingly compelled to incorporate substantial bodies of more flexible light troops into their order-of-battle to cope with the surge in engagements in urban areas and other constricted terrain where the indiscriminate musketry salvos and ponderous, unwieldy linear tactics of the heavy infantry proved hopelessly inappropriate.[12] Just as in the 1780s force structures had to adapt to meet these new conditions, by the 1980s geographical evolution was seen to be having significant repercussions for force-to-space ratios and other aspects of military planning. In built-up and wooded areas, the effective range of direct-fire, flat-trajectory weapons was truncated. Armoured units had less scope for manoeuvre and indeed, if employed *en masse*, might find making contact with the enemy increasingly difficult as their available approach routes became clogged. In fact in enclosed terrain such forces would not only be unable to exploit their strengths but could prove very vulnerable; channelled into relatively narrow spaces, they would be difficult to control and would be sitting targets for enemy fire, which might even be delivered from quite close quarters by concealed foot troops equipped with armour-piercing missiles.

All of this pointed to a need for greater mobility and dispersion; more emphasis on tactics and on the strategic concept of 'manoeuvre by fire'; smaller but more capable – perhaps purely professional – forces, with high-calibre officers and NCOs trained in the supervision of independent actions; more infantry instead of tanks for the siezing and retaining of positions; and a range of active and passive defences to help counter the opposition's improving long-range attack systems. Both NATO and the Warsaw Pact recognised the need for adjustments to their forces, but the Russians were quickest off the mark. Rather than create brand new units or try to pack yet more capabilities into their existing tank and motor rifle divisions,[13] they elected to retain them but with an altered organisation. In the 1930s and 1940s, the Red Army had employed mobile corps and brigades for operational and tactical manoeuvre, and, especially after 1962, Soviet theoreticians showed mounting interest in reviving this approach.[14]

Eventually corps consisting of carefully tailored brigades with contrasting blends of tank and mechanised infantry units were devised as blueprints for the entire Army. These could then be adapted in line with prevailing economic, political and military guidelines. By switching brigades around for example, an army could be made to look less tank 'heavy' and thus more 'defensive', when in fact the aim might be to make it more suited to a given military objective which could be offensive. One planned division for instance comprises ten infantry and only six tank battalions. This furnishes it with both an enhanced ground-holding capacity and, especially in enclosed terrain, a very powerful assault capability. Likewise the reintroduction of *ukreplennyi raion* – fortified areas – and fortification-construction units by the Russians should not be interpreted as a purely defensive measure: during the Great Patriotic War, fieldworks were often used as hinges and launchpoints for offensive manoeuvre.

At the time of writing it would be difficult to disagree with the assessment of East–West relations given by Richard Perle in testimony to the US Senate's Armed Services Committee in January 1990. A former assistant secretary of defense, he argued that it was 'simply no longer possible to imagine a cohesive Warsaw Pact, led by Soviet troops, forcing its way through the centre of Europe in a massive invasion'. Indeed the Warsaw Pact is formally defunct as a military alliance. Equally some NATO commanders have been left uncertain as to the future mission of their own forces and, perhaps, in which direction they should face. Nevertheless Soviet military power remains an important consideration for our purposes. Because it was the perceived threat of aggression from this quarter that brought NATO into being and because, even after the full implementation of the first Conventional Armed Forces (CFE) Treaty, the Russians will remain the greatest single military power in the Atlantic-to-the-Urals (ATU) region, despite improving relations many NATO and other states will still regard the USSR's armed might as their major, potential security problem – at least as far as the ATU area is concerned. When all is said and done, it is not as though the danger of Magyar expansionism, for example, was ever seen as particularly pressing by the Western powers, and emerging designs for NATO's force dispositions make the alliance's principal concerns quite apparent.

Secondly, even diminished Russian military capabilities furnish a useful yardstick when measuring the potential effectiveness of *Raumverteidigung* and other 'Just Defence' concepts. After all, even when Soviet and Warsaw Pact military power was at its zenith, these postures were advanced as realistic policy options. If the military challenge they might face now and in the future is so different to that of the past that they have ceased to be suitable, then that only highlights their fundamental inflexibility. If on the other hand it is to be assumed that there is not even a danger of military attack from within the ATU region, then what is the rationale for any sort of defence against one?

This is a basic problem with 'Defensive Defence' concepts. They assume a degree of mutual trust which, if it existed, would make defence capabilities beyond those necessary for internal security quite irrelevant. Indeed if a state's principal foreign policy objective is to appear utterly benign, then a state of total disarmament is logically the least menacing posture it could adopt. But except for a few radicals who favour 'passive resistance' to any attack or occupation, few advocates of 'Just Defence' are prepared to go this far. Yet implicit in their decision to prepare to fight is the belief that they might actually be attacked, which reveals their true perceptions of their proposed security 'partners'. That countries like Sweden and Switzerland can be armed to the teeth and yet regarded as unthreatening by their neighbours can only be adequately explained not just in terms of the nature of their military preparations but also their long-standing, scrupulous respect for international law and for the rights and interests of individuals and other states.

We should however say something about 'non-violent resistance'. As we saw in Chapter 3, this approach has been advocated by elements of the 'Peace Movement' since its inception. The Quakers and other religious denominations have been particularly prominent in this regard, as have individual socialists and pacifists such as Ernst Friedrich. Throughout history there have been examples of extraordinarily brave men and women who, irrespective of the consequences for themselves, have steadfastly clung to such principles.[15] However passive resistance does have severe limitations. Above all, it tends to depend on how ruthless the opposition are prepared to be in pursuing their objectives. Professor Raymond Aron once ridiculed it for assuming that 'the age of massacres and exterminations is definitely over, and that a nation which puts down its arms will be neither deported nor reduced to slavery nor purely and simply exterminated'.[16] The gory crushing of the Chinese pro-democracy movement in 1989 suggests that age is still not over, while the experience of occupied Denmark in the early days of the Second World War is another particularly glaring example of the regular failure of passive resistance and civil disobedience techniques. Such outcomes are scarcely surprising however. As in all conflicts, the will to endure punishment to achieve a given goal is of paramount importance. But this type of contest is intolerably uneven; too much if not all of the suffering has to be sustained by one side.

Similarly guerilla warfare has been suggested as a means of resisting occupation. This can lead to many of the problems involved in passive resistance however. Many occupying powers have adopted a policy of '*oderint dum metuant*' – let them hate us as long as they fear us. Acts of resistance have frequently been met with retaliation which, in an attempt to deprive the partisans of popular support, have often been directed against innocent third parties as much as those directly responsible. For example, in 1942 in response to the assassination of Reinhard Heydrich, head of the *Sicherheitsdienst* of the SS in Czechoslovakia, the Nazis exterminated 3000 people, including every male in the village of Lidice.[17] Likewise in 1944, the *Waffen* SS massacred 642 men, women and children at Oradour-sur-Glane in the Haute-Vienne region of France in reprisal for the harassment of occupying troops by the local resistance, while, 30 years before, as these Germans' forefathers swept through Belgium and north-east France, almost every village and town experienced terror as a deliberate policy: innumerable hostages were taken; settlements and the magnificent library at Louvain were burnt to the

ground 'not as a punishment but as a deterrent'; and on the orders of
Generals von Bülow and von Kluck, 150 civilians were executed in
Aershot, 612 at Dinant and 384 at Tamines.[18]

Especially in the Second World War, such policies enjoyed considerable success. Whilst neutral countries like Sweden were harangued for the immorality of a stance which kept them out of the
struggle,[19] the populations of the occupied countries adopted, for the
most part, an attitude of 'anything for a quiet life'. Active resistance
was prosecuted by relatively tiny numbers of citizens, who in so doing
often incurred the wrath of the majority for perpetuating a seemingly
hopeless struggle for which the entire community was made to suffer.
The supporters and members of the French *Maquis*, for example, had
as much reason to fear some of their own countrymen as they had the
Nazis. Indeed in addition to those, as commemorative plaques all
over France record, '*fusillé par les Allemands*', more than a few were
gunned down or betrayed by collaborators among their own people.
Such experiences however were not unique to France, nor to the
Second World War. For guerilla warfare, like *Raumverteidigung*
concepts, might have, as Professor Adam Roberts has commented, a
non-provocative character *vis à vis* foreign states, but is

> extraordinarily provocative . . . once an opponent is not merely a
> foreign state but also an occupying power. The image of a terri-
> torial defence struggle might not be so different from the image of
> the Peninsular War in Spain and Portugal from 1808 to 1814 as
> recorded by Goya in his series of lithographs entitled 'Disasters of
> War'.[20]

Certainly the potentially horrendous costs and destructive and protracted nature of this form of conflict cannot be stressed too strongly.
Any type of war in a congested and urbanised region like Central
Europe threatens to lead to immense structural damage and loss of
life. But the concepts of civilian resistance[21] and 'the nation in arms'
carry with them additional dangers. As Clausewitz warned:

> By its very nature, such scattered resistance will not lend itself to
> major actions, closely compressed in time and space. . . . Like
> smoldering embers it consumes the basic foundations of the enemy
> forces. Since it needs time to be effective, a state of tension will
> develop . . . [which] will either gradually relax, if the insurgency is
> suppressed in some places and slowly burns itself out in others, or

else it will build up to a crisis: a general conflagration closes in on the enemy, driving him out of the country before he is faced with total destruction.[22]

However, although there have been intermittent instances of guerilla operations alone compelling an occupying power to withdraw, generally this type of resistance is more irritating than decisive unless carried on in conjunction with operations by regular forces. This was made very clear in the Spanish *Guerra de la Independencia* of 1808–14. Moreover, as the Spanish discovered in the wake of that war, once a population has become accustomed to employing violence for political purposes, the process can spill over into domestic politics and prove difficult to stop; most of the guerilla leaders who had fought so bravely against the French in the Peninsular War, for example, were later executed by the very king they had helped restore, for fighting to secure internal reform. Lastly we should note the need for outside logistical support in maintaining a lengthy guerilla war. The British provided this to the Spanish during 1808–14 and for many of the European resistance movements between 1940 and 1945; the Americans and others later did the same for the Afghan *mujahadeen* between 1979 and 1989. Who would or could have provided it had Western Europe ever fallen under Soviet occupation during the Cold War era must remain an open question.

Whatever the precise nature of the defence might be however, by shunning the capacity for retaliation 'Just Defence' ensures that the battlefield can *only* be one's home territory. As we saw in Chapter 1, it has been argued that a strategy that lacks the potential for inflicting punishment on an aggressor is weaker in deterrence terms than one which combines defence with retribution and the threat of escalation, while Clausewitz insisted that the 'flashing sword of vengeance' must be an integral part of defence if it is to be effective. Indeed to many commentators the basic problem with most of the purely conventional defence options that NATO might adopt is just that they are too much concepts of defence rather than of deterrence. Even if NATO's first and last political objective is the defence of its members – an objective which Gorbachev for one seems to have acknowledged is sincerely sought and which is, to an extent, *structurally* imposed on the alliance's military forces by a rigid hierarchy of political control and by a lack of sustainability for any kind of grand strategic offensive – that is not a reason for eschewing any and every type of offensive capability. Apart from rendering the task of calculating the costs and

benefits of aggression far harder, even a limited capacity for counterstrokes against an attacker's homeland can bring vast operational
dividends. It obliges him to think defensively as well as offensively,
and to devote at least some resources to protective missions. Furthermore, as he cannot be absolutely certain where an attack might fall,
he has to endeavour to be universally strong. This can absorb quite
significant resources which could otherwise be devoted to his offensive.

As we saw throughout Chapter 1, NATO's deployment in the past
has owed far more to politics, inertia, economics and history than to
any operational considerations, be they defensive or offensive. Indeed NATO's 'offensive' capabilities have been geared not to the
mounting of invasions of an opponent's territory but to rendering any
incursion into its members' homelands more manageable militarily
speaking. Unlike Huntington's conventional retaliation strategy,
concepts like FOFA have not sought to go beyond the regional defeat
of an aggressor. They are intended to reduce the tempo and weight of
his offensive either through interdiction or, in the case of tactical
nuclear arms for example, by compelling him to disperse his units,
thus making them less able to both secure or exploit a breakthrough.
If this option is to be totally renounced, then the main defensive line
will have to be sufficiently strong to resist whatever forces can be
concentrated against it; and even with interdiction attacks, that has
always appeared an unattainable goal for NATO.

If for instance NATO were to forego any capacity for offensive
counter-air operations, then the following repercussions could be
expected. First, an aggressor could devote the resources which would
otherwise be needed for the protection of his own airforces and fields
to supporting his offensive. These might include command, control
and intelligence-gathering units, surface-to-air (SAM) missiles, air-
defence fighters and ground forces used for base perimeter security.
Second, unmolested by suppressive attacks, his rotary-and-fixed-wing
aircraft could maximise their sortie-rates. Together these two factors
could decisively swing the battle in the attacker's favour. Even if the
numbers of aircraft at his disposal were not especially large, the
'force multiplier' effects would be considerable. He might very easily
establish air supremacy which, as has been demonstrated in virtually
every major war since 1939, yields enormous benefits. Indeed it is
improbable that even the strongest of ground defences could withstand attacks backed by substantial airpower, particularly if its own
supporting air defence relied on SAMs. These have effective range
ceilings – beyond which many aircraft can operate with impunity,

especially if equipped with stand-off weaponry – and, as we shall see, suffer from other, exploitable technical weaknesses. Indeed recognising this, even the Swedes, who in many respects are quite enamoured with territorial defence concepts, have preferred to entrust the bulk of their air defence missions to *Viggen* aircraft rather than SAM batteries.[23] Unlike missiles, planes are discriminating, reusable and can engage numerous targets over a variety of ranges. In any case, the surface of the earth can be pictured as the coastline of the air. Just as the most cost-effective way to protect a coast is not by dispersing guns and vessels along its full length – as has been suggested by 'Defensive Defence' advocates[24] – but by controlling the surrounding seas, so too is securing command of the air far preferable to scattering batteries and planes all over the earth's surface.

The Swiss too – who again put considerable emphasis on territorial defence – have recognised the limitations of purely static resistance. Fixed defences can furnish stable weapon platforms, cover, and scope for observation and concealment. But they can be pinpointed even before hostilities commence and are vulnerable to long-range counter fire. Similarly whilst built-up areas, for example, can offer a defender certain advantages, these are not as great as they sometimes appear. Besides the obvious problems posed by the presence of large numbers of civilian inhabitants, many conurbations are not ideally oriented for defence; they lie parallel to, rather than straddle, possible attack axes. Moreover, whereas forests are often rooted in shallow soil strata, making the digging of trenches and other defensive positions very hard, too many buildings are insufficiently robust for sustained defence. As can be seen from any photo of battle-scarred Beirut, multi-storey constructions for instance too easily fold in on themselves when hit by shellfire. In fact it is often easier and safer to defend ruins. This is an important consideration for, as NATO exercises in the Kassel area of Germany in 1986 highlighted, steadily improving road networks are making even quite cluttered areas porous to tanks and self-propelled artillery which can be used to focus substantial firepower on buildings from relatively close quarters.

In any case their basic permeability makes the defence of woods, built-up areas and other intricate terrain manpower-intensive. An entire battalion might be required to adequately protect a solitary village of modest proportions, for instance, while the problems of controlling dispersed fighting of this nature are considerable. Nor should it be forgotten that artificial and natural barriers can impede and restrict the movements of friendly ground forces as well as hostile ones; few mines, for example, can as yet reliably distinguish between the two, and friendly units endeavouring to withdraw or advance will find choke-points, rivers and other obstacles equally indiscriminating. The favoured option is therefore to use settlements and other strongholds as pivots for manoeuvre; forces will fight from rather than in them, and this calls for tanks and other vehicles capable of manoeuvre under fire. The Swiss for example are blessed with a defensive geography *par excellence*, which they have reinforced with the most advanced man-made fortifications in the world. Yet they still see the need for nearly 1000 *Leopard* and other main battle tanks to cover areas of open terrain and lock horns with invading armoured forces.

The supporters of 'Defensive Defence' are, as we have noted, reluctant to contemplate any fighting within population centres and have endeavoured to exclude major conurbations from their *Raumverteidigung* models. Indeed assailing urban areas is a notoriously time-consuming and gory process which demands a plenitude of infantry especially. Tanks can be helpful in the reducing of strongholds, but are generally poorly suited to street fighting: they are rather bulky for operations in such confined spaces and, when the hatches are closed, the crew has very restricted vision; at short ranges the limits on the depression and elevation of their guns make it virtually impossible to bombard the cellars or upper storeys of buildings; and their relatively thin top armour, coupled with the increased opportunities for attack from above that fighting in streets presents, makes them far more susceptible to destruction by even short-range anti-armour weapons. Thus, particularly for an aggressor seeking a rapid victory in order to head off escalation or to avoid a long war in which economic power might prove decisive, the besieging of cities and so on is unlikely to be attractive. On the other hand, given the highly developed and urbanised nature of much of the heartland of the NATO region – especially western Germany – it seems that in the event of war it would be virtually impossible to totally evade engagements in built-up areas.

In many senses however, the 'Just Defence' movement's distaste for the economic, societal and structural destruction implicit in urban warfare spotlights one of the great paradoxes in their reasoning. The West German theorists in particular have, as we have seen, been primarily motivated by their fear of the consequences should deterrence fail. 'Flexible Response' includes the explicit threat to use nuclear weapons. This could only lead to the devastation of Germany – an 'irrational' situation, as NATO was and is supposed to defend Germany, not preside over her destruction. Conventional defence strategies were thus seen as preferable, and a plethora of variations on the 'Defensive Defence' theme was duly advanced. Yet as noted above, the sort of protracted conventional conflict favoured by the West German theorists was likely to prove only marginally less damaging for their country than nuclear war.[25] But if 'Flexible Response' was to be rejected on the grounds of its assumed consequences, why should the virtually ineluctable repercussions of 'Defensive Defence' be any more acceptable, particularly as they might still culminate in the use of nuclear firepower anyway? When for example, in an effort to justify 'Non-Offensive Defence', John Grin and Lutz Unterseher maintain that 'in the nuclear age, the party that [conventionally] counterattacks would have to reckon with the risk of nuclear retaliation, however irrational and self-defeating such a reaction would be',[26] does it not occur to them that a purely defensive operation might provoke the selfsame response from an aggressor, especially if he is losing?

Henry Kissinger once observed that some of America's European allies wanted 'the *appearance* of nuclear support so that the Soviets never challenge their vital interests. [But] whether they are actually prepared to face the consequences of nuclear war is ambiguous'.[27] This is particularly true of many supporters of 'Just Defence'. On the one hand they have a visceral dislike for nuclear arms and even the thought of their use whilst, on the other, many expect the US to provide some form of final, nuclear but non-threatening guarantee for their security. Nuclear deterrence apparently has its merits after all.

Horst Afheldt, for example, argued in 1978 that the mission of his proposed technocommandos would be to make an attack on and occupation of NATO territories by the USSR 'politically and militarily as costly as possible'. Their 'credible, nonnuclear, limited-range' defence would prevent a *fait accompli* and give the US time to mobilise not only its conventional but also its nuclear forces, especially its submarine fleet.[28] (Nuclear strike capabilities based in Europe or the US would only invite pre-emptive attacks, he insisted, and, if used against invading forces, would also be destroying that which NATO sought to defend.) The submarine force would then be used in a 'rational strategy of threat or coercion'. Only targets would be menaced whose destruction the Soviet government would find 'unacceptable'; and, Afheldt suggested, this meant jeopardising their hegemony in Eastern Europe. 'Every nation of the Warsaw Pact that took part in an active attack on NATO would be admonished: "After warnings to give the local population opportunity to evacuate the target areas, NATO will begin with minor attacks on the economic infrastructure."' Although in a later work he was to dismiss any threats to use nuclear weapons as 'blackmail' and lacking in credibility,[29] if these warnings went unheeded, Afheldt continued, and if the countries concerned did not desist from participating in the attack, their economic infrastructure would 'if necessary' be destroyed. The Soviet response to this ultimatum, he assumed, would be in kind; but as their forces would be occupying German territory, their margin for threatening German targets would be correspondingly diminished. A political dialogue would therefore *have* to be resumed.[30]

Leaving aside the incredible selfcentredness of this policy and its utter impracticality – as Chernobyl demonstrated in 1986, even the most 'minor' of nuclear bombardments would have appalling repercussions for the whole continent – its logic is fundamentally flawed. NATO is a nuclear-armed alliance. Any attack by the Warsaw Pact on it would have run the risk of nuclear retaliation, however small that danger might actually be. If the Russians were prepared to accept that risk in the first place, they would either be acting totally irrationally – in which case they could neither be reasoned with diplomatically nor deterred – or they would perceive themselves to be in such a dire situation that war – even one that might culminate in nuclear obliteration – was the only possible way out. In his case, the use by NATO of nuclear weapons would be part of their calculations and assumptions. If they were undeterred by that at the outset, why should they suddenly be overconcerned by it at some subsequent stage, particularly as all that was under immediate threat was not their own country but an expendable military glacis? In any event, having been warned that the conflict was about to become nuclear and having fairly concluded that they would have nothing to lose by striking first, might the Russians have not done just that?

Afheldt assumed that their objective would be to occupy his country and that they would therefore be unwilling to see it devastated. But in devising their military strategies, the supporters of 'Defensive Defence' all too often take such a narrow scenario as a postulate. Consequently their political and military calculations are too inflexible to cope if confronted by some other challenge. Having embarked on a world war, it is far more likely that the Russians' aim would have been something infinitely grander and urgent than the mere acquisition of territory and population: the breaking of NATO's military power and political will. Faced with a desperate need to achieve this, they might indeed have used nuclear weapons; and if, as Afheldt claimed, the loss of some economic potential in the territories of their vassal states would have been 'unacceptable' to the Russians, how would the West German government have viewed the razing of, say, Cologne?

Equally, how might Germany's neighbours, especially Britain and France? After all, the quickest way to end a war is to lose it; and even if, as Afheldt maintained, his suggested approach would have bought time and created a stalemate in which negotiations could have been opened,[31] what would they have been about? To everyone they would have looked like a tacit admission of defeat by West Germany; to the Russians, who presumably had concluded before starting the conflict that there was no progress to be made by talking, they would indeed have heralded the capitulation they sought – and if that was not quickly proffered, they would have dismissed them as a time-gaining ploy aimed at involving the USSR in a prolonged *Zermürbungskrieg* which, given its economic inferiority, it could not hope to win. For NATO the only successful outcome would be the restoration of the *status quo ante*. How, given the military stalemate, would that have been achieved? Indeed would the two blocs not have faced much the same situation they confronted immediately before hostilities commenced, namely fight or capitulate? And as the Russians had already decided that the latter would be intolerable, would the outcome not be escalation? What would Afheldt have NATO negotiate, apart from the terms of its own surrender?

In any case it is very unlikely that conventional defence plans like Afheldt's would or could succeed in holding off a determined attack. He first envisaged, in 1978, a force of 10 000 technocommando units dispersed across an area of around 200 000 square kilometres. (Major connurbations would be avoided.) Each unit would thus have to cover about 20 square kilometres and would comprise some 20 men for anti-armour operations and a further 16–19 for air defence and other tasks. Their principal armament would be *Milan* type portable anti-tank rockets, and target-seeking missiles with a range of at least 25 kilometres. Afheldt expected each unit to account for a statistical average of three enemy tanks in combat. By 1988 he was advocating a very similar scheme but based on the work of Eckart

Afheldt.[32] Light infantry teams would man a *Raumverteidigung* of 70–110 kilometres in depth. A network of static, small, single-shot rocket-launchers with a maximum range of 40 kilometres would furnish the defence's firepower, though a few mobile units would also be deployed until such time as the defensive net could be completed. Each square kilometer of the *Raumverteidigung* should, Afheldt suggested, contain 5 rocket-launchers, each with a range of 40 kilometres. Thus if an attacker penetrated the border on a 50-kilometre front, his units would instantly come within striking distance of 12 500 missiles. If he continued to a depth of 100 kilometres, '100 000 missiles would be available to the defender to destroy the attacking forces'.

This sounds impressive, but it is really utterly implausible. To begin with, it is impossible that a defence of such density could be afforded. An average of one missile-launcher per square kilometer would be difficult to achieve, let alone five. Even then a host of other problems would ensue. Who would maintain all these launchers and their sophisticated, target-seeking missiles? Would they be kept armed at all times? If not, where would the warheads be stored, how and when would they be distributed, and how would they be kept safe from the elements, inquisitive children, saboteurs, terrorists and vandals? After all a solitary blaze at a warehouse in Donnington, Shropshire during 1988 effectively destroyed all of the wartime tank-spaces and other back-up equipment of the British 'Army of the Rhine'. Indeed what would a civilian population which is increasingly environmentally aware make of these proposals, not to mention the people living up to, say, 35 kilometres beyond the border? Would they really find living among scores of minefields and under the muzzles of these thousands of rocket-launchers palatable? And would the governments of neighbouring states really perceive this potential to saturate *their* side of the frontier with fire as unprovocative and benign?

Secondly, how effective would the system be operationally? Any defender faces the initial problem of having to guard everywhere whilst retaining enough strength for the main battle wherever it occurs. But a *Raumverteidigung* is especially feeble in this regard, for it is questionable whether adequate man- and firepower could be concentrated anywhere. An attacker with any sense would disregard most of the web, cutting a number of very narrow, converging axes which would enable his forces to mingle with hostile units and population centres. This would make the continued use of indirect fire by the defence an increasingly hazardous and impractical under-taking. As it is, for technical reasons we will examine shortly, the accurate coordination and delivery of long-range fire can be an immensely complex – and expensive – business; perhaps a third or more of all the missiles activated could be expected to malfunction and many others would be wasted if only in 'overkill'. Meanwhile, *desant* operations and airpower could be employed by the attacker to clear a path for his ground units which, by combining, say, infantry assaults with concentrated artillery fire, could overwhelm an anti-tank orientated defence all too easily.[33]

In fact this homogeneity threatens to prove a fatal flaw. The effectiveness of modern combat forces is largely derived from the synergism achieved by integrating contrasting types of units and weapons. This enables them to cope with a range of challenges and environments. Infantrymen for example are used not just for the holding of ground but also for assault and for giving armoured units close support against anti-tank defences. Fixed- and rotary-wing aircraft are also incorporated into the scheme of things, being used both offensively and defensively. The essentially monotonous *Raum-verteidigung* models are the antithesis of this approach. The few 'spider' units in the web cannot be everywhere and, if committed against major assaults, are likely to prove too puny to have much impact; by the 1980s NATO had concluded that very substantial forces were needed for efficacious counterstrokes. So all too often the static light infantry units would have to fight alone. Although con-stantly threatened with encirclement, they would have no means of guarding their flanks and rear, and their ammunition would quickly be exhausted in any firefight. In any case, apart from their strictly limited and single-threat-focussed firepower, units of less than 40 men also suffer from a lack of redundancy; after a few casualties had been sustained, the whole force would be effectively *hors de combat*.

Indeed, although the small size and dispersed nature of the de-fending units can make targeting and observing them more problem-atic, once combat is actually joined these characteristics can become positive drawbacks. Firstly, a target is a target. Unprotected troops are woefully vulnerable to any kind of firepower, even that of smallarms, and a modern Soviet motorised infantry division, for instance, has 25 times the firepower of a comparable division of the Second World War.[34] In fact the unarmoured, lorry-borne infantry which played such an important role in that conflict has really had its day; shells designed to splinter into colossal numbers of fragments, fuel-air explosives and submunitions used *en masse* are capable of killing and injuring personnel on an unprecedented scale, even if they are scattered across relatively large areas. Only troops sheltered in armoured vehicles or ensconced in sealed bunkers with ceilings at least a metre thick can survive in this environment. Whilst far from indestructable, vehicles do allow for manoeuvre under fire – including retreat if necessary – whereas the fixed position can be more easily targeted, is unlikely to withstand modern, deep-penetration warheads, and is incapable of ferrying its garrison to a place of safety; once their position is overrun, they face surrender or extermination.

Equally this lack of mobility multiplies the problems of logistical sustainability. If required, platforms like tanks can move to acquire more ammunition or whatever is wanting. Static defences on the other hand must by definition be kept supplied with everything they need. This entails either having adequate stockpiles with every combat unit or finding some secure method of distributing supplies in quantities commensurate with consumption. In a rambling *Raumverteidigung* containing thousands of scattered combat teams, neither of these options would be viable. As one SACEUR once remarked, if 'Defensive Defence' means 'no more mobility, I'm not sure that is any defence'.[35]

This raises two, largely interlocking considerations: logistical sustainability and the maintenance of morale. The Americans' deployment of substantial armed forces to the Persian Gulf during the summer of 1990 highlighted the vast quantities of *matériel* necessary to nourish military operations of any size. In high-intensity combat, a typical heavy division can be expected to devour some 1000 tonnes of ammunition, spares, rations, fuel, water, lubricants and other supplies every day. Although some technical innovations – such as the Dismountable Rack Off-Loading and Pickup System (DROPS) now in use with the British Army – have eased certain problems encountered in resupply, broadly speaking the trend towards automatic weapons and ever more mechanisation has compounded the difficulties involved immensely. Indeed the pattern that has emerged over the past 200 years is alarming: a commissariat officer with Wellington's army at Vitoria in 1813 noted that, in a day's fighting which resulted in just 8000 enemy casualties, some 3 675 000 rounds of musket and 7000 of artillery ammunition were expended;[36] in the opening weeks of the Great War, the Germans, despite having allocated five times as many shells per artillery piece as in 1870, found themselves running short; during the Second World War, a typical plane-mounted cannon could discharge some 1200 rounds every minute, whereas today the figure is nearer 6000; while the 105 millimetre howitzer currently in use with several NATO Armies is capable of unleashing a shell every ten seconds.

Scarcely surprisingly, peacetime stocks of ammunition and other essentials have failed to keep abreast of these escalating, potential demands. Furthermore modern equipment is so costly that accumulating adequate stockpiles is prohibitively expensive. Simply procuring the range of weapons that is necessary to keep the term 'multi-role aircraft', for example, from being a misnomer is difficult enough. In fact, despite guidelines calling for enough supplies for 30 days of combat, the alliance's collective reserves are well short of the quantities of *matériel* required, and only the US could even contemplate sustaining a major conventional war for this sort of period. The Russians on the other hand have amassed sufficient stockpiles for 60–90 days of combat and, as we shall see, their industry is largely geared to replenishing these at short notice. The West's economy by contrast, though much bigger is essentially designed for the meeting of consumer needs in peacetime; it would require 180 days at least to switch to a war footing and get into a position to satisfy the military's requirements.[37]

The surge in the consumption of *matériel* is partly a result of the expansion of combat both in terms of time and space that is another consequence of the application of modern technology. Much of the so-called Seven Years' War, for example, was made up of periods of complete military inactivity; the armies and fleets stayed in their camps and harbours awaiting those few months of the year when weather and other considerations made military operations practical. In recent years however, just as the advent of electronic detection systems transformed maritime warfare, the nature of land combat is undergoing a revolution because of technological innovation. Operations can now be conducted around the clock. Darkness and bad weather no longer guarantee cover for recuperation and resupply. The increasing transparency of the battlefield, coupled with the growth in effective homing munitions and long-range delivery systems, means that, as one Soviet marshal has pointed out, combat can be immediately extended not just to the border regions but throughout the length and breadth of a country.[38] Fighting threatens to be more widespread, exhausting, confusing and complex than ever before. Stimulating drugs will be as much a part of the soldier's kit as traditional rations. Opportunities for sleep, eating, evacuation, repairs and maintenance work will be rarer, yet the wear and tear on equipment and personnel far greater.

All of this puts a premium on improved logistical lifelines, partly because no amount of sophisticated technology can make up for a lack of ammunition, but also because an army still 'marches on its stomach'. Napoleon insisted that 'In war the morale is to the material as three to one', while Clausewitz's opinion, that 'Morale elements are among the most important in war',[39] has been repeatedly borne out by experience in combat and even in manoeuvres. One of the most revealing studies of what actually underpins morale in military forces was undertaken by two former members of the Psychological Warfare Division of the Supreme Headquarters, Allied Expeditionary Force, Europe (SHAEF) during the Second World War. Through extensive interrogation of German prisoners of war, they compiled a collection of results which have very grave implications for the advocates of *Raumverteidigung* concepts.[40]

As we noted in Chapter 1, much of the American interest in doctrinal reform during the 1980s was inspired by disillusionment with the almost passive nature of the US Army's 'Active Defence' approach. A very similar debate took place within the French Army after its defeat by Prussia in 1870–1. French doctrine, it was perceived, had been too submissive for there to have been any other outcome. *École de Guerre* instructors such as Lucien Cardot argued that too little attention had been paid to the question of morale, the offensive spirit, initiative and Henry Bergson's concept of *l'élan vital*. This made a great impression on a whole generation of French cadets, among them Ferdinand Foch, and within thirty years the offensive was firmly embodied in French manuals as the *ne plus ultra* of military operations; passive defence was to be 'rejected absolutely', for it was 'doomed to certain defeat'.[41] With the benefit of hindsight, 'Just Defence' supporters like Horst Afheldt might ridicule this 'cult of the offensive' as strategically and tactically inept. But its underlying, subtler aim was and is too important to dismiss. It recognised that sustaining the troops' morale in a static *bataille d'usure* was harder than in one of manoeuvre and, above all, that the object of military operations must not be reduced to achieving a stalemate rather than a victory. This was the perceived weakness of the US Army's 'Active Defence' doctrine and it was this that the introduction of *Field Manual 100–5* and *Air–Land Battle* sought to rectify; the initiative and 'agility' – a mental attribute as much as a physical one – were portrayed as essential to success.

Whatever the tactical and strategic merits of this *modus operandi* might be, according to the SHAEF psychology professors' findings, from a morale-sustaining point of view at least the prescriptions of the 'cult of the defensive' are palpably inferior. Firstly, whilst certain very distinctive groups of soldiers like the International Brigade of the Spanish Civil War have been primarily motivated by their devotion to major political goals, the vast majority of personnel – especially in nonprofessional armies – are barely interested in such grand matters. When questioned about the political opinions of his men, one captured *Wehrmacht* sergeant, for example, laughed and replied:

When you ask such a question, I realize well that you have no idea of what makes a soldier fight. The soldiers lie in their holes and are happy if they live through the next day. If we think at all, it's about the end of the war and then home.[42]

In fact it would seem that the steady satisfaction of certain primary personality and material needs plays the key role in maintaining a unit's cohesion and will to fight. These include esteem, affection and companionship, as well as adequate leadership, food, medical care, ammunition, weaponry, clothing and concern on the officers' part for the individual soldier's welfare and survival.[43] Whenever the meeting of any of these requirements was seriously disturbed, the SHAEF studies revealed, the determination to resist likewise disappeared. The main sources of disruption were found to be: the dilution of the sense of comradeship due to indiscriminate influxes of recruits of diverse ages and backgrounds; the loss of psychological solidarity within a unit as a result of its physical dispersion; threats to the safety of the soldier's hometown; a failure to see the role of unit and personal missions because of an inordinately complex strategy or army organisation; loss of leadership; prolonged breaks in the supply of food and other essentials; and, last but not least, circumstances where the threat to individual survival seemed greatest and where the prospects for tactical success seemed utterly bleak, as under concentrated artillery or air bombardment, for instance.[44]

From their very nature it is clear that *Raumverteidigung* models of the type favoured by the 'Just Defence' movement are inherently susceptible to many of these demoralising agents. We have already noted the difficulties involved in keeping their garrisons adequately supplied, and these could only worsen as the battle progressed and parts of the net became encircled. Similarly the tactical dispersion of the troops and their passive, defensive approach could pose morale problems of immense proportions. Concerning the latter, Alistair Horne has noted the insidious destruction that this type of doctrine inflicted on the defenders of the Maginot Line[45] for example, while, with regard to the former, as the SHAEF psychologists observed on the Western front in 1944–5,

> the tactical situation of defensive fighting under heavy . . . artillery bombardment . . . forced soldiers to take refuge in cellars, trenches, and other underground shelters in small groups of three or four. This prolonged isolation from the nucleus [of their unit] . . . for several days worked to reinforce the fear of destruction of the self, and thus had a disintegrative influence. . . . A soldier who was isolated in a . . . concrete bunker . . . and whose anxieties about physical survival were aggravated by the tactical hopelessness of his situation, was a much more easily separable member of his [combat] group than one who, though fearing physical destruction, was still bound by the continuous and vital ties of working, eating, sleeping, and being at leisure together with his fellow soldiers.[46]

Likewise the effective command and control of these defensive webs and their supporting 'spider' units would be very difficult. Even if the buried communications network envisaged in most models proved capable of coping with the varied and vast demands that would be placed on it, the coordination of thousands of essentially independent units would be an awesome task. Because of their dispersed mode of fighting, light infantry have traditionally had a larger proportion of officers and NCOs.[47] But these have to be of high calibre and are simply not available in sufficient numbers to direct several hundred thousand men in this style of combat. Yet without close supervision the units are likely to prove ineffective. Besides the problem of demoralisation, how, without some form of centralised control, would *all* the rocket troops in a given area be restrained from launching *all* their missiles at just one target as soon as it came into range? And who would have effective control over where and when the 'spider' units were committed? What priorities would they adopt, and would they harmonise with those of the net defenders, including those for logistical support?

The local-based nature of the defence would also be likely to have its drawbacks. Troops who have an intimate knowledge of a given region can of course put this to good tactical use. However many soldiers would be reluctant to see their home towns destroyed and their loved ones jeopardised as a result of stubborn resistance. The SHAEF psychologists found that

> When the area of the soldier's home was occupied by the enemy or when the soldier himself was fighting in the area, there was a strong disposition to desert homeward. One such soldier said: 'Now I have nothing more for which to fight, because my home is occupied'.[48]

Similarly another who had surrendered prematurely remarked that, after a period in a bunker without much to do, 'The men often discussed capture. Conversation usually started about families: who was married and what was to become of his family'.[49] Likewise others frequently commented that defeatism and the desire to surrender arose 'not from discussions about the war in its political and strategic aspects, but rather about the soldiers' families'.[50]

For reservists, who not only have to suddenly undergo the transformation from civilian to soldier but also cope with the change from peace to war, influences of this kind could have especially debilitating effects on morale. In any case such troops are not particularly suited to light infantry operations, and reliance upon them to undertake this type of work is yet another flaw in most *Raumverteidigung* models. Reservists are often enthusiastic and are perfectly capable of performing many missions. But as Winston Churchill once remarked, 'Wars are not won by heroic militias', and 'tank hunting' is a job that only elite infantry are sufficiently trained and disciplined for. Even for them, as any British Royal Marine would confirm, executing this sort of mission on the modern battlefield promises to be a formidable task.[51] Indeed it is partly in an effort to get round the morale and other problems encountered in trying to engage hostile armour at short ranges with man-portable anti-tank weapons that many 'Defensive Defence' theorists favour the use of long-range, indirect-fire systems. However this is scarcely a solution. Such armaments tend to be more sophisticated, heavier and bulkier. They therefore have to be mounted either on a vehicle or in a bunker fitted with a suitable recoil-absorption apparatus. This, together with their need for intricate and costly targeting and guidance mechanisms, makes them much more expensive and easier to detect and counter. Above all however, indirect fire is too often dangerously inapplicable once the defence has actually been penetrated and the battlefield becomes a tangle of friendly and hostile forces. Thus line-of-sight armaments are preferable, even though combat at shorter ranges usually calls for good quality personnel.

In any event the mobilisation of reservists and other troops would entail several problems. Carl Conetta and Charles Knight have asserted that 'Because the net battalions are relatively static, mobilising them in times of crises would entail little or no provocation'.[52] But this is unconvincing. Any 'crisis' meriting mobilisation would presumably involve a real risk of armed conflict and it would clearly be in the interests of any state contemplating military action to try to prevent or pre-empt any measures that might thwart their own. The advocates of 'Just Defence' have often disparaged deployment procedures – notably the Schlieffen Plan and similar pre-First World War schemes – as being, together with arms-races, the major causes of war. As we have seen, that is a very doubtful claim. But even if one were to accept it, that would not make such military imperatives any less ineluctable or exigent – even if the aim was unambiguously defensive. By the very act of preparing to fight, a country signals that it expects either to attack or be attacked. War has a reciprocal nature, and to claim that the mobilisation of one's own forces is clearly benign whilst the same move on the part of a potential adversary is provocative and destabilising seems eclectic to say the least.

But the danger of being hoisted with their own petard is not the only one the supporters of 'Defensive Defence' would face should mobilisation of their *Raumverteidigung* models ever prove necessary. As the American experience in the Persian Gulf crisis of 1990 demonstrated, summoning reservists to the colours is a disruptive and expensive business. The quicker the matter can be resolved and the troops sent home, the better. Moreover as, irrespective of the technology involved, getting one's blow in first can have both military and political attractions, *Blitzkrieg* tactics like those used by Iraq against Kuwait in 1990 have much to recommend them: the defence might be overpowered before it can muster its strength and the world is then presented with a *fait accompli*. Even in countries where localised, territorial defence has a high profile and where mobilisation can theoretically be achieved relatively swiftly, the time periods required remain appreciable. Sweden, for example, needs 72 and Switzerland 48 hours. Moreover many Swedish and Swiss towns lie close to coastal or land frontiers and are thus particularly vulnerable to a *coup de main*.

Neither of these countries are, however, 'front line' states. They are protected by friendly buffer zones and would in any case be unlikely to be the ultimate objective of an attack; it is more probable that their territory would be violated by forces heading elsewhere. Furthermore, should they ever have to engage in protracted conventional warfare, they, like the other major unaligned states in Europe, would benefit from favourable geographic conditions. Those in Switzerland have already been mentioned, while Sweden, Finland and Yugoslavia all enjoy considerable strategic depth. Finland's area, for example, is only slightly smaller than the whole of Germany but contains few vulnerable concentrations of population. Such conditions make the defence policies of these countries far more viable than they would be in crowded Central Europe for instance. Indeed it is noteworthy that the states which proved most adept at conducting defence in depth during the Second World War were all relatively underdeveloped, not heavily urbanised and contained large, natural bastions such as forests and mountains.[53]

Indeed the common assumption on the part of 'Defensive Defence' theorists that their prescriptions are generally applicable in space and time is misguided. As Professor Adam Roberts has concluded, some aspects of territorial defence have considerable potential, but they 'cannot completely replace existing forces, doctrines and alliances, nor can they entirely supplant nuclear deterrence. Switzerland cannot be slavishly copied by . . . Germany or any other country'.[54]

Similarly the few members of the 'Just Defence' cult who have turned their attention to the question of naval power commit essentially the same error. It might indeed be feasible for some states to rely on coastal defence forces. Others however, like the UK and USA, cannot. The core of British military power in the past has been maritime muscle, which has been used in the support of both British and allied armies operating in Europe and on other continents. The same is essentially true of the USA. If, as is suggested by the 'Defensive Defence' movement, this capacity for power projection is dismantled, how will island nations like the British come to the assistance of their allies, police international sea-lanes and guard their own vital interests? In any case, adequately protecting a coastline with garrisons and static gun-emplacements can be a Herculean task; the innumerable coves and straits that make up, for example, the Danish sea-shore around Jutland alone have a total length in excess of 7000 kilometres.

Indeed ultimately maritime security must rest not on the defence of mere coastlines but on the control of whole sea areas and the preservation of freedom of navigation. Who, under a 'Defensive Defence' regime, would undertake this? It is not, after all, as though NATO has much choice in this regard. The very title of the alliance stresses the significance of the sea. Whereas to the Russians, for instance, 'blue water' naval capabilities and substantial merchant fleets are of very secondary significance, for NATO they are an imperative. The economies of its members are largely dependent on raw materials, notably oil, which are imported by ship. Likewise, in the event of conflict, 75 per cent of all Russian reinforcements and war stocks could be moved by railways, with much of the balance going by road. NATO would *have* to transport 90 per cent of its reinforcements and *matériel* by sea.[55]

When all of these threads are drawn together, it is apparent that 'Defensive Defence' is an inferior military doctrine when compared with 'Flexible Response'. In seeking to look non-provocative and benign, the former sacrifices far too much in the way of military efficiency and dependability without necessarily securing either of these objectives. Even if such a defence could be made to work satisfactorily, it would not make armed conflict any less probable or destructive and could not even guarantee to obviate the danger of nuclear war – the 'Just Defence' lobby's principal objection to 'Flexible Response'. Overall the concept fails to take adequate account of the fact that the various members of NATO have both differing views of the requirements for deterrence and contrasting opinions on what military objectives would be appropriate if deterrence were to fail. Indeed, given that 'Defensive Defence' can by its very nature only pose very restricted risks to any would-be aggressor, it has to be evaluated more as a war-fighting strategy than one for war avoidance.

In this key regard it is very doubtful that it would improve on 'Flexible Response': it would be no better suited to the sustaining of a forward defence against either a limited incursion or a reinforced attack; and besides being unlikely to secure much time for formulating responses, would so circumscribe the nature of any retort as to make it insignificant anyway. 'Just Defence' cannot threaten an adversary with escalation. It almost overlooks what the peacetime role of armed forces is: namely to convince any potential opponent that a recourse to war as an instrument of policy, even defensive policy, would be counter-productive because the conflict would either be lost or prove prohibitively costly. In fact forces structured for 'Non-Offensive Defence' could not even be expected to retake lost territory and restore the *status quo ante*.

That presumably is the minimal hope if not objective of any *defence* policy, and, as we saw in Chapter 2, some 'Defensive Defence' theorists, notably Albrecht von Müller, have incorporated a capacity for retaliatory action into their models in an attempt to close this glaring gap. Obviously however, this runs contrary to the postulates of 'Just Defence'; forces which are capable of mounting substantial counterattacks to regain lost ground are equally capable of attacking and seizing the territory of neighbouring states. Attempting to get round this contradiction, advocates of the SAS blueprint, for example, have argued that the counteroffensive strength of such 'spider' units within the defensive web 'derives from their interaction with the net; outside of it their offensive potential quickly diminishes'.[56] But surely the same is true of NATO's current ground forces? They are firmly under the political control of representative, democratic governments which are unlikely to sanction anything other than defensive operations and, more to the point, their extremely restricted logistical sustainability renders them incapable of going beyond limited ripostes anyway; they are structurally incapable of invading, though not of attacking.

This is an important point, if only because it clarifies what the Russians mean when they speak of a 'defensive strategy'. From conversations with his then counterpart, Marshal Akhromeyev, Admiral Crowe, the former head of the US JCS, concluded in the wake of it formal announcement in 1987 that their 'new doctrine means that the Soviet Union will initially remain on the defensive for about 20 days while trying to negotiate a peace. If that fails, Soviet forces will have to launch a "counteroffensive"'.[57] This interpretation harmonises entirely with the views and ideas expressed in the Russians' own military literature. In fact, if their writings on operational, strategic and tactical issues are surveyed as a whole, its is clear that they are formulating something similar to *Air–Land Battle* as far as doctrine is concerned and are trying to devise the best force structures they can for carrying it out.[58] Economic and other pressures have set the tempo for this process, but it is being primarily driven by the ineluctable need to adapt to the constantly evolving nature of warfare and the prospect of an increasingly assertive political leadership which might refuse to authorise a pre-emptive conventional offensive. It is *not* to be seen as the adoption of 'Defensive Defence' as defined by either the mainstream school of thought in the West or its few disciples in the East. In fact the vast majority of Soviet theorists embrace a Clausewitzian view: an initial defensive phase in military operations would allow time for full mobilisation which should then be followed by a 'crushing retaliatory blow'.[59]

Indeed much of the Soviet debate on 'Defensive Defence' has surrounded four possible variants advanced by Andrei Kokoshin and Major-General V. Larionov in articles they wrote in 1987 and 1988.[60] The first of these models reiterates the traditional Soviet view that the best means of defence is an all-out attack. The second scenario also calls for a decisive invasion of the enemy's territory, but this is to be preceded by a defensive operation. Roughly analogous to the Battle of Kursk in 1943, this model is the one most favoured by Russian analysts. However the third, in which the counteroffensive would conclude with the restoration of the *status quo ante*, also enjoys some support and appears to be undergoing serious appraisal.[61] The fourth model, that of 'Just Defence' as espoused by most Western theorists, seems to have found little backing. It is therefore probable that the Russians' future strategy and its declared objectives will not be greatly dissimilar to those of 'Flexible Response'.

As we have seen, Clausewitz maintained in *Vom Kriege* that the defensive, providing it served as a prelude to a decisive counterstroke, was superior. This aspect of his reasoning however was rejected by most military staffs as the Nineteenth Century wore on, and by the Twentieth had been widely discarded as obsolete. The Russians now seem poised to return to Clausewitzian orthodoxy in this regard: they see the defensive, as an initial phase, as offering some operational advantages. That this is not a step towards 'Defensive Defence', however, is adequately evinced by their total rejection of its tenets on the operational, strategic and tactical levels. For them the attack remains the only decisive action, and their forces will continue to be structured for the delivering of counterblows which will expand 'into the realm of actual strategic offence'. The only question left unresolved is how far such an offensive should be allowed to go. Indeed this approach is very much in keeping with the methods of the great 'defensive' commanders of history. The 'Iron' Duke of Wellington, for instance, was perhaps unsurpassed in his mastery of such operations. Nearly all of his engagements in the Peninsular War were characterised by a defensive action which heavily exploited terrain, man-made obstacles and the other advantages which Clausewitz argued the defence could capitalise on. Yet he repeatedly employed audacious tactical ripostes to help overthrow attacks, and most of his 'defensive' battles culminated in a general counterstroke which, circumstances permitting, would develop into a strategic offensive. The Russian Kursk operation of 1943 has evident parallels.

As far as the tactical and strategic levels are concerned, the prescriptions of 'Just Defence' are nonsense in Russian eyes. This is scarcely surprising. Pure defence is simply not viable. Attack capabilities are needed to establish an effective forward defence and recover lost territory. This much is conceded by the proposals for 'spider' units found in most 'Defensive Defence' models, but it is clear that, whilst constituting worthwhile targets for pre-emptive strikes, these forces would be too feeble to carry out such missions efficaciously. Likewise the web units would suffer from an array of drawbacks. Designed to be virtually immobile, each one would be unable to influence the fighting in all but its immediate vicinity. The great majority of them would thus constitute a waste of precious resources. Bearing in mind Napoleon's maxim that a single battalion often decides the day,[62] this could prove fatal. Even after CFE I, the Russians for example, should they so desire, are still likely to be able to move perhaps 40 divisions against Central Europe at comparatively short notice. There is an accepted rule of thumb that an attacker needs a numerical superiority of three to one to succeed. With the disintegration of the Warsaw Pact and the signing of CFE I, the numerical balance has probably tilted decidedly in NATO's favour, but an overall supremacy of this magnitude still remains beyond the grasp of any foreseeable combination of states. Nevertheless a *local* supremacy of at least three to one and, against a dispersed *Raumverteidigung*, possibly as much as eight to one is attainable.

However it is doubtful that such a preponderance of forces would in practice be necessary. To concentrate against any incursion, the few, scattered 'spider' forces available to the defence as a whole would have to be capable of lateral movement at speeds and over distances hitherto uncontemplated. Only airborne units could have the prerequisite mobility, and even they would require the support of an excellent command, control and communication system, not to mention the organic staying power to repel the attack and retake the lost territory. Balancing these conflicting needs would be as technologically challenging as it would be expensive, and it is difficult to see how the emerging force's structure could possibly be presented as unthreatening to neighbouring countries.

As far as the web elements of the defence are concerned, several very serious weaknesses can, as we have seen, be identified. If called on to defend his patch of the *Raumverteidigung*, the 'minuteman' could not, given the array of morale and material problems he would face, be reasonably expected to do so, and even if he did, would be unlikely to secure anything other than a posthumous gallantry award. Too many 'Just Defence' theorists assume that these net infantry would, once attacked, fight on to the bitter end, continuing to resist fanatically even when the enemy's spearheads have driven through or bypassed their positions. In practice, had these troops not already been killed, wounded or captured, it is grossly improbable that they would have either the will or the means to go on resisting. Their ammunition, personnel reserves and other resources would quickly be exhausted in any engagement and, once their battle station was turned or penetrated, overwhelming demoralisation would be virtually inevitable: there would be no prospect of resupply, relief, medical care for the injured or even escape. As innumerable official studies into the effectiveness of 'stay behind' units have concluded, even crack troops like the British Special Air Service – who incidentally tend to operate in groups appreciably larger than those proposed for the predominantly reservist combat teams found in these webs – would be ill disposed towards further fighting under such circumstances, while the collapse of Iraq's army in 1991 only accentuates the point.

But this highlights a fundamental problem with these *Raumverteidigung* blueprints: they are far too divorced from mankind's accumulated experience of war and its nature. Horst Afheldt for example asserts that each of his technocommando teams will destroy an average of three enemy tanks in combat. There would, he claims, not be a battle but

> a series of decentralised combat actions all following the same tactical pattern. The statistical efficiency of these . . . is well known. Combat would be replaced by a series of minor actions of known statistical efficiency.[63]

Extrapolations of this kind are as abstract as they are absurd: nobody has constructed a country-sized area defence, let alone operated one in actual combat conditions. So how can they have a 'known statistical efficiency'? In any case, war is far too complex and unpredictable to be neatly packaged into a computer model. As Wellington once commented, 'I have fought battles enough to know that, even under the best arrangements, the result of any one is not certain'.[64]

In fact what relevant evidence we do have suggests that Afheldt's prescriptions and their like are recipes for disaster. In recent military history for instance we find something very similar to his proposed *Raumverteidigung*: the so-called 'Weygand Line' employed by the French in the closing stages of the Battle of France. After the Maginot Line – which embodied in concrete the very defensive posture and mentality that 'Non-Offensive Defence' espouses – had been outflanked, General Weygand abandoned the ruinous 'continuous front' philosophy and attempted to save the situation by forming a new defence behind the Rivers Somme and Aisne. It consisted of 'hedgehogs': troops entrenched around natural or man-made bastions bristling with 75 millimetre artillery batteries which were to be focused 'like revolvers' on the advancing Germans. Behind this 'chequerboard' defence were *groupements de manoeuvre* scraped together from the few remaining units of allied armour.

Initially at least the French did inflict appreciable losses on their attackers. Rommel's *Panzer* regiments, however, quickly changed their tactics to cope with these new conditions: they moved cross-country to avoid the 'hedgehogs' which were then subdued by follow-on infantry forces. The results were spectacular. Rommel bounded forward, advancing on 17 June alone some 240 kilometres. In the entire French campaign, his division only lost 42 tanks damaged beyond repair and a little over 2000 casualties. He captured, on the other hand, 97 648 prisoners, 458 armoured vehicles, 277 guns and 4000 trucks.[65]

We must of course be cautious when drawing conclusions from this precedent. Technology for instance has changed since Rommel's time and, as the proponents of 'Just Defence' regularly argue, would now make concepts like Weygand's far more viable and effective. But how valid are such claims, especially following the 1991 Gulf War?

2. 'DEFENSIVE DEFENCE' AND EMERGING TECHNOLOGY

'I shoot the Hippopotamus with bullets made of platinum,
Because if I use leaden ones, his hide is sure to flatten 'em.'
(Hilaire Belloc, *The Hippopotamus*)

Besides maintaining that defence – from an operational point of view – is generally superior to attack, the 'Non-Offensive Defence' movement has argued that current technological trends are also proceeding in favour of the former rather than the latter.[66] Not all proponents of alternative defence postures are mesmerised by the wizardry of emerging technology; some favour reliance on sturdy, simple and, above all, proven weapons and equipment. But many of the proposed models do depend, to a greater or lesser degree, on its exploitation for their feasibility.

Broadly speaking what these models envisage is the integration of a number of technological advances to yield an awesomely complex and formidable conventional war machine controlled by staffs from one or more 'electronic hilltops'. The models include computerised battle management networks, comprising sophisticated sensor, communication, data-processing, surveillance and target-acquisition systems; stand-off attack missiles and intelligent mines; and light infantry units equipped with a variety of 'smart' anti-armour and -air weapons. Dispersed, concealed and, where possible, protected in hardened bunkers and emplacements so as to deny any opponent significant targets and enervate the effect of his fire, the elements of the defence would none the less have the ability to concentrate coordinated firepower against any point within their own web and, typically, up to 40 kilometres into the enemy's territory beyond.

As we saw in Chapter 3, throughout the course of recent history firepower has steadily secured ascendancy over shock-action on the battlefield as technology both enhanced the range, accuracy and destructive power of weapons and refined the capabilities of the target-acquisition systems that guide them: warships engaged each other at ever greater ranges; the development of increasingly sophisticated missiles and aircraft allowed firepower to be delivered with speed over distances of tens, hundreds and thousands of miles; while automation, entrenchment, mechanisation and armoured protection joined with new explosives, rapid-fire smallarms, guns, grenades, mortars, barbed-wire and chemical agents to secure the gradual demise of traditional, close-order infantry attacks and the dashing but equally vulnerable horse artillery and cavalry. Apart from to a few specialist units like commandos, the skills of close-quarter combat had become anachronistic and essentially of minor importance by the early days of the Second World War. In their place all foot troops adopted something more akin to what, in the eighteenth and nineteenth centuries, had been the preserve of *Jäger* and other light infantry units: the tactics of the sniper, in which the objective was to inflict damage from a distance while exploiting stealth, terrain, dispersion and concealment to minimise the risk to oneself.[67]

By wedding sophisticated anti-armour weaponry to these classical qualities of the light infantryman, the architects of the various area defence models hope to create a David who, armed with a high-technology sling, will prove capable of defeating that Goliath of twentieth century offensive operations, the tank. They argue that whereas improvements to the firepower, mobility and protection of armoured vehicles have been relatively marginal, the capability to locate, target and destroy these metallic monsters has increased dramatically. Modern surveillance techniques are making the battle-field increasingly 'transparent', with the result that any movement betrays one's position to the enemy. Given the accuracy and lethality of emerging weaponry, this threatens to prove literally fatal; once detected the target will be subjected to unerring fire, which will destroy it.

Whilst many experts would counter this claim with the view that a capacity for mobility – especially rapid, evasive movement – actually increases one's chances of survival in such a potentially hostile environment,[68] 'Defensive Defence' advocates are broadly persuaded that static, positional warfare is, because of emerging technology, now superior to concepts stressing manoeuvre. They therefore feel that, if pitted against highly mechanised and armoured forces like those on which the USSR in particular has traditionally relied, their *Raumverteidigung* models will emerge victorious.

This approach is however somewhat eclectic. Too many of the emerging technologies in question are just that; they are still at best in the development stage and are unlikely to have a substantial impact on warfare for some years yet. To compare these weapons of tomorrow with those of today and conclude that the latter will probably prove inferior is scarcely helpful and not a little disingenuous. Given certain trends which will be discussed later, the tank for example might well be nearing obsolescence. For the moment however it remains effective and, as we shall see, there are technological and other developments which promise to prolong its life into the next century. Indeed, whilst there is widespread talk of a 'revolution' in military technology, the process is generally likely to be one of incremental rather than abrupt, wholesale change. There are several political, economic and technical reasons for this, but let us begin with a glance at some of the equipment and weapon systems involved. For in order to assess their potential and shortcomings, one must have some knowledge of how they work.

First, the ability to miniaturise components has, together with advances in large- and very-large-scale integrated circuits, permitted the development of microcomputers which are capable of performing immense numbers of operations every second. Formerly computers were much larger, heavier instruments, their dimensions growing in proportion to their complexity. Now however, microelectronic components can be accommodated in quite small spaces, allowing a solitary missile, for instance, to contain sophisticated guidance controls and targeting sensors. Similarly microcomputers with digital and signal processing functions are being incorporated into various surveillance systems, allowing numerous targets to be tracked simultaneously and the information about their movements disseminated to battlezone commanders virtually instantaneously. The fastest of all computers today perform around 100 million operations per second; and, if attempts to develop so-called 'neural' computers succeed, even this figure could be multiplied several times over. That said, such high levels of processing pose very formidable development and validation problems. For instance the automatic recognition of vehicles from infrared (IR) images was seen as having great promise during the 1970s, but it was not until the late 1980s that suitable microelectronics had evolved for this potential to be exploited on any scale. Developing a neural computer, with colossal numbers of interconnections and the capability to undertake innumerable tasks simultaneously, will be an expensive and time-consuming matter.

Yet the need for ever more sophisticated processing systems is likely to be insatiable as the amount of data being fed into surveillance networks, for example, continues to expand. The American Precision Location Strike System was for instance designed to yield 'real-time' targeting data on hostile emitters such as radars, jamming devices and communication networks. The programme was eventually cancelled however, as analysing and processing so many signals proved impossible. Similarly the British *Nimrod* rival to the American E-3A Airborne Warning and Control System (AWACS) had to be abandoned when, despite the expenditure of £1000 million on the project, the on-board computers still failed to meet the necessary specifications. Computers and other microelectronic circuits have moreover proved susceptible to various malfunctions. In the 1970s, electronic chips in US *Minuteman* missiles burnt out in what became known as the 'purple plague'. More recently the memories of guidance and other systems have sustained damage because of faulty circuits and , as any home computer buff will know, can be erased by an abrupt loss of power. 'Bugs' are common in software and, without special protection, most modern electrical circuits are very vulnerable to the destructive effects of the electro-magnetic pulse that accompanies any nuclear explosion. Lastly, the computer 'hacker' and 'virus' have come to pose a threat. In February 1990 for example, three West Germans were imprisoned after being convicted of selling information to the Russians; they had extracted it from Western military databases with the aid of a home computer and a telephone.[69]

Wellington once commented that 'All the business of war . . . is to endeavour to find out what you don't know by what you do: that's what I called "guessing what was at the other side of the hill"'.[70] Some 175 years after Waterloo this observation has lost little of its validity. As we saw in Chapter 3, it was largely to their superior ability to obtain information and to coordinate and control their forces that the Germans owed their spectacular success in France during 1940; and today, modern, integrated intelligence systems are regarded as offering a potentially decisive advantage in war. Accordingly they are given high priority. As ground-based radars cannot 'see' below 50 metres or over the horizon, they cannot reveal what is on 'the other side of the hill'; so airborne platforms are increasingly favoured, as is the use of space satellites. The American Joint Surveillance and Target Attack Radar System (JSTARS), for instance, aims to furnish 'real time' monitoring and identification of both moving and stationary targets at ranges of over 50 kilometres. Likewise the British, French and Russians are developing similar radar systems and sophisticated, integrated communication networks. Britain's Airborne Standoff Radar, for example, will be employed in battlefield surveillance operations, supplementing the *Ptarmigan* communication system in use with her ground forces in Germany. For their part, the French have the RITA battlefield communication system and are developing *Orchidée* (*Observatoire Radar Cohérent Héliporté d'Investigation des Eléments Ennemis*) for introduction in the mid 1990s.

In a rambling *Raumverteidigung* studded with combat units, the rapid collation and dissemination of intelligence would be a *sine qua non*. But accurate information plays a vital role in any military operation, and accordingly great attention is paid to both acquiring it for friendly forces and to denying it to those of the enemy. Indeed electronic deception and jamming techniques are playing an ever greater part in warfare. Radar observation for instance can be frustrated by a variety of devices: the reduction of the radar signature of aircraft for example, by diminishing their cross-section and by using 'radar-absorbent' materials in their construction; the deployment of metallic 'chaff' or powerful jammers to blur radar reception; and the unleashing of anti-radiation missiles which home in on the radar's own transmissions. The bat-shaped American F 117-A Bomber is regarded as the classic example of 'Stealth' technology, though terrain 'hugging' is currently the commonest way by which aircraft evade radar detection. This can be countered to an extent by airborne surveillance systems. But spotting a rapidly moving, low-flying target is one thing, engaging it is another. Indeed down-to-earth radar observation does have its limitations. 'Clutter' – radiation reflected from the ground – clouds images, and at long distances even relatively large targets like moving tank columns appear minute. Distinguishing them from other vehicles and their surroundings is very taxing. Phased-array radars – which consist of a static 'matress' made up of scores of small aerials rather than the traditional large, rotating dish design – can monitor hundreds of targets in a given area and can thus perform the work of an entire network of steered dishes. Some have ranges of up to 5000 kilometres, giving considerable warning time of impending developments. Even sophisticated radars can however be thwarted – and not just by man. Over-the-horizon systems for example bounce their beams off the ionosphere and can experience interference caused by the aurora borealis and australis.

Equally however, jamming technology is not free from problems. The Airborne Self Protection Jammer, for example, was described by the world's top electronics experts in the 1988–9 edition of *Jane's Avionics* as possibly 'the most significant US electronic warfare system in the current decade'. Yet by 1990 the programme was four years behind schedule and costing well in excess of its estimated price. Despite thirteen years of development, it was moreover performing disappointingly. Intended to electronically deceive hostile radars, it proved incapable of detecting, identifying and countering even quite old systems.

Besides radars, sensors such as IR devices have made significant advances in recent years, and this has had important repercussions for missile design in particular. IR sensors passively detect the infrared or heat energy given off by all objects, distinguishing between them by thermal contrast. Focal plane arrays, consisting of blocks of detector elements crammed together like the aerials of phased-array radars, are among the most significant microcomponents recently developed. Just as one phased-array radar can do the work of several dishes, a focal plane array permits a scene to be focused by a solitary viewing lense onto a bank of IR detector elements, each of which then scrutinises a tiny portion of the scene. This maximises the quantity of infrared energy received and thus permits far sharper image resolution. The more detector elements, the better the thermal picture that emerges.

This is the advantage of the focal plane array. Formerly IR technology was rather bulky and a typical sensor could not be fitted into a missile of under 30 centimetres in diameter. Now however much smaller spaces are required. Air defence missiles like *Stinger* and *Sidewinder* simply lock on to a 'hot spot' in the target such as the plane's engine, which contrasts vividly with the relatively cold and uncluttered background formed by the sky. More complex imaging IR seekers can convert IR impulses into electronic signals which, amplified and processed, produce black and white video imagery: a red hot object like a tank engine, the exhaust gases of which might be at a temperature of 800 degrees celsius, appears white against its cooler, darker surroundings. Such video imagery can be obtained even in darkness, smoke or other conditions of poor visibility. It allows for greater target detection ranges, and for smaller, lighter system designs.

Capitalising on such advances, technologists have been able to devise weapons carrying several types of sensor. This has led to a growth in stand-off weapons which need either very accurate targeting information and navigation devices or an organic ability to search out targets and attack them. Combinations of IR seekers and millimetric wave radars are particularly common. Again however these weapons have their limitations. Typically, IR scanners can 'see' up to five kilometres, but they must be kept cool to avoid 'noise' – unwanted IR radiation within the sensor itself. This calls for built-in cryogenic mechanisms, usually employing liquid nitrogen as a coolant. Moreover IR recticle seekers are fairly ineffective at tracking single targets on the ground. This is because a typical X-band scanner has, at a range of one kilometre, a beam width of 100–150 metres. So even if the target has quite a large radar cross-section, there is still a great deal of background 'clutter' to be coped with, which might include burning hulks, sun-warmed rocks, IR flares fired as decoys by the opposition and, especially once battle is joined, friendly tanks and vehicles. (Indeed Soviet theorists particularly have argued that mingling with the enemy in a fluid, fragmented battle is one means of countering the effectiveness of such high-precision weaponry.[71]) Furthermore, although digital processing techniques can assist in the recognition of targets against complex backdrops and can tune a weapon's flight path in the final approach phase, inevitably the missile can only be programmed to deal with a restricted number of targets and surroundings. This makes it vulnerable to comparatively simple counter-measures like alterations to the outline shape of potential targets; and even if these can be overcome, terminal guidance still needs to be of an exacting standard, especially against well protected targets like tanks.

Besides being employed as weapons to dazzle or damage electro-optical and optical observation systems – including the human eye – lasers are widely used as rangefinders, target designators and terminal guidance mediums for armaments, including the American *Hellfire* missile and *Copperhead* artillery shell. Semi-active versions utilise a passive seeker which homes in on a beam that is reflected off the target. Others ride down a beam with the aid of a rear antenna. The end of the trajectory tends to curve however, making for inaccuracy. Except for the latest carbon-dioxide rangefinders, which are expensive, laser penetration can also be affected by heavy rain, snow, smoke or fog. Moreover the opposition might focus on the platform or soldier illuminating the target. These furthermore have to get sufficiently close to their quarry, yet their very proximity can severely circumscribe use of the weapon system. *Copperhead* for example has a minimum range of one kilometre, but its employment against moving armour, for instance, would demand exceptionally rapid coordination between the batteries firing the shells and the spotters illuminating the targets. Lasers are therefore best deployed on platforms which can perform both functions, and against static or slow moving targets. However as the American raid on Libya in 1986 illustrated, even then the accurate placing of laser-guided projectiles under combat conditions can prove problematic.

Besides active ones like lasers, passive sensors have significant military applications. We have already noted the use of IR seekers in missiles for example, but there are also devices which detect other forms of energy. These include acoustic, pressure, electro-magnetic and chemical sensors. Fitting such devices into warheads not only makes the weapon more expensive, heavier, bulkier and more complex, it also means that the sensors are destroyed when the warhead detonates. It can therefore be cheaper and generally advantageous to separate the two. A web of sensors bonded together by a buried grid of fibre-optic cables would, for example, be feasible. However the size of area covered would of necessity have to be limited. Firstly, to monitor any given patch of terrain a combination of contrasting sensors would be required. Seismic devices for instance can usually detect people up to 50 metres away and vehicles at up to ten times that distance. But they cannot distinguish between, say, a light vehicle nearby and a more distant but heavier one. Additional data is required, calling for combinations of sensors. Secondly, they would have to be deployed in packs of sufficient density so as to avoid 'blind spots' and, lastly, would have to be integrated with immensely sophisticated computers capable of processing the colossal amounts of information they would convey.

Even then people would have to interpret the results and decide on an appropriate response. An 'automated battlefield' of the type depicted by Frank Barnaby[72] not only sounds a little too much like playing *Space Invaders* but also overlooks the need for human accountability both in war and peace. If war, as Clemenceau said, 'is too important to leave to the military', then a situation in which mankind would have *completely* entrusted his fate to machines seems utterly repugnant. Even in the nuclear missile age we have held back from such a step lest war 'by accident' might indeed become feasible. Equally, criss-crossing a relatively small, evacuated 'killing zone' with tripwires and other sensors might be justifiable in certain circumstances. But the notion of extending the project to cover entire inhabited regions, especially in peacetime, would seem both impractical and open to abuse. Even those citizens who rather take civil rights for granted could well get a mite upset at the thought that 'Big Brother' might not only be watching but listening and smelling too. In any case, furnishing sufficient numbers of sensors and then maintaining them and their nodal computers could prove far costlier than deploying them on even thousands of warheads. Nor would sensor networks be any less vulnerable to countermeasures and deception than other electrical technology. Although there are scatterable devices which can plug gaps in nets caused by, say, artillery fire, preventing 'blind spots' once battle had commenced would be increasingly problematic, as would the process of distinguishing friend from foe.

The exploitation of the various technological advances outlined above has led to an assortment of developments which the proponents of 'Defensive Defence' have eagerly seized upon. The ability to deliver fire remotely – and thus at minimal risk to oneself – is however foremost among these. The technical problems encountered in trying to strike at distant targets, especially mobile ones, increase in direct proportion to the range, but modern avionics and near 'real time' targeting devices promise to help overcome them. Although some advocates of defensive strategies remain sceptical about the effectiveness of such high technology and would prefer to rely on simpler, cheaper and more robust weapons, even their models depend to a considerable extent on an ability to destroy targets at ranges of up to 40 kilometres.

There are already weapon systems which are theoretically capable of doing this. The Multiple Launch Rocket System (MLRS), for example, can saturate an area as far as 30 kilometres away with scores of submunitions. In under a minute it can unleash twelve rockets laden with such devices, achieving in effect the same amount of firepower as three entire battalions of American eight-inch artillery pieces. 'Smart' terminally-guided submunitions (TGSM), which are either aerodynamically controlled by fins and wings or by lateral motors that adjust their trajectory and altitude, are potentially even deadlier, for unlike unguided projectiles they are fitted with millimetric radars or IR seekers which enable them to lock on to selected targets. Early tests of two prototype weapons of this genre, the SADARM TGSM and the *Skeet* self-forging fragment, proved disappointing however. After ejection from the delivery missile, these weapons spin on their axes, tracing a spiral path across the ground with their sensors. Having chosen a target, they fire armour-piercing fragments through its comparatively thin, top armour. But in the 'Assault Breaker' tests organised by the US Defense Research Project Agency in 1983, only one out of eleven TGSM packages enjoyed any success, destroying, under *optimal* environmental conditions, five stationary M-47 tanks, which incidentally have a comparatively large IR signature. The *Skeet* fared even worse in the trials, failing to hit any of the targets.[73]

Admittedly these tests involved immature technology which has since undergone improvement. Nevertheless they underline the need for *very* considerable progress before some of the more elaborate concepts for the long-range acquiring and destruction of moving targets especially can be transformed into realities. Clearly however, even the unguided submunition has great potential, whatever its delivery system. A squadron of *Harrier* ground-attack planes, for example, can saturate a square kilometre of ground with some 18 500

BL-755 bomblets in a couple of minutes, the hollow charge of each bomblet being designed to penetrate the top armour of a Russian T-72 tank. Indeed studies undertaken in the early 1980s suggested that to destroy 60 per cent of an armoured division – taken as consisting of 600 tanks, 500 other armoured vehicles, 50 artillery batteries and 500 airdefence and wheeled vehicles – would require , 2200 *successful* aircraft sorties if conventional, 250-kilogram gravity bombs were used. Alternatively 300 strikes with unguided submunitions would achieve the same results, or as few as 60 sorties if *Skeet* and similar weapons could be made to work. Even if 10-kiloton nuclear warheads were employed, destruction on this scale would call for 10–25 weapons.[74]

The US Army's Tactical Missile System (TACMS) is designed to disperse anti-personnel and anti-armour mines at ranges of up to 70 kilometres. Indeed mines are among the cheapest and most effective devices available for sealing off territory. They can be scattered quickly, are very destructive and are immensely difficult to spot, especially from rapidly-moving armoured vehicles. They also employ an assortment of trigger devices and sensors: electro-magnetic, acoustic and pressure. Mines which will permit the safe passage of friendly forces while remaining lethal to the enemy's are also under development. However 'smart' self-activating and directing mines which, powered by little engines, roll or hop around battlefields in search of targets are among the many examples of high-technology gadgetry that, as yet, perform better in theory than in practice.

The weapon that lies at the heart of most *Raumverteidigung* models is however the short- and medium-range anti-armour missile. The 1973 Arab–Israeli War highlighted the growing efficaciousness of these, and a variety are currently in service. As 'hand-held' and 'man-portable' weapons, they have to have negligible recoils and their projectiles must travel relatively slowly so as to permit trajectory correction. Accordingly they inflict damage not through the kinetic energy of the missile itself but rather by employing shaped-charge warheads which, exploding next to the target, direct a 'slug' of molten metal and extremely hot gases through its armour. Travelling at up to three kilometres per second, the 'slug' incinerates the crew and detonates fuel and ammunition stocks as it diffuses through the tank.

Typical examples of this type of weapon include the *TOW*, *Milan*, *Dragon* and *Bofors Bill* systems. The last of these weighs 77 pounds, is carried by two men, has a range of 2000 metres and, to avoid having to penetrate heavy side or frontal armour, employs a 'flyover' missile which, once above the top of the target, is detonated by a proximity fuse. Nevertheless the weapon is capable of piercing up to 700 millimetres of homogenous armour. Similarly the *Milan* is also crewed by two men. It weighs 81 pounds and has a maximum range of 1900 metres. It is a direct-fire weapon, the latest version being able to penetrate as much as 750 millimetres of armour. The *Dragon* on the other hand weighs 57 pounds and can be fired by one man. It is another direct-fire system with a range of 900 metres, and the latest model can cope with up to 700 millimetres of armour.

The American *TOW* (tube-launched, optically-tracked, wire-guided) missile has also been produced in several forms. The Improved variant (*ITOW*), which has been operational since 1981, was fitted with an upgraded warhead and a probe to optimise penetration. The *TOW II* which succeeded it was also equipped with a better warhead and guidance mechanisms. In 1987 however, the deployment of reactive armours – which will be discussed shortly – led to the *TOW IIA*. This had a 'tandem' warhead configuration to maximise penetration, but concern about the long-term effectiveness of direct-fire missiles against ever improving frontal and side armours persisted. Accordingly the *TOW IIB* is a top attack weapon like the *Bofors Bill*, its dual canted warheads being detonated by magnetic and proximity fuses once it is above the target.

Further significant refinements to the *TOW* are unlikely. Because of the dimensions of its firing-tube, the missile's diameter is restricted to 150 millimetres; so the US Army has decided to introduce a new, third generation of armaments better able to accommodate future technological changes. The Advanced Anti-Armour Weapon System programme is concerned with developing both medium (AAWS-M) and heavy (AAWS-H) weapons to replace *Dragon* and *TOW*. The AAWS-M should be available by 1996. Weighing 42 pounds including its reusable control and launch unit, it will be one-man-portable, have a range of 2000 metres and be a 'fire and forget' missile whose tandem, shaped-charge warhead will guide itself to the target with an imaging IR seeker. The warhead will be capable of piercing 750 millimetres of homogenous armour, but will follow a shaped trajectory for top attack. The system's anticipated reliability and easy maintainability are expected to offset its initial high cost. For the AAWS-H, an assortment of potential candidates has been scrutinised. The Fibre-Optic Guided Missile (FOG-M) was rejected, but will be utilised in forward area defence; it will be used to engage helicopters and armour at ranges of 10–30 kilometres. The missile's speed and flight pattern give its operator 10–20 seconds to find and focus on a target, images of which are relayed from a warhead-mounted camera through fibre-optic cables to a video display. The operator, using a joystick, can thus steer the weapon as required.

A ground-based variant of the *Hellfire* missile which is currently deployed on US *Apache* helicopters is, along with the Hypervelocity Missile (HVM), a possible heavy anti-armour weapon of the future. The existing *Hellfire* employs a laser guidance system to deliver a shaped-charge warhead at supersonic speed and at ranges of up to 8000 metres. The land-launched version will incorporate a millimetric wave radar, an imaging IR seeker, digital autopilot and an improved warhead. The HVM will also exploit supersonic speed to thrust a metal dart through armour. It will probably require, however, a minimum range of one kilometre to allow the projectile to attain the requisite velocity.

This raises an important point about anti-armour systems. They seek to neutralise any assailants before being knocked out or over-run. According to Soviet calculations for example, an anti-armour defence deploying ten weapons on a front of one kilometre will currently destroy at least five and perhaps as many as eighteen of an attacking force of twenty tanks.[75] If however the number of anti-armour weapons is halved, then the survival rate for the tanks increases dramatically. The accuracy, lethality, sustainability and rate of the defenders' fire clearly influence such calculations, as do factors affecting their own vulnerability – the environment, the amount of suppressive fire, morale and so on. To date, armoured engagements have typically occurred at ranges of less than 1000 metres. Even during the 1967 and 1973 Arab–Israeli conflicts, where many tank battles took place on relatively level and open country-side, ranges were usually between 300 and 800 metres. In built-up, wooded, enclosed or undulating terrain like that found in much of western Germany, moving targets are screened for much of the time. At ranges of less than 500 metres, mobile tanks might be visible for 40 per cent of the time, but at between 500 and 1000 metres this figure falls by half, while at over 2000 metres an anti-tank battery might only have a view of its target for 15 per cent of the time. In whatever period is available, the missile's operator has to acquire a target and aim, fire and guide his weapon towards it. Missiles typically travel 1000 metres every 3–4 seconds. However a *Dragon*, for instance, covers 240 metres before it can be 'gathered' – brought under control by the operator – and although *Milan* and *TOW* can be reined in more quickly, this does mean that missiles have optimal minimum ranges. 'Fire and forget' weapons which lock onto targets after launch are better able to tackle opponents taking evasive action, but to do this they need longer initial ranges and wider guidance bandwaves.

As most of the available 'man-portable' anti-armour systems are line-of-sight, direct-fire weapons, all of this imposes obvious limitations. It can prove difficult to focus a missile – and keep it focused – on a target, and while doing so the operator is vulnerable to counter fire. Further, although an infantryman has been defined as 'something you hang things on', the term 'man-portable' is something of a misnomer; these weapons are currently bulky and, with their day- and night-sights, batteries, cryostats and firing platform, can weigh as much as 50 kilograms. They are moreover very noisy and have a disturbing backflash which prevents them being discharged in confined spaces. Improved technology will of course eventually rectify many of these shortcomings. But for the time being at least, these weapons are not as invincible as many people believe; and the designers of armoured vehicles are constantly looking for means to make them still less so.

As long ago as the 1960s, Khrushchev, while observing Soviet military forces on manoeuvres, was struck by the growing vulnerability of tanks to missiles. 'When I saw how the tanks . . . were put out of action in no time', he recalled. 'I felt sick. After all', he continued, 'we are spending a lot to build tanks, but if – God forbid, as they say – a war breaks out, . . . [they] will get burnt out before they have reached the line to which the high command ordered them'.[76] The Israelis came away with similar impressions after the 1973 war; the tank appeared to be on the verge of obsolescence. However, as they subsequently demonstrated, it was not. By altering the structure and tactics of their ground forces, and by exploiting ingenuity, new materials and technologies, the Israelis increased both the direct and indirect protection of their armoured vehicles. The life of the tank was thus prolonged.

The Israeli invention of reactive armour for example did much to improve the survivability of tanks threatened by shaped-charge warheads. Reactive armour consists of boxes of low-grade explosive bolted onto the tank's surface. It can be fitted in about 30 minutes and a typical application of 40 panels adds roughly one tonne to the tank's weight. When the 'slug' from a shaped-charge warhead penetrates one of these boxes, the low-grade explosive detonates. The blast, which includes fragments of the exploding panel, disperses the 'slug', grossly enervating its penetrating power and rendering it incapable of piercing the underlying main armour.

The Russians were quick to copy the Israelis' idea. Although reactive armour offers no protection against the armour-piercing, high-velocity, tungsten and depleted-uranium darts which, fired by other tanks, cannot be 'spoofed' or decoyed and penetrate armour at speeds of several kilometres per second, it was a cheap and quite effective way to guard tanks against a whole family of weapons. Indeed, to overcome it, new missiles like the *TOW IIA* detailed above had to be developed. These carry two warheads in tandem, the smaller, leading one being designed to detonate the reactive armour, leaving the way clear for the second, main charge which followed a splitsecond later. The obvious countermeasure to this was to have several layers of reactive armour – and up to three have been seen on Soviet T-72 tanks. However the ineluctable need to keep the tank's size and weight down imposes limits. In particular their turrets have to be light enough to rotate, so dense top armour is out of the question – an Achilles' Heel which, as we have seen, several of the latest anti-armour weapons seek to exploit. Furthermore reactive armour might be 'stripped off' with heavy machinegun fire and, in exploding, can be hazardous for friendly infantry around the tank. It is not however the only type of protection available to armoured vehicle designers. Composite and ceramic armours can be very effective, and lighter but tougher versions are in the offing. Similarly a French–American consortium is trying to develop a 'responsive' armour, and even the feasibility of using electro-magnetic fields for protection is being explored.

When combined with appropriate operational concepts and tactics, motivation, experience and leadership, the impact of the types of technology discussed above can be impressive. Having noted the effectiveness of SAMs and anti-tank missiles in the 1973 Middle East War, Laurence Martin felt moved to write in the following year that

> It would be disastrous to fall once more into the typical Western (and particularly American) fallacy of seeing salvation in a technological superiority that has always proved transitory, but at present it really does seem possible that the coming generation of weapons will inherently favour the defence.[77]

Yet by 1980, Israeli tank divisions, restructured to take account of the lessons of that war, had a significantly enhanced capability for suppressing anti-armour defences with firepower, while individual tanks had been fitted not only with reactive armour but also with improved, interior protective devices to help mitigate the effects of shaped-charge warheads. When the Israelis invaded the Lebanon in June 1982, the benefits of these measures became apparent. It was perhaps in the air, however, that the blending of modern technology with the Israelis' tactical skill and combat experience payed its highest dividends. Unmanned *Scout* remotely-piloted vehicles (RPV), equipped with electro-optical sensors and digital communications, were launched into the Bekaa Valley to reconnoitre the Syrian airfields and SAM batteries in the vicinity. Cheap, unguided drones which can electronically mimic fighter planes were also deployed. Compelled to keep their target-acquisition radars switched on in order to engage this apparent threat, the SAM sites were then themselves attacked with missiles which homed in on their own radar beams. In the meantime Israeli E-2C spy planes monitored Syrian air space, warning their own fighters of any impending attacks, while a Boeing 707 airliner, specially modified for electronic warfare, joined with suitably equipped CH-23 helicopters in jamming Syrian communications.

Within a few minutes of commencing the attack the Israelis had inflicted tremendous damage on the seemingly fearsome SAM batteries. Indeed by the end of the operation around 30 had been destroyed. Thanks to the advanced avionics of the Israeli planes and the precision-guided munitions they had at their disposal,the numerous Syrian airdefence cannon and man-portable rockets could scarcely influence the fighting either; the attacking planes were able to operate at ranges and altitudes beyond the reach of these weapons. Nor did the Syrians' own combat aircraft enjoy much success; 85 of their *Mig* fighters were destroyed, whereas the Israelis lost just two planes. The element of technical surprise had been as, if not more, important than operational surprise.

Subsequent conflicts, notably that between the UN and Iraq, underlined the threat to unprotected infantry from a gamut of increasingly efficacious anti-personnel weapons. Besides the usual mines, grenades and fragmenting shells, fuel-air munitions proved especially deadly. A detonator within a warhead disperses an explosive in a fine mist over a wide area. Having been permitted to mingle with the oxygen in the atmosphere, this is then ignited by a second detonator. As the explosion derives the necessary oxidising agent not from within the charge itself but from the natural air around it, weight for weight such combustibles are much more powerful than conventional explosives. In fact, in terms of blast and shock impact, they are comparable to low-yield nuclear detonations. Propylene oxide vapour, for example, is, when mixed with air, five times as potent as Trinitrotoluene (TNT). The effect, even on dispersed troops, can be horrendous, and pressure-sensitive devices – such as delicate electronics, mines and sensors – are no less vulnerable.

Several conclusions can be drawn from all of this. First, whilst emerging technology does show great promise, massive progress is needed in surveillance, munitions, delivery systems and information processing before a lot of concepts can be converted into realities. High technology projects have been notorious for slipping back in terms of time and performance but rising in cost; and predictions made in the mid 1980s of, for example, a fully 'automated battlefield' within twenty years[78] seem more than unlikely to be fulfilled. Generally research for and development of a weapon takes between seven and ten years, after which it might remain in service for as many as forty. Life-cycle costs are an important consideration, while the necessity to avoid placing excessive emphasis on a single specific undertaking which might not come to fruition, together with the need to incorporate potentially costly projects into budgets and planning cycles, ineluctably leads to procurement on an incremental basis. There is moreover a forgiveable tendency among the military to depend on force structures and equipment, not to mention doctrines, with which they are familiar and whose strengths and weaknesses they have recognised. They have to draw on the lessons of history, but at the same time discard those precedents which changed circumstances have rendered obsolete. The temptation to prematurely adopt some new innovation is strong, but it is a risky enterprise that can end in either spectacular advantages or dismal and expensive if not dangerous failure.

At a time when defence budgets are contracting severely, value for money is of ever greater importance. According to a 1989 National Audit Office Report, unreliability alone increases the support costs of the British Ministry of Defence, for example, by over £1000 million per year – some five per cent of the total defence budget – while a March 1990 memorandum compiled by the Comptroller and Auditor General for the Commons' Public Accounts Committee identified nine defence projects which were up to five years behind schedule and were already responsible for some £2000 million in overspending. Indeed eleven major programmes were exceeding their original estimated costs by 25–200 per cent, often because of serious failures in new technology. These included the EH-101 anti-submarine and utility helicopter; the *LAW 80* light anti-tank missile, which incidentally both the Ministry's Lord Trefgarne and a 1989 Commons' Select Committee Report conceded had already been rendered obsolete by reactive armour innovations; the *BATES* Battlefield Artillery Target Engagement System, which is a classic example of a software-dependent, long-range targeting device whose estimated cost and development timetable have both been greatly exceeded; and the *Skynet* communications satellite, which has been badly delayed by the repercussions of that glaring and tragic failure of advanced technology, the *Challenger* Space Shuttle disaster.

So in equipment procurement there is a need to balance affordability, dependability and robustness against a certain amount of redundancy, diversity and flexibility to cater for contrasting and possibly unforeseen environments, scenarios and challenges. There is also the question of whose equipment should be purchased. As we have seen, American products tend to dominate the high-technology weapons market. A decision on, say, a new main battle tank involves, besides the sort of considerations listed above, alliance objectives such as standardisation and compatibility of forces, as well as domestic political and industrial considerations; jobs, a lucrative export trade and the retention of a key strategic manufacturing capacity are all at stake.

Such choices moreover have to be made in an international environment which is increasingly porous as far as the exchange of know-how and technology is concerned. The acquisition by middle-ranking powers of advanced military hardware, such as missile systems, and the proliferation of chemical and nuclear plants which could be turned to developing military capabilities, are good illustrations of this.[79] With the extension of trade relations between East and West and the concomitant acceleration of economic integration, imbalances in technical expertise will be levelled out. Much of the Soviet military equipment that appeared in the 1970s and 1980s, for example, was clearly copied from Western designs and often exploited technological breakthroughs made by others. More generally however, maintaining a technological edge over potential and putative adversaries is becoming increasing difficult, and any lead that is secured often proves ephemeral. Indeed one can pay a high price for being the pioneer who must shoulder the initial costs of research and development.

Seen in this context, the faith in an enduring and marked technological supremacy which characterises so much of the thinking of 'Defensive Defence' advocates is misplaced. 'Whatever happens we have got the Maxim Gun and they have not' scarcely applies anymore – even if one substitutes 'Atom Bomb' for 'Maxim Gun'. In any comparison of military power, countries might indeed enjoy leads in certain, possibly crucial, fields, but elsewhere they might be trailing. Nor should the relative capacity for producing up to date equipment be accorded any less consideration. In the 1930s, for example, it was not merely the sophistication of German aicraft that troubled the French and British, but the rate at which they were manufactured; in 1939, for instance, Germany's productivity in this regard was five times that of France.[80] Clearly this had implications not only for any initial balance of forces but also for the sustaining of capabilities once war actually commenced.

The American arms industrialist Martin Marietta once observed that by the year 2054 the entire US defence budget will purchase just one tactical aircraft which will have to be shared by the Air Force and the Navy three and a half days per week, except for leap years, when it will be made available to the Marines for the extra day. Joking aside, the spiralling cost of military equipment, coupled with diminishing defence budgets, does threaten to sharply limit procurement in the future. Authors such as Jon Connell have been very critical of what they regard as unnecessary 'gold-plating', which has sent prices soaring without always securing a commensurate increase in capabilities. He would prefer to see dependence on adequate numbers of proven, simple, cheap weapons, arguing that for a similar expenditure NATO could furnish itself with a robust conventional defence.[81]

This view does rather ignore the decisive advantages which some technological innovations have given one side over another in combat, notably during the 1991 Gulf War and the Israeli Bekaa Valley operation of 1982. It does however have some merit. The 'Defensive Defence' lobby, on the other hand, too frequently wants to have its cake and eat it. 'Effective non-provocative defence will be relatively cheap', we are told by an advocate whose proposals are suitably representative.[82] However we are then presented with a shopping-list of prerequisites which typically includes: fortified border zones 'saturated' with ground-based sensors, hardened troop emplacements, mine fields and anti-tank obstacles, usually encompassing up to 50 000 square kilometres of precious real estate; airborne, satellite and other aerial surveillance systems operating in conjunction with sophisticated computers and a buried fibre-optic network to provide command, control, communications, intelligence and targeting data on an automated but decentralised basis; a judicious mixture of anti-armour and -air missiles and guns for close-combat, plus large numbers of longer-range systems capable of delivering precision fire from up to 80 kilometres away; large numbers of helicopters tailored for particular roles; ground-attack and single-role interceptor aircraft; adequate garrisons throughout the country 'to deter attacks by airborne forces and to defend coastal areas'; 'very mobile' squads of local troops to cover the entire forward defensive zone; mechanised infantry units to give them support when and where necessary; a coastal defence fleet; sufficient manpower, stocks of spares, ammunition and supplies to maintain the dispersed defending forces for a protracted period of high-intensity conventional warfare; and, last but not least, strategic nuclear forces of adequate size, power and sophistication to 'neutralise' those of the other side, even though their possession would be grounded on a no-first-use policy – a posture which is presented as 'totally consistent with the universally recognised right of self-defence, and is therefore morally acceptable and unambiguously legal', whereas preparing NATO troops to use nuclear weapons is regarded by 'civilised societies' as quite the opposite.[83]

I am not an expert on morality. I do however find this eclectic approach to nuclear deterrence intellectually unconvincing. To publicly foreswear the first-use of nuclear weapons – which, as Sir Hugh Beach once remarked, is a ruse that is 'declaratory, unverifiable, and not altering the price of fish by one kopeck',[84] – would, even if taken seriously, just undermine deterrence, which calls for both an evident capacity and willingness to inflict damage on any aggressor. So long as nuclear forces exist, no amount of unilateral self-restraint can guarantee they will not be used; even if one party holds back, there are no grounds for assuming the other will follow suit. Indeed, if confronted with a lack of headway against the sort of impregnable conventional shield postulated by the 'Just Defence' lobby, is there not a danger that a desperate attacker might then resort to using nuclear armaments? This after all was the choice of the Americans in 1945 in preference to taking on a fanatical Japanese defence in depth. Indeed can conventional weaponry, however sophisticated, suffice to deter war?

Debate on that point seems destined to continue. What is clear though is that 'Defensive Defence' stances are potentially very expensive, in part at least because of their reliance on sophisticated technology. By applying modern scientific solutions to military problems, it is now theoretically possible to do almost anything. But one must be prepared to pay the price, both for the equipment itself and for the sought-after, skilled technicians needed to maintain and, in many instances, operate it. Procuring adequate numbers of state-of-the-art anti-armour weapons for all those penny packets of light infantry could, for example, devour an inordinate proportion of any available budget, leaving very little over for the numerous other essential elements, including the basic infrastructure – the fortified border zone. If past experience is anything to judge by, these promise to be prohibitively costly. To have any credibility at all, they would have to be at least twenty kilometres deep and would require some means of preventing opponents either outflanking or simply flying over them; after all, a shield is worthless if it cannot be manoeuvred to protect any part of the body. Even if that were feasible, the resources needed to build such a defensive belt would be immense. The Maginot Line incoporated the latest innovations in fortification architecture.[85] It was an astonishing engineering feat and its cost nearly bled inter-war France white. Started in 1930, by 1935 it was only partially finished, had already cost more than twice the original estimate and was a year behind its completion date. Its German counterpart, the so-called 'Siegfried Line', a far less ambitious project, but nevertheless one calling for the construction of 14 000 bunkers, took over a year to build and consumed more than twenty per cent of Germany's annual cement production.

Up until the end of the Cold War, the obvious place for a fortified border zone of this description lay through the heart of divided Germany. The West Germans however, with an eye on the eventual reunification of their nation and its lands, resisted any such proposal even when the military threat from the East was at its peak. Subsequent events vindicated both their optimism and this policy. Today it is unthinkable that any new, significant fortifications would be erected in Europe. Customs controls are being relaxed, and those border defences that do exist are being torn down. In an increasingly urbanised and industrialised landscape criss-crossed by ever more communication links and other physical signs of growing economic and political harmony, there will be diminishing scope for their return, even if an increasingly integrated and environmentally-aware European community was prepared to sanction it. All that one might expect to see in this regard is the establishment of restraints, like those on the US–Mexican border, to prevent a prosperous Germany in particular suffering a mass influx of unwanted 'economic refugees' from the East.

In any case it is not clear that static, positional warfare would necessarily prove superior to manoeuvre concepts. Knowing one's exact position can be useful when it comes to coordinating long-range fire, for example, and hardened emplacements can offer their occupants some protection. On the other hand the location of such fixed positions can be pin-pointed even before hostilities commence and it is unlikely that they could all be made to withstand the latest deep-penetration shells and warheads, not to mention gas and fuel–air explosives. If the rapid destruction in 1914 of the subterranean forts around Liège – which, designed by Henri Brialmont, the greatest military architect of the era, were popularly regarded as the most perfect and formidable defences in Europe – by German howitzers did not underline the limitations of such bastions, then the capture, by paratroops landing on the roof, of the awesome successor to these self same forts, Eben Emael, in 1940 certainly did.[86] Of course subduing fixed defences can be costly in both time and casualties. But if mobile targets are now to be regarded as vulnerable to long-range fire, then sedentary ones must be more so; and efforts to increase their survivability through hardening and other measures ceases to be cost-effective after a point and only renders them still more conspicuous.

Above all, any obstacle only becomes a real barrier to an attacker when it can have sufficient firepower focused on it. So the type and number of weapons deployed in and around a *Raumverteidigung* and the capability to accurately coordinate their fire are of crucial importance. As we have seen, advanced technology does have something to offer in this regard, but it is not a panacea. For one thing it contains the seeds of its own destruction. Most of these weapons are sequential systems: they rely on a chain of mechanisms working in succession. If one link in the chain fails, then so does the whole; and the more sophisticated the device, the more links there are to malfunction. A human hair, grain of sand or drop of water can wreak havoc in computers and other exotic electrical circuitry, while constant use and rough handling inevitably take their toll. Nor need breakdowns stem from organic sources. As noted, high-technology can be countered with various, often inexpensive, devices and measures, and can be affected by environmental factors. A mix of systems is therefore essential to ensure that at least some will function under whatever circumstances prevail, as are adequate numbers of technicians capable of maintaining, repairing, and operating such labyrinthine electronics. Specialists of this calibre are in short supply, difficult to recruit and even harder to retain.

Moreover there are just too many unknown quantities involved in all this. Nobody can be certain what, for instance, the *overall* effect of large-scale electronic warfare would be, with hundreds of jammers and so on transmitting simultaneously. Indeed the precise calculations and extrapolations that hold up so well in a laboratory or operations briefing room frequently wither in the face of the rough-and-tumble realities of battle, where confusion, fear and 'friction' in general 'makes the apparently easy so difficult'.[87] Anxious to peddle their wares, manufacturers have understandably sought to present their latest gadgetry in the best possible light; demonstrations and tests have been conducted under contrived conditions which bear little relation to those found in actual combat. Even then, however, performance expectations have often proved excessive. In fact a failure rate of 25–30 per cent is regarded as normal for most high-technology under campaign conditions.[88] When for example Texas Instruments' AAWS-M design was tested by the US Army in February 1989, it was successful in fourteen out of twentytwo firings against stationary and moving tanks in daylight, darkness and smoke. Company officials blamed the failures on '"low-tech" problems with batteries and rocket motors as well as some software problems with the seeker's automatic tracker'.[89] In so doing, of course they sought to excuse their sophisticated missile system. Ironically however, they merely underlined that even comparatively simple, proven technology cannot be absolutely dependable. Cold weather for instance adversely affects human beings, oil, radios and batteries. We must not be Luddites in our attitude to emerging technology, but anybody who has wrestled with a recalcitrant internal-combustion engine on a freezing winter's morning will know what I am getting at.[90]

What does all this imply for future combat trends? To date the close battle has been confined to the line of sight – the reaches of the human eye assisted by optical, thermal and radar systems, but constrained by weather and terrain conditions. Technology promises to extend the battlefield and make it more transparent. Achieving strategic surprise will consequently become harder, and will be effected more through political deception and technological means like electronic warfare than through traditional techniques such as camouflage and concealment. Indeed technical surprise through some innovation or brand new technology might compromise any defence, but the advocates of *Raumverteidigung* concepts have compounded the danger by orientating their models too much towards one particular threat: the tank.

Other considerations aside, this is a little ironic, for so many supporters of 'Just Defence' insist that the tank is already obsolete. Frank Barnaby for example points out that 'it is virtually impossible to hide some sixty tons of hot metal . . . from the sensors of intelligent missiles', and that 'the best tank guns are not very effective beyond about two kilometres; even small anti-tank missiles, like TOW, are effective at longer ranges'.[91] There is an element of truth in this. Yet as we have seen, modern combat units are not exclusively made up of one weapon system, but a whole variety operating in close cooperation; any opponent thus faces a spectrum of challenges. Secondly, because of topographical and other restraints, the close battle has usually been conducted at relatively short ranges where guns can be more flexible than missiles and where anti-tank teams are themselves vulnerable to an assortment of threats. Indeed the modern, automated, smoothbore tank cannon, with its high muzzle velocity and resultingly flat trajectory, has a first shot hit probability at typical engagement ranges in excess of 80 per cent. This compares very favourably with the performance of guided anti-armour missiles whose penetrating power is also weaker. Modern tanks, such as the Russian T-80, can in any case fire missiles through their barrels, and thus combine their mobility and protection with the missile's longer reach. Moreover, whilst armoured vehicles might be becoming more visible to thermal contrasting devices, there is no guarantee this trend will persist indefinitely. Compared with the US M-47 tank, for example, the Soviet T-62 has a much smaller IR signature because of the configuration of its engine and exhaust system; and thanks to the tireless efforts of the creative scientific community to which the distinguished Dr Barnaby belongs, vehicle protection is moving away from solid metallic armours that conduct heat very well to materials which do not. Further, even if the missile locates its target and is not decoyed, there still remains the hurdle of actually piercing these increasingly sophisticated defences.

Indeed, for the duration of the 1990s at least, platforms like tanks are likely to retain their current edge over anti-platform systems. The tank remains an optimum mixture of firepower, protection, mobility and all-weather capabilities, and seems bound to undergo further refinements. New materials will assist in restricting size and weight without sacrificing protection, while automation will reduce manning requirements and, again, dimensions. Engines with better power-to-weight ratios will improve agility, while generally lighter, smaller vehicles will ease the problems of avoiding detection and of strategic mobility. The new generation of French armoured cars and similar light-weight platforms mounting relatively heavy guns are tangible evidence of this trend.

In the longer term however, it is possible that the penetrating power of third generation anti-armour weapons such as TRIGAT and the AAWS-H will prove too great for passive armours on any practical scale. Coupled to improved guidance and target-acquisition devices, this might lead to the ascendancy of anti-platform systems. Yet even this will not necessarily secure the total demise of tanks, manned aircraft and so on. In thinning out their tank units, for example, the Russian general staff who have so often correctly anticipated the impact of technological innovations, including those pioneered by the West, are preparing for a situation in which tanks will be less useful than before. Such restructuring is of course presented as a move towards a more defensive posture and is inspired at least in part by financial restraints; but it would be naïve to assume that operational considerations have been entirely disregarded. As V.G. Reznichenko remarked in 1987:

> Under the influence of modern weapons . . . the combat formation of forces on the offensive is destined to consist of two echelons: a ground echelon, whose mission will be to carry out the penetration of the enemy's defence and develop it in depth, and an air echelon created to envelop defending forces from the air and strike at their rear areas.[92]

The platform which the Russians, among others, have identified as the tank's successor in many roles and which will make up the bulk of this 'air echelon' is the helicopter. Its incorporation on a large scale into their armed forces has been underway for some years, and even a cursory glance at its characteristics reveals why. Just as in the 1920s and 1930s mechanisation endowed all types of land forces with greater mobility, so too has the rotor-wing aircraft the potential to transform every dimension of military operations: firepower, mobility, command, reconnaissance and supply. The modern helicopter possesses as good an all-weather and day and night operating capability as most ground vehicles; it can overfly minefields, rivers and other natural or man-made obstacles; it can lift substantial loads and

yet cover great distances at up to 250 kilometres per hour, permitting
both the sudden concentration of firepower or *matériel* and the
dispersal of its own logistical support facilities; it can land almost
anywhere and, as it can approach a given point from any direction,
exploiting the terrain to conceal its movements, it can achieve considerable tactical surprise. Indeed, because of these features, even a
relatively small unit of helicopters can be a potent force. It can
remain unobserved, far to the rear of the battle zone if desired, until
required. Then at short notice it can be deployed to cover or threaten
a comparatively vast area.

However, like any platform, helicopters do have their limitations.
They are rather vulnerable, though their robustness is steadily
improving, as is their agility. Mast-mounted sights and the employment of increasingly sophisticated 'fire and forget' stand-off missiles
are also giving them sufficient reach to strike at targets without
unduly exposing and thus jeopardising themselves. There are moreover various endeavors afoot to further refine the helicopter. The
current generation of conventional rotorcraft designs is unlikely to be
dramatically improved on in some regards, for, as in the design of any
weapons platform, the need to find an optimum balance between
speed, range, protection, firepower, manoeuvrability and signature
size imposes constraints. But many of the new technologies outlined
above are being incorporated into rotorcraft to give them ever
greater potential.

Through the use of low-weight materials such as toughened ep-
oxies, metal matrix composites, reinforced thermoplastics and
aluminum-lithium alloys, airframes, power plants, rotorhubs, gear-
boxes and bearings will all be lighter but sturdier. Engines, for
example, will weigh up to 30 per cent less, but will be more powerful
and, through the use of variable-cycle configurations which provide
both shaft energy and propulsive thrust, and transmissions with
high-ratio conformal gearing, will create less noise and vibration,
making for a platform that is more comfortable and stable as well as
harder to descry. Tilt rotors and advancing-blade designs promise to
further enhance endurance and hover capabilities, pushing dash
speeds up to as much as 450 kilometres per hour, while fly-by-wire or
-light active control mechanisms will allow high-velocity, nap-of-the-
earth flight to be safely accomplished without excessively straining
the pilot or machine. Indeed the principal advances in helicopter
design will be with regard to elusiveness and survivability in general.
Stealth technology, higher speeds, better handling and low-level

flight capabilities will all assist in this, and robuster construction will improve crash and damage tolerance. Rotorcraft will become more difficult to detect and, if spotted, harder to destroy.

The need for improvements to its survivability highlights the helicopter's main drawback. Whilst it can help in the holding of ground, it cannot undertake that mission itself. It has to be done by land units which have the necessary firepower and protection for firefights; helicopters are really 'hit and run' forces. This underlines the need for a mix of forces if combat operations are to be successful. Neither rotorcraft nor any other type of unit should be expected to perform tasks for which they are ill-suited and in which they would be at their most vulnerable. Consequently the tank and other armoured vehicles cannot yet be dismissed as obsolete as some have suggested. Clearly many roles might now be far better fulfilled by helicopters and the armoured division might indeed come to suffer from 'aircraft carrier syndrome', whereby an ever greater proportion of its resources have to be devoted to self-defence tasks. Nevertheless the tank might have to be retained as the only means of executing certain essential missions, even if higher attrition rates have to be assumed.

Such broadly complimentary applications of new technology is a well established trend which seems unlikely to take on a revolutionary rather than evolutionary character for the time being at least. Nor is it necessarily the case that emerging technologies favour the defender more than the attacker. The basic problems they respectively face in combat have rarely contrasted all that much, and we are poised on the threshold of an era in which technological developments promise to further erode any distinctions that do exist. Light infantry, for example, have been cited as forces which lack offensive capabilities. Yet, as we saw in Chapter 3, they have been employed in the past to spearhead assaults and, supported by modern equipment like helicopters and anti-armour missiles, are now acquiring a very potent attack capacity, especially on enclosed terrain and against forces deployed in reduced densities.

The fact is that what determines whether a given weapon is defensive or offensive is the manner in which it is used. People will fight with whatever implements technology puts at their disposal, and those belonging to putative opponents will always appear threatening. Bernard Brodie once observed that 'The history of military technology thus far has encouraged the doctrine that to every new weapon there is inevitably deployed some "answer"'. Just as President Reagan hoped that his Strategic Defense Initiative (SDI) would shield people from the ultimate weapon, the nuclear-armed, inter-continental ballistic missile, so too have the 'Just Defence' lobby sought to present a technological 'fix' to the problem of conventional war. Reagan of course was pilloried, either because of his unbounded faith in such untested and prohibitively expensive technology or because to many, especially in the 'Peace Movement', SDI was part of a nefarious American plot to extend the arms-race and end the stabilising threat of mutually assured destruction; from behind its impregnable shield, the US would be able to launch nuclear attacks with impunity. It was soon palpable that the project would never fulfil Reagan's expectations however. For a fraction of the cost it could be effectively countered and, at best, would only furnish a limited, point defence system.

But SDI and people's varying reactions to it perfectly illustrate the significance of perceptions. How would an attempt to build an impregnable conventional defence be regarded by a country's poten-tial adversaries? Would it not be likely to provoke some reaction – an arms-race or possibly even the pre-emptive strike which the advo-cates of 'Just Defence' identify as one of the greatest threats to peace? Indeed is it not ironic that, as has long been the case with nuclear weapons, many of the more recent technical advances – notably the ability to deliver long-range fire with great accuracy – which they condemn in some circumstances as destabilising are in others portrayed as the keys to security? Today, technology is no more likely to obviate the possibility of war than it was in the time of Bloch and Nobel. Even the threat of nuclear annihilation cannot guarantee that. On the contrary, as Alfred Thayer Mahan surmised over 100 years ago in his *The Influence of Sea Power Upon History*: 'The unresting progress of mankind causes continual change in the weapons; and with that must come a continual change in the manner of fighting'.

3. THE IMPACT OF ARMS-CONTROL AND DOMESTIC POLITICAL AND ECONOMIC FACTORS

'It is not armaments that cause war, but wars that cause armaments.'
(Salvador de Madariaga, *Morning Without Noon*).

As we saw in Chapter 3, there was considerable debate in European military circles during the period 1871–1914 as to whether or not technological advances had rendered successful offensive operations impossible. The broad conclusion that general staffs came to, however, was that, although losses would inevitably be greater than in previous wars, with sufficient man- and firepower opponents could still be overwhelmed.

Such a solution is no more available to NATO's strategists today than it has been throughout the history of the alliance. As highlighted in Chapter 1, the arbitrary allocation of resources to defence is something which Western liberal governments could not indulge in precisely because they were the creation of and answerable to democratic, pluralistic societies with a free press and other influential institutions. Today, economic, political, social and demographic trends are not propitious for any expansion in the military capabilities of the NATO states, nor is any being sought. On the contrary, whilst there is talk of a 'leaner but meaner' force structure, budgets are being slashed and units dismembered. Meanwhile, in the countries that once made up the Warsaw Pact, disarmament is still more in evidence as newly-elected, representative administrations feverishly channel resources from their bloated defence establishments to those sectors of their economies which provide basic goods and services to their enfranchised, impatient and increasingly acquisitive citizens.

East–West disarmament is supposedly being formalised and regulated through the CFE process at Vienna, where consensus has already been reached on numerically balancing certain key categories of forces. Further reductions might be negotiated and endorsed in the future. However arms-control agreements could be described as 'a security policy by other means'; and, given the recent revolutionary changes in the European political and strategic environment, it might be argued that the need for arms-limitation accords between NATO and its former, putative adversaries has lost its urgency if not its rationale. Whilst one might question whether there has ever been a serious Soviet 'threat' to Western European security, that the Russians and their erstwhile allies possessed formidable military capabilities which *could* have been employed directly – and, as we saw in Chapter 1, were utilised indirectly – in pursuit of political objectives is indisputable. Even before the signing of CFE I however, it was evident that this capacity was being significantly reduced and that NATO member states would, without a formal agreement if necessary, reciprocate. Although there is no hard and fast relationship between the numbers of weapons and the likelihood of war, this development, together with the radical changes in other non-military attributes of the former Eastern Bloc, has done much to change people's perceptions in this regard and has created an atmosphere in which further disarmament treaties will be expected. The Soviet 'threat' is receding, very largely of its own volition, and other potential opponents are beginning to appear more menacing. Should NATO's arms-control initiatives not now be directed more towards them?

Regrettably there is no guarantee that these putative foes could be enticed into making any such agreements. Arms-limitation where it seems most needed is not necessarily available, whereas further accords with the Russians are probably negotiable but not quite as desirable. Nevertheless CFE I will furnish a solid base of legal obligations and verifiable, numerical balances on which future treaties could be founded and, very importantly, has already endowed the Soviet military withdrawal from Eastern Europe with a political legitimacy it would otherwise have lacked.

A characteristic of the CFE negotiations so far has been the emphasis placed on cutting those capabilities which are seen as essential for conducting sudden, large-scale offensive operations, the aim being to increase mutual confidence by reducing the capacity for a surprise attack. Such reasoning of course lies at the heart of 'Non-Offensive Defence' postures. But it should not be assumed that this trend is a calculated move towards military stances of this *genre* by either NATO or the Russians. True, in his speech before the UN General Assembly in December 1988, Gorbachev argued that some Soviet divisions were being reorganised and 'after a major cutback of their tanks . . . will become clearly defensive'. But as we have seen, there are alternative, technical and operational explanations for this, and moreover the Russians have always refused to describe their forces and doctrine in any other way. For example in a 1989 article, General Yazov, the Defence Minister, maintained that

> The formation of our doctrine was carried out in the course of the struggle to consolidate Soviet power. From the very outset its nature was defensive and aimed at the protection of our socialist Fatherland. . . . [It was necessary] to defend it by force of arms against attacks from internal counter-revolution and external forces seeking to eliminate the proletariat's revolutionary gains. . . . Thus in its political aspect, Soviet doctrine has always been of a defensive nature. . . . At the same time, it used to be laid down by the military–technical side of the doctrine that . . . the Armed

Forces . . . had to have all the capabilities necessary for routing the enemy, including and indeed primarily by means of decisive offensive actions. . . . We believed that the warring parties . . . would strive to achieve objectives mainly by means of the offensive. The higher the Armed Forces' capability for such actions, the more reliably . . . would the other side be deterred from hostile actions and the better the circumstances for preserving peace.[93]

Even General Yazov had to subsequently concede that:

this postulate contained a certain contradiction: the political aspect of Soviet military doctrine retained its exclusively defensive orientation, whereas on the military–technical side its offensive elements predominated, primarily in the field of strategy, operational art and tactics – and hence also in certain areas of military organisation.[94]

It was precisely this paradox that, together with the fashion in which the Russians intermittently used their military power, troubled NATO; declarations of intent, such as no-first-use of nuclear arms, are all very well, but what a potential opponent judges *could* be done is what counts. In fact as General Lushev, Commander-in-Chief of the Warsaw Pact, acknowledged that same year, the incipient restructuring of Russian forces was aimed not at a complete removal of offensive capabilities as espoused by 'Just Defence' proponents but at their restriction in accordance with 'defence sufficiency'.[95] In short, the capacity for massive surprise offensives was to be diminished, not the capacity for attacks *per se*.

Furthermore, as we have seen, the move towards 'defence sufficiency' on the Russians' part has been influenced more by economic factors than anything else. Even before Gorbachev came to power it was palpable that the cost of keeping such vast military establishments was crippling investment, research and industrial development to an extent that endangered social cohesion and stability. Like Germany in the 1930s, the Russians were confronted with either trying to make these armaments pay their way through war, or reducing defence expenditure and pursuing a more modest and conciliatory foreign policy. They chose the latter. As the threat they had seemed to pose receded, NATO states too lost little time in cutting back on military expenditure, even before any formal CFE treaty had been concluded: early in 1990 the Germans abandoned a new law to increase the *Dienstzeit* for conscripts from twelve to fifteen months and, as part of the terms for German reunification, pledged to reduce their armed forces to 370 000 personnel; in America, where military spending had helped swell budget deficits to massive proportions, the Pentagon announced plans to decrease expenditure and manpower by at least 25 per cent over five years; the Dutch decided to plunder £800 million from their defence budget during the same period; France, also suffering from a fiscal squeeze, embarked on a review of her forces and weapon development schemes and trimmed national service from twelve to ten months; while in the UK, where rising inflation was already badly eroding the purchasing power of the defence budget, the desire to secure a 'peace dividend' before an approaching general election led to the continuation of the 'long retreat' of British defence policy, with the Rhine Army and the RAF in Germany being cut by half. Given the demographic troughs and the need for austerity measures that were affecting most Western states by the late 1980s, at least some of these changes had been on the cards for a while. A degree of military restructuring was inevitable. The challenge was to achieve it in a controlled and balanced manner, and to decide what affordable mix of forces would best preserve peace with security.

The seeming contradiction between Russian military capabilities and stated objectives conceded by General Yazov underscores a serious conceptual problem relating to 'Just Defence' postures, namely what constitutes such a stance. As we saw in Chapter 3, the difficulty in distinguishing between 'offensive' and 'defensive' weapons proved a major obstacle in the Geneva Disarmament Conference of 1932–4, and the CFE I talks at Vienna were plagued by similar difficulties. The tortuous discussions over what platforms were to be defined as 'tanks', as opposed to 'armoured combat vehicles', are a classic illustration, as are the differences over what constituted a 'strike aircraft' and how that was to be distinguished from an 'air-defence fighter'. One could suggest equally pertinent but subtler questions. An AWACS aircraft, for example, can alert a defensive network to an impending aerial attack. But alternatively the same equipment could be utilised to coordinate assaults on an opponent's airfields, for instance. Similarly, long-range refuelling tankers can be employed to replenish escorts acting in a defensive mode, but can also be used to sustain offensive actions in an adversary's territorial waters or airspace. Just as General Yazov insisted that Soviet forces and doctrine have always been 'defensive', so too has NATO portrayed its 'offensive' capabilities in such a fashion; its airpower for instance was acquired to suppress enemy incursions – a 'defensive' mission. And if one agrees to limit, say, strike aircraft numbers, what guarantee does one have that somebody will not replace 'air defence interceptors' with unrestricted quantities of SAM batteries and employ these ostensibly 'defensive' planes in securing control of an enemy's airspace instead of their own?

Indeed whether a cannon is a 'defensive' or 'offensive' weapon would rather seem to depend on whether you are standing in front of it or behind it. It is a matter of perception. Likewise the operational manner in which a given piece of equipment is utilised is crucial. In the Falklands War of 1982 for example, the British used *Milan* anti-armour missiles – which are defined by most 'Just Defence' advocates as 'defensive' armaments – to 'soften up' Argentinian fieldworks before storming them. Moreover what is viewed as constituting security varies from state to state; it is a subjective judgement, and one country's security is too often another's insecurity. Thus while CFE I's emphasis on cutting certain types of capabilities on the Central Front might do much to satisfy the Germans and Poles for instance, the Norwegians feel that other weapon categories and equipment are more applicable to their corner of the world, and are therefore of greater concern. That is not to say that reductions in Soviet armoured, mechanised and air units will not benefit the Norwegians at all, it is just that, because of their geostrategic position, they are equally if not more disturbed by the Russians' fleet air arm, naval infantry and capacity for amphibious and maritime operations in general.

Other points should also be made about the CFE process and disarmament as a whole. First, parity in numbers does not necessarily mean parity in capabilities, any more than arms-control means security. Agreements fixing common force ceilings on quantities of key weapon platforms need to be carefully dovetailed, otherwise excluded categories might become the focus for new, destabilising arms-races. Far from being abolished, offensive military power could simply take on a different form. Either way, future competition might revolve as much around quality as quantity. In any case the inexorable collapse of the Warsaw Pact made a mockery of plans for a numerical East–West force balance before the ink had even dried, leading to Soviet calls for compensatory cuts in German forces especially. These *were* achieved, if only by the back door of the reunification treaty. But it is not clear where within the territory of the Warsaw Pact signatories the Russians are actually going to be permitted to base the 3200 tanks, for example, that they are allowed under the provisions of CFE I. Likewise differing national perceptions of security requirements and military priorities will make the preservation of symmetry within NATO – or any successor organisation – increasingly difficult; there is too little consensus over what threat is to be confronted.

Indeed we now appear to be moving from a state of high military preparedness and stability to one of lower military preparedness and an increased risk of instability. Radical cuts in nuclear arsenals are especially alluring, but it seems to me for one that the improbability of such weapons being used by any rational government increases in direct proportion to their overall numbers; a capacity for retaliation and guaranteed destruction on an unacceptable scale is an important element in promoting mutual deterrence. Given the new political alignment of Eastern Europe, short-range nuclear weapons are clearly redundant, but the ability to hit targets in the USSR has to be preserved for the time being at least. As to the claim made in NATO's July 1990 *London Declaration On A Transformed North Atlantic Alliance* that its nuclear forces are now to be 'truly weapons of last resort', one can only wonder whether they were really ever anything else, particularly in the age of nuclear parity.

The limitation of conventional force sizes could also create as many problems as it solves, especially for the supporters of 'Just Defence' postures. *Raumverteidigung* models for example are essentially manpower intensive. A slump in the numbers of young men available for military service was being experienced in virtually every Western country by the end of the 1980s, and several states, notably West Germany, were planning to increase conscription periods in an endeavour to meet the resultant shortfalls. Despite such measures however, it was clear that the hundreds of thousands of troops needed to make area defence feasible were simply not going to be available.[96] (In fact, some studies – including perennial British Army explorations into the possibility of sealing off the 500-kilometre Irish frontier – suggest the number of personnel required for a credible area defence of the German border, for example, could be in excess of eight million.) Now, although reunification has largely solved any foreseeable manpower problem for the Germans, their forces – air, land and sea – are capped by treaty obligations. This, together with the numerical restrictions imposed by CFE I and the reunification agreement's clauses forbidding the garrisoning of NATO units on the territory of the former *Demokratische Republik*, threatens to circumscribe the scope for territorial defence schemes very considerably. Moreover any intermediate force structure must be capable of accommodating any future cuts in strengths, armaments and deployments that are negotiated. An accord on short-range missiles, for instance, could demolish several of the assumptions on which the viability of *Raumverteidigung* models is founded.

As it is, the reductions so far endorsed will have considerable repercussions for NATO strategy, notably on the commitment to the forward defence of German territory. Even under the old 'layer cake' arrangement of national corps the spread of units was somewhat uneven, with the largest and best forces being concentrated in the more naturally defensible Central Army Group area, while the more open and vulnerable North German Plain was relatively weakly held. Lower force densities on the Central Front will inevitably have an adverse impact on force-to-space ratios and enhance the need for mobility and reach on the battlefield. Although light infantry deployed in towns and forests might serve as pivots for mobile forces, the emphasis will clearly be on manoeuvre rather than static, positional warfare. As we have noted, suitably equipped and organised, even light units are capable of offensive action and, in an environment where they will face a diminished threat from powerful armoured formations, could prove especially efficacious. In fact in a number of Western Armies programmes already exist for the creation of hybrid units which, through the exploitation of the latest technology, will have the firepower of a modern heavy division but the strategic and tactical mobility of a light one.[97] Similarly the Russians are, as we have seen, remolding their forces and operational methods to take account of these new circumstances.

The potential importance of airportable and other light forces is already being acknowledged in emerging blueprints for NATO's order-of-battle in the 1990s. These bear some resemblance to suggestions made as long ago as 1973 by Kenneth Hunt.[98] The traditional 'layer cake' deployment of national corps running from North to South will be superseded by a 'current bun', comprising a multinational screening force predominantly composed of light troops behind which powerful but airmobile divisions will be deployed as rapid-reaction reserves. Still further back will be headquarters and other *cadres* around which reserve corps will congeal in the event of a major emergency. Because of German political sensitivities, the bulk of the armies' heavy equipment will probably also be stored in these rear zones, if not outside the theatre altogether, and generally NATO forces will have to endeavour to be seen and not heard. Indeed the plan owes much – perhaps too much – to the political desire to make their presence more palatable for both the Germans and the Russians.

Broadly speaking however, the trend is towards maximising the potential and value for money of whatever forces remain in being. Consequently, whilst their numerical strength will be reduced by the Vienna process, their combat capabilities will be as great if not greater than before: older equipment will be scrapped and newer kit, possibly transferred from allies, will take its place. Aircraft, for example, will be of the multi-role type, there will be more professional personnel rather than conscripts, and there will be a general search for flexibility to enable contrasting environments and missions to be coped with. Postures like 'Just Defence' which deliberately seek to limit military options are unlikely to be embraced. But maintaining up-to-date, well-equipped units with a high degree of mobility will be expensive and, whilst the 1991 Gulf War will distort some countries' calculations in the shorter term, defence budgets are set to fall rather than rise. Moreover, in deciding exactly how any defence cake is to be apportioned among NATO members in the wake of the CFE I agreement, several thorny issues arise. For example, particularly with regard to air and naval forces which require large, sophisticated and costly infrastructures, relatively small countries like the Benelux states, Denmark and some members of the erstwhile Eastern Bloc might deem it economic nonsense to try to preserve an amplitude of military options, especially if, because of national priorities and treaty-imposed numerical restrictions, the forces concerned can only be of negligible size. Adaptability might make them more cost-effective, for dedicating equipment and personnel to narrow, specialised tasks is obviously expensive and does not always yield a capability commensurate with the proportion of national resources invested.

Especially in the light of accords limiting the size of forces however, role-specialisation and burden-sharing between states might ease the problems involved. This approach can have its drawbacks though: collaboration too often entails all the impediments and costs of management by committee, which can diminish any financial savings achieved; burden-sharing can easily become an excuse for burden-shedding; and, if one member of a syndicate suddenly withdraws from role-specialisation arrangements, its former partners can be left deficient in some crucial regard. In any case, as the Persian Gulf crisis of 1990 showed, the tailoring of units to particular environments and roles can cause severe practical problems should 'out-of-area' missions ever have to be undertaken. Many of the Western forces dispatched to Saudi Arabia were designed to fight Soviet armour in the temperate climes of Central Europe, not Iraqis in the sand and heat of the desert. Light infantry and 'spider' units geared to the protection of a particular patch of a *Raumverteidigung* would be even more inflexible in this regard, and this could have serious repercussions for the military capabilities of NATO, UNO forces or any other body expected to enforce the 'new world order' as and when required.

Indeed, whilst the retention of national forces across the spectrum of capabilities means that resources are thinly, perhaps inefficiently, spread, it does afford the state concerned the scope to deal with its peculiar local and other security problems without having to turn to its allies. National sovereignty is thus not entirely dependent on others and on their willingness to carry on performing allotted tasks which might not necessarily be in their own interests. These points are particularly well illustrated by the case of Greece and Turkey. Given their general interests and geostrategic positions, they appear to be perfect candidates for a close, military partnership. Unfortunately their past disputes over Cyprus in particular have not only prevented them from cooperating much but have even made them potential belligerents. So much so in fact that, although they are both members of NATO, the Greeks are reluctant to see their forces cut as part of a CFE treaty unless the Turks do the same, whereas the latter, confronted by an increasingly bellicose Iraq and large, sophisticated Soviet forces, would prefer to build up their own military strength rather than diminish it.

Thus collaboration can have its political limitations, whatever its economic attractions might be. Yet it can help the process of alliance integration and lead to greater standardisation of equipment – the lack of which has been a long-standing and costly flaw in NATO's forces. Indeed if the multi-national units now envisaged for the Central Front, for example, are to be any more viable than the ill-fated 'Multilateral Nuclear Force' of the 1960s, common weaponry and equipment, tactics, communications and language will be essential. At the same time these forces will have to be structured in a manner which will permit both the accommodation of any future negotiated reductions and the temporary withdrawal of national contingents should that prove necessary. Indeed integration below the brigade level is probably impossible, at least for the foreseeable future.

Finally we should metion some problems attached to verifying and enforcing the arms-control agreements concluded at Vienna. First, verification is an expensive business and will erode any savings made on defence expenditure in the short to medium term. Besides data-exchange mechanisms and expert inspection teams, a range of monitoring equipment – including satellites, an assortment of ground-based sensors and airborne radar systems[99] – will be needed to assist in ensuring that the numbers of restricted weapon platforms in the ATU area do not exceed the limits prescribed by treaty. What will happen if they do, or if compliance is broken in some other way, is unclear however. Demilitarised and weapon-free zones, for example, are all very well, but if a state's forces possess the necessary lift capacity and mobility they can easily move into them. The Russians for instance have sufficient tank-transporters to move several entire divisions at once. Indeed, as we have seen, some potentially crucial capabilities are receiving less attention than others, while it would in any case be virtually impossible to enforce arms-control measures in some fields. For example, monitoring a country's chemical industry to prevent the clandestine manufacture of weapons is difficult enough, but how can arms-control be applied to that key capability of the modern battlefield, electronic warfare? Similarly when even relatively small technical refinements can dramatically alter the characteristics of, say, missiles or ostensibly 'light' armoured vehicles, how are limits and definitions enshrined in accords to be given durability? And how does one prevent the abuse of the provisions and exemptions regarding, for instance, stored, training and reserve equipment, or civilian transport helicopters and lorries which differ only from their military cousins in the colour of their paintwork?[100]

Calling as it does for a cut of between five and fifteen per cent in selected platforms, CFE I will not itself have all that dramatic an impact on NATO's forces. Even before the Vienna process yielded any fruits, it was clear that demographic and economic trends were pointing to some restructuring and curtailment of procurement plans. What might have more substantial repercussions is the atmosphere of expectation that the unprecedented progress in East–West disarmament has given rise to, and national perceptions of threats, security and military requirements. In this regard there will be some divergence between individual European states and between the two continental pillars of the alliance. The US for example will bear many of the CFE I reductions, but will maintain military capabilities and units commensurate with its global commitments and needs. The limit imposed on troop strengths in Europe is increasingly regarded by the Americans as more of a ceiling than a floor. Indeed by the mid 1990s their air and ground forces stationed there may well have dwindled to well under 100 000 personnel. Many European countries, on the other hand, will have contrasting requirements: 'out-of-area' operations will be of secondary if any significance; concepts of security and 'defence sufficiency' will vary from capital to capital; and, with the decline of the common threat and the concomitant breakdown of the East–West military confrontation, defence priorities are likely to undergo permutation.

All of this will have consequences for force structures and for the manufacture and procurement of military equipment at a time when the 'military–industrial complex' is already experiencing appreciable change. Since the 1970s the position of the defence conglomerates as a very distinct and in many senses privileged sector of Western economies has been abraded. Governments have progressively applied competitive tendering and other commercial techniques to defence procurement, removing the special institutional arrangements and immunity from market forces that have been the hallmarks of this trade for much of the post-war era. Simultaneously, measures such as the Single European Act, financial deregulation and other alterations to trade markets have, together with the growth of cartels and multi-national corporations, eroded the sovereignty of individual states, creating a more interdependent economic order. Up till recently the defence sector was protected as an essential one which both helped to preserve peace and powered technical innovation in the economy as a whole. However, as far as the second of these factors is concerned, the general trend towards electrical rather than mechanical technology has led to the eclipse of the defence sector by the civil. Indeed the former now increasingly tends to benefit from the spin-off from the latter's efforts, especially in such fields as space exploration and computers.

Historians and economists still remain divided over whether research and development resources invested in military projects generate much in the way of general economic advancement.[101] In Britain, where in 1988 for example the Ministry of Defence consumed £1191 million out of £4500 million spent by the government on research, the debate has been particularly fierce. But this is a long-standing issue which has affected many states. During the nineteenth century especially, military imperatives evidently stimulated growth, industrialisation, innovation and competition; and, as we saw in Chapter 3, those who could not or would not endeavour to keep up in the race rapidly fell prey to those who did. Above all, the Japanese realised that they would have to create a social, industrial, scientific, bureaucratic and economic infrastructure like that found in the industrialised world if they were to be practitioners rather than victims of colonialism. Their success in doing so was remarkable. However the constant fear of being overtaken made for instability; and in 1941, sensing that time was running out and that war was the one route to salvation, Japan was to turn on Britain and America in a desperate bid to secure military and economic hegemony in the Pacific.

With the advent of nuclear weapons, arms-races seemed to take on an especially menacing aspect. The 'Just Defence' movement, among others, have, as we have seen, been very critical of this and other technical developments, albeit in a somewhat syncretic manner. What is clear however is that by the 1970s the Russians were failing to hold their own in competition with the West across the whole gamut of economic activity. Their highly centralised economy was primarily designed to facilitate any switch to wartime production that should prove necessary. Thus their ability to swiftly mobilise resources for war was superior to the West's. Yet as we noted throughout Chapter 1, the main challenge facing both blocs in the post-war world was not to prove that of actually waging a conflict but sustaining the wherewithal to do so in peacetime without causing fatal distortions in the economy. The USSR failed to cope with this test and consequently found itself approaching its zenith as a military superpower. Too used to massive injections of labour and cheap, raw materials, the Russian economy suffered a steady decline in output as the growth rates of these resources fell off during the 1970s and 1980s.[102] At the same time SDI and other Western projects hailed the beginning of another phase of intense technological rivalry. Even if 'Star Wars' did not come up to President Reagan's expectations, it was palpable that the spin-off from SDI could, together with quantum leaps in computing capabilities and in other fields of electrical engineering, only lead to an ever more pronounced Western ascendancy. So long as competition had largely been over mechanical rather than electrical technology, the Russian economy had had some chance of matching or copying Western innovations. But given the relentless application of multifarious sensors, avionics and other convoluted circuitry in weapon designs, the Russians could not hope to keep abreast of developments. As Brezhnev admitted in *Pravda* in October 1982: 'Technological advances necessitated by future military requirements might be beyond the sophistication of the economy'.[103]

Apart from pleading for a ban on the creation of non-nuclear armaments 'based on new physical principles, whose destructive capacity is close to that of nuclear weapons',[104] Gorbachev could only respond to this danger by regenerating and remoulding the ailing Soviet economy. In discussions with his military advisers, he seems to have persuaded them that only this would hold out the long-term prospect of Russia retaining her position as a great military power.[105] By 1985 some three quarters of her total production comprised capital goods; consumer items accounted for only 25 per cent. Statistics released in 1989 conceded that twelve per cent of national income and fifteen per cent of overall expenditure was being devoted to defence, though some Western estimates and subsequent comments by Soviet officials suggest that these figures were well below the real levels. For instance Oleg Bogomolev, a prominent economist in the Congress of People's Deputies, stated in April 1990 that some 20–25 per cent of the GNP was being consumed by the armed forces.[106] Gorbachev duly announced plans to slash military production by 30–50 per cent by 1995 and, within a similar timescale, boost the defence sector's production of consumer goods to 60 per cent of total output; two out of five main tank manufacturers, for example, were already producing agricultural tractors, and such diversification was to be expanded.

This was to prove easier said than done however. The introduction in January 1989 of self-financing in industry, for instance, did not lead so much to profitability through greater efficiency as to higher prices, while the funding of large government spending deficits by the printing of money only served to exacerbate this inflationary trend. Imports were sucked in and, given a lack of hard currency to pay for them, the Russians had to default on some of their overseas debt repayments which, between 1984 and 1986 alone, had tripled in size.[107] Meanwhile at home, informal trade barriers were erected as cities and regions tried to limit the sale of goods and foodstuffs to local inhabitants only. Jokes about Gorbachev abounded. He could, it seemed, change the world and win the Nobel Peace Prize; but he could not make sausages.

Those parts of the Soviet economy that had built an awesome military machine and permitted the sending of scores of cosmonauts on impressive space missions had always been held in high esteem. They were the repository for the best administrators, technicians and scientists and appeared to be far more productive and successful than any other public enterprise. This however was largely illusory. The defence industry was just as wasteful and inefficient as any other, cushioned, as its Western counterpart had often been, from market forces. The State Order system of placing contracts meant procurement was not done on a 'shop around' basis, and even if it had been, the highly specialised nature of most companies and products severely limited scope in this regard. In trying to create a more streamlined, cost-conscious and civilian-orientated defence sector, Gorbachev encountered the same problems that pervade the rest of the Soviet socioeconomic order. Too many industrial and bureaucratic *apparatchiks* had a vested interest in preventing *perestroika* and, as was highlighted by Sergei Andreyev in an article in the Leningrad monthly *Neva* in January 1989, sought to hinder or thwart it either by disregarding the directives of central government or by containing and combatting their impact with local measures.

Nor did all of the military share their president's reforming zeal. Whilst most agreed that revitalisation of the industrial base and *konversiya* – defence conversion – were essential if the USSR was to remain a great military power, the implications for the armed forces in the meantime were grave. Admittedly, through *glasnost, perestroika* and sweeping disarmament measures, Gorbachev prompted a thaw in East–West relations which led to a peace windfall, an influx of vital technology, credit and managerial expertise – notably the package agreed on at the Houston Economic Summit of July 1990 – and markedly retarded both the development and deployment by NATO of the new, threatening generation of weapons. On the other hand the Soviet armed forces suffered an abrupt loss of intimacy with the Party and the country's ruling elite. Accustomed to being at the heart of decision-making, the general staff found itself increasingly marginalised, robbed of its almost exclusive control over military doctrine and force structures, obliged to accept changes within its own hierarchy and to the conscription laws, and compelled to make rapid and massive cuts in manpower and equipment. By definition the military were the one group most dedicated to the protection of their socialist fatherland and its values. Inevitably they proved a bastion of conservative opposition to reform. The victory of the Red Army and

Communism in the Great Patriotic War had not only secured the military a special place as the heroes of Soviet society, but had also been used to justify just about everything from the command economy to the Party's monopoly on power and other privileges. Given the USSR's faltering economy, her one major claim to being a superpower lay in the size of her armed forces. Now Gorbachev was dismantling them and, moreover, the *cordon sanitaire* which, at enormous cost, the Red Army had won in Eastern Europe.

Besides those who remained sincerely uneasy about the threat they perceived from the West, there were many who were disillusioned and disgruntled by the way all of this was handled. Thousands of Soviet troops were withdrawn to the USSR, only to find that there were no proper facilities for them and their dependents. By 1990 there were around 180 000 military families waiting to be reunited in proper married quarters, for example. Similarly there were no schools for the children, while for their fathers the future seemed equally uncertain in a country which no longer wanted their professional services and which, thanks to *glasnost*, was becoming ever more critical of the armed forces' shortcomings. Some officers even formed a trade union, *Shield*, in an attempt to protect their interests. Meanwhile, in the East European countries they had vacated, there were disputes over the value of facilities they had handed over to the indigenous populations; open hostility towards Russian troops became common and, to the embarrassment of West Germany especially, Red Army deserters took to fleeing to the West and asking for political asylum.[108]

Increasingly the military became a hotbed of resentment and dissatisfaction. Yet Gorbachev needed them. Unrest in Baku, Vilnius and Erevan had to be dealt with by the Army, which did little to ameliorate its already ambivalent attitude to his reforms. On 25 February 1990 the curious manner in which troops were mobilised in Moscow to control a 'dissident' rally provoked speculation about the danger of a coup. The rumours were dismissed by Alexander Yakovlev, one of Gorbachev's closest colleagues, but relations between the military and its political masters palpably underwent some changes hereafter. The nature of the May Day Parade was evidently a sop to the Army, and various other conciliatory gestures were made. Nevertheless, during the period May–July 1990 the Soviet attitude in the CFE negotiations markedly hardened, apparently because of pressure from the general staff, while at the Twentyeighth Party Congress there was ample evidence among their 300 delegates of the forces'

mounting sense of alienation and concern: Major-General Ivan Ni-
kulin accused the politicians of staging an 'unbridled disarmament
race'; General Albert Makashov harangued them for standing by
while 'traitors' undermined the services' fighting effectiveness; and
when, in a letter to the newspaper *Komsomolskaya Pravda*, 47 liberal
scientists, military personnel and politicians warned the national
leadership of a threatening alliance between reactionary Party members and senior members of the forces, there was uproar.

Although at the self same conference Gorbachev routed his opponents and effectively completed his transformation of the institutions and upper echelons of Soviet government – a process which, by
means of regular purges of the politburo and other reforms and
machinations, had been underway since 1988 – this was an incom-
plete victory. If *perestroika* is to be carried through, then he will have
to secure adequate support along the full length of the administrative
ladder. This will be a very difficult and time-consuming process, and
years if not decades will pass before the benefits of change become
really apparent. Indeed, at the time of writing, Gorbachev has
already been in power for some five years and the reform programme
he has initiated will of necessity have to continue after his passing.
His successors are unlikely to completely abandon it however, partly
because there is no viable alternative – even if the Gorbachev
revolution were reversible, the ways of the *ancien régime* were
patently no better, and were in many respects worse – but largely
because he is as much a symptom of change in the USSR as a cause of
it. His rise to power and success to date could only have been
achieved with the consent and active support of a very substantial
part of the ruling elite. Indeed he can be regarded as the product of
developments that have been sedately under way for several decades,
and rather less placidly since the early 1980s.

The attempts of successive Soviet administrations to transform
their country's backward, predominantly agrarian economy into one
that could rival capitalism's technological, industrial and commercial
prowess were bound to spawn changes in society which the Party
would have to adjust to or risk destruction. As the means of production altered, the demand for educated, skilled workers and bureau-
crats ineluctably grew, while, equally inevitably, the acquisitive and
inquisitive nature of these professionals conflicted with the Party's
endeavours to maintain a cohesive and controlled society. The social
order, if not socialism, was coming to an end; and now the real
debate within the USSR is about whether Gorbachev's reforms,

notably the economic package approved in October 1990, will proceed sufficiently far and fast.

Somebody once defined a communist as a person who has abandoned hope of becoming a capitalist, and clearly Gorbachev and his successors face major difficulties as an increasingly better informed and acquisitive population restlessly awaits the tangible benefits of reform. Until these appear in their shops and pay-packets, *perestroika* will lack substance to a degree that no amount of glittering *glastnost* can compensate for. Indeed in this regard Gorbachev has already played most of his cards; his spectacular achievements in foreign policy now need to be balanced by more in domestic matters. Whatever he does, however, we should not lose sight of the fact that his overarching concern is to preserve the power and influence of the USSR. Whether he can do that and simultaneously tackle her immense domestic problems remains to be seen.

Many of the difficulties confronting the USSR in the process of *konversiya* are likewise being experienced in the West as the enormous martial establishments of the Cold War unravel. With military budgets being plundered and forces reduced, the defence and related sectors in Western economies face contraction. In the shorter term, the costs involved in moving units to new accommodation or demobilising them will offset any peace dividend, as will those of verifying CFE I; the price of withdrawing a solitary infantry battalion of 600 men from the British Army of the Rhine and rehousing it in the UK has been estimated at £55 million for example. Thereafter however, and particularly when the current equipment cycle begins to draw to a close and the prospect for substantial savings grows, the decline in defence-related expenditure promises to be sharper.

It would be a little perverse if the end of the Cold War did not bring some form of peace dividend for Western electorates, who in any case will anticipate one. However for many people disarmament will entail little but economic and social upheaval. In places as far apart as Fort Dix in New Jersey and Koblenz in Germany the impact of defence expenditure reductions on the local economy threatens to be devastating if it is not already proving so. The second of these places for example has, together with 37 other towns in an area bounded by it, Hammelburg, Göttingen and Kassel, traditionally played host to the III Corps of the *Bundeswehr*. In 1988 some 12 000 military personnel were garrisoned in Koblenz and spent some DM 500 million there. 3246 local people were employed on bases, while businesses in the region supplied the troops with, among other products, 2.8 million bread rolls, 1500 pigs, 154 beef cattle, and DM 0.5 million in fruit and vegetables. Similarly Fort Dix, a major training camp through which some 35 000 soldiers pass each year, poured $1 million into the local economy every day in 1989. Around 4000 civilians actually worked at the fort, while a further 8000 locals depended on it indirectly for their employment. Investment in facilities, such as schools for the soldiers' children, ran into millions and imposed considerable burdens on local authorities.

Given the commitment to reduce Germany's forces to 370 000 personnel and the Pentagon's plans to implement major reductions, it is evident that towns like Koblenz have much to lose. Equally the withdrawal of thousands of foreign troops from Germany will, whilst welcome in some senses, have significant financial repercussions which will be distinctly disagreeable. For instance, according to figures compiled by the Cologne *Institut der Deutschen Wirkschaft*, in 1988 US forces in Germany spent some DM 10 000 million locally. German savings on defence will be necessary to help meet the enormous costs of reunification. Indeed this consideration must at least partly explain Chancellor Kohl's willingness at Stavropol in July 1990 to give the Russians a pledge to substantially diminish Germany's forces, irrespective of what was being proposed in the CFE I negotiations. As throughout NATO, the talk in German military circles is of making their Army *'Kleiner, aber feiner und professioneller'*. In the communities where this process may end in unemployment and dereliction, however, the usual aphorism is: 'We all want disarmament – but not here'.

The threat to jobs that disarmament will bring is one that is being recognised in most Western countries, but especially in the US, Britain, France and Germany where defence enterprises constitute very significant parts of the economy. In Britain, for example, the industry had sales totalling £11 000 million in 1989, nearly a quarter of which were exports, and roughly a million employees. Workers organisations, notably the Confederation of Shipbuilding and Engineering's twelve unions, which have 250 000 members dependent on defence expenditure for their employment, began to take fright in early 1990 and approached the European Commission for help and guidance, while the Labour Party busied itself with plans for establishing a defence diversification agency, should it win the next election. Needless to say it was not just the workers who were concerned about the industry's future. On one day in June 1990 alone, the share values of leading armament companies slumped by £150 million as investors, anticipating spending reductions of at least two to five per cent in real terms over the next few years, shifted their funds elsewhere.

This highlights what will prove a major problem with diversification. Even if we leave aside the incredibly naïve view that plant designed to manufacture, say, missiles can suddenly start producing dishwashers instead, the full extent of the difficulties involved do not seem to have dawned on many people. Restructuring will be an extremely costly affair. Capital will be needed for the conversion of machinery and factory buildings, and the retraining of employees. But where will this finance come from? In the past the rationale for a sizeable defence sector was largely provided by a military threat which has now greatly receded. How, given falling demand for their products, are defence-orientated companies going to attract the necessary investment? Will shrunken domestic consumption be sufficiently profitable to repay capital loans, or will companies have to attempt further expansion in the crowded and highly competitive markets overseas?

Such problems have been experienced by neutral countries, notably Sweden, for some time.[109] But they now appear destined to become more widespread. At the time of writing, restructuring of the NATO states' defence industries seems to be proceeding along two tracks: companies are attempting to diversify either within the defence sector itself or by moving into civil products; and a massive take-over and merger process is under way, aimed at eliminating competition and thus maximising market share. This last development is encountering resistance from protectionist policies. However some sectors already appear to be dominated by international cartels and this trend is likely to grow. The problem with this process is that it is essentially market-led and is thus prone to culminate in excess capacity in some areas and a dangerous lack of it in others. The link between one force structure and another is made up of equipment development and procurement programmes that might stretch out over ten or twenty years and absorb an appreciable slice of a country's GNP. But already one sees a growing reluctance on the part of many enterprises to get – and stay – involved in expensive, risky, high-technology projects like the European Fighter Aircraft; and if they do, the costs incurred can lead to smaller but no less important schemes being squeezed out. Rapidly rising unit costs are a common

problem as things stand, but a switch to 'Defensive Defence' strategies in which very limited numbers of some weapons platforms,
notably tanks and aircraft, would be procured, would exacerbate the
problem enormously.

There is also the concern that any tapering off in defence research
and development will lead to a decline in spin-off benefits for the civil
economy. As we have seen, it is far from clear how great these
actually are. It is evident that, at times, military requirements have
stimulated investment and development which, in the case of railways for instance, has had far-reaching and advantageous repercussions for much of society. On the other hand, a lot of
military-related production is just too *sui generis*.[110] The Russians'
current attempts to fashion tractors out of old tanks illustrate the
point well enough. They make *dreadful* tractors; they are far too
heavy for most agricultural purposes and, in a country where energy
resources are increasingly costly and restricted, their inordinate
fuel-consumption is particularly prohibitive. Likewise customised
defence industry machine tools have extremely narrow applications
when compared with, say, basic computer software.

In the longer term the two are inextricably connected but, for the
duration of the 1990s at least, economic rather than military power
seems destined to play the leading role. European integration; the
costs of German reunification; the American budget deficit; the
penury of the Russians and East Europeans; all of these factors
suggest that the concern and resources of governments are now likely
to be focused primarily on economic development. And it is from
this, as opposed to a cash windfall from the cutting of military forces
in the shorter term, that any substantial peace dividend might come,
especially for France, Britain and the USSR. Restructuring costs, the
financial repercussions of the Gulf War, debts and inflation will, after
all, already have accounted for much if not all of these immediate
savings before they are even made. But whereas in West Germany
and Japan the proportion of government research and development
funds spent in 1988–9 on civil rather than military projects was 87.5
and 96.5 per cent, in France and Britain it was only 62.4 and 52.0 per
cent respectively.[111] Given the comparatively limited spin-off benefits
from so many modern defence innovations, the opportunity costs
involved here could prove very substantial over a prolonged period.
Clearly some governmental direction will be essential if future force-
structure plans are to be matched with a commensurate and appropriate manufacturing capacity, but the end of the Cold War offers

several NATO states, notably Britain, some scope to redress the balance within their economies, take advantage of the economic opportunities of the next few years and thus create the wealth which, if they are to remain significant military powers, will be essential in the future.

5 Concluding Remarks

'There is no simple formula for peace, and no single act that will assure peace. Any who preach that are dangerously deluded. Only the combined result of many efforts at different levels, and at many places, will assure peace. In these efforts everyone has a part to play. The stakes are the greatest for which men have ever played.'

(John Foster Dulles)

With the end of the military, political and ideological division of Europe which has dominated East–West relations since the Russian Revolution and the Second World War, the continent stands on the threshold of an ear of great opportunity. The process of European integration is gathering pace; in the wake of the Single European Act, total economic and monetary union can, although some countries might have justifiable reservations about it, only be a matter of time. As tariffs and protectionism end with the creation of a unified market, the present array of national currencies of differing relative values, for example, will become an anachronism that can only complicate and obstruct the mechanics of free trade; the very logic of the situation points to their supersedence by a single currency of some kind, administered by a central bank. Indeed in October 1990 the vast majority of the EEC states declared this to be one of their goals. Similarly they speak and act increasingly as one in their relations with the rest of the world, and once their economic interests become completely interwoven, it would be surprising if this embryonic political cohesion did not take on a formal, institutionalised shape, such as a European confederation, which must at some point begin to concern itself with security matters. In fact an assortment of potential foundations for this is already in being. It only remains to be seen whether it will be the CSCE, the EEC, NATO or the Western European Union.

But as we have noted, the creation of an efficacious security organisation will be no easy task. As highlighted by the UN's attempt to respond to the Kuwait crisis of 1990–91, coordinating the political and military efforts of disparate states is easier said than done. Any new body must, in my view, include the US and must preserve or satisfactorily replace the integrated, military command structure that is NATO's greatest asset and the key to effective defence planning.

This will entail the harmonising of a number of conflicting interests and will raise some very thorny legal, political, economic, ideological and military problems, not the least of which will relate to the design, doctrine, command, purpose and strategy of the armed forces. With the dramatic improvement in East–West relations, many in the 'Defensive Defence' lobby perceive that their time has come in this regard. But this is, I believe, an illusion. European states will, for the foreseeable future, concern themselves more with economic rather than military power. In these circumstances, mustering the political will to devote the necessary resources to *any* kind of security effort will be difficult; arguing for the sort of massive investment that the 'Non-Offensive Defence' postures call for would be as futile and counterproductive as it would foolhardy. Moreover, even if electorates were prepared to support a stance that would impose very considerable burdens on them and their environment, doubts would persist as to its military and political relevance. For it is apparent from the signing of the CFE I Treaty and other concrete measures that, today, neither NATO nor the former Eastern Bloc feels especially menaced by the other's military power. Indeed both sides have now, I would contend, made their strategies *vis-à-vis* each other as 'defensive' as they are likely to for some time yet. What strategic options they have left they will be anxious to preserve, and cost-effectiveness alone dictates that future forces must be as flexible as possible, not constrained by *Nichtangriffsfähigkeit*.

In fact the end of the Cold War has demolished much of the rationale for 'Defensive Defence' as it is classically defined. It always appeared parochial, but now seems dangerously so. Whilst the USSR retains immense military capabilities, its very willingness to make major arms-control accords and the other strands of its more 'defensive', conciliatory policies suggest that this 'threat', if it has not disappeared, is now more manageable. Others however are far less so. Technical developments are constantly making the world a smaller place, and the greatest challenges to the interests and security of the NATO states are now emanating from once-distant regions of the globe. Non-intervention policies and the military prescriptions of 'Just Defence' offer no viable solution to these problems. On the contrary, a regime that precludes any form of power-projection is liable to prove quite impotent in the strategic and tactical environment of tomorrow. As battlefield depth increases, so too does the need for greater 'reach'. Border fortifications of the type advocated by the SAS and others offer little if any protection from incoming missiles – be they armed with conventional, chemical, biological or nuclear warheads – and in any case are comparable to a screening force: the real battle begins once they have been penetrated. Again, *Raumverteidigung* models are inherently feeble in this regard. Their web defences contain numerous physical and psychological weak-spots and would be likely to prove very porous to attacking forces. Yet the construction of this basic infrastructure could be expected to devour so many resources that it is doubtful whether much, if anything, would remain for the provision of 'spider' units, even if military budgets were to be larger than is conceivable.

Indeed the attractions attached to 'Defensive Defence' are almost exclusively political. Even they, however, are specious, depending for their viability on a continuing confrontational scenario in which neither peace nor war ever breaks out; for 'Just Defence' both lacks credibility as an efficacious military posture and is too rigid to adjust to arms-control initiatives, technological evolution, the realignment of states and other mutations that, as was most graphically high-lighted in 1989–90, can transform the international and strategic scene. NATO's current approach of 'Flexible Response', on the other hand, is both militarily and diplomatically more accommodat-ing. It *will* need some refinement in the wake of the revolutionary changes that have occurred in Europe of late, but remains an essen-tially effective stance which has helped preserve peace with security. 'Non-Offensive Defence' would be unlikely to achieve as much and would certainly not make war potentially any less destructive. Far from being a strategy for tomorrow, it would appear to be a concept founded on the permafrost of the Cold War; and as the one melts away, so will the other.

Notes and References

1 NATO and the Quest for Alternatives, 1949–89

1. See, for example, D. Gates, 'American Strategic Bases in Britain: The Agreements Governing Their Use', *Comparative Strategy*, vol. 8, no. 1 (1989) 99–124.
2. *Western Security: The Formative Years*, O. Riste (ed.) (Oslo: Norwegian University Press, 1985) pp. 158, 160.
3. Ibid., p. 48.
4. Ibid., pp. 257–8.
5. Ibid., pp. 259–60.
6. See C.J. Bartlett, *The Global Conflict, 1880–1970: The International Rivalry of the Great Powers* (London and New York: Longman, 1984) pp. 305–6.
7. *Western Security*, p. 261.
8. Quoted in M. Howard, *Studies in War and Peace* (London: Temple Smith, 1970) p. 159.
9. B. Liddell Hart, *Deterrent or Defence: A Fresh Look at the West's Military Position* (London: Stevens, 1961), p. 23.
10. A. Roberts, *Nations in Arms: The Theory and Practice of Territorial Defence* (London: Macmillan/IISS, 1986 edition) p. 254.
11. See D.N. Schwartz, *NATO's Nuclear Dilemmas* (Washington: Brookings, 1983), p. 51.
12. *Western Security*, p. 257.
13. W. Hayter, *A Double Life* (London, 1974) pp. 120–4, 151–2.
14. 'Sayings of the Week', *The Observer*, 30 September 1979.
15. Bartlett, *The Global Conflict*, p. 339.
16. See *Foreign Relations of the United States*, (FRUS) (Washington: GPO, 1979), 1951, I, pp. 42–4, 107–8, 166–72, 180–1; III Part I, pp. 451–6.
17. Ibid., 1951, I, pp. 124–7, 182–206.
18. See *Documents of the National Security Council, 1947–77*, P. Kesaris (ed.) (Washington: University Publications microfilm, 1980): NSC 162, 30 September 1953; NSC 5501, 7 January 1955.
19. NSC 6017, 17 November 1960.
20. *The Guardian*, 9 August 1982.
21. See W.W. Kaufmann, *Planning Conventional Forces, 1950–80* (Brookings, Washington, 1982).
22. Quoted in *Western Security*, p. 257.
23. See, for example, J. Record, *Revising US Strategy* (Washington: Pergamon/Brassey's, 1984) pp. 29–35.
24. Ibid., pp. 44–5.
25. A. Arbatov, 'Parity and Reasonable Sufficiency', *International Affairs* (Moscow), no. 10 (1988) pp. 80–1.
26. V. Zhurkin et al., 'Reasonable Sufficiency', *Novoye Vremya*, no. 40 (1987) p. 13.

27. See 'The Future Tasks of the Alliance' (Harmel Report, December 1967), in UK Secretary of State for Foreign and Commonwealth Affairs, *Selected Documents Relating to Problems of Security and Cooperation in Europe, 1954–77*, Cmnd 6932 (London: HMSO, 1977) Document 7, pp. 49–52.
28. R.L.L. Facer, *Conventional Forces and the NATO Strategy of Flexible Response* (Santa Monica, California: Rand, 1985), p. 33.
29. See, for example, *Western Security*, p. 286.
30. Record, *Revising US Strategy*, Appendix A, p. 99.
31. Ibid., Appendixes C–F, pp. 101–4.
32. D.T. Yazov, 'On Soviet Military Doctrine', *RUSI Journal*, vol. 134, no. 4 (1989) p. 1.
33. *The Absolute Weapon* B. Brodie (ed.) (New York: Harcourt Brace, 1946) p. 76.
34. See, for instance, C. Gray, 'Nuclear Strategy and the Case for a Theory of Victory', *International Security*, vol. 14, no. 1 (1979) pp. 54–87. For nuclear war's probable implications for Britain, for example, see British Medical Association Board of Science and Education, *The Medical Effects of Nuclear War* (Chichester: Wiley, 1983), and S. Openshaw, P. Steadman and O. Greene, *Doomsday: Britain After Nuclear Attack* (Oxford: Blackwell, 1983).
35. B. Brodie, *The Implications of Nuclear Weapons on Total War* (Santa Monica, California: Rand, 1957) p. 1118.
36. H. Afheldt, 'New Policies, Old Fears', *Bulletin of the Atomic Scientists*, vol. 44, no. 7 (1988) p. 24. For entertainingly jaundiced views of this issue see S. Tiedtke, 'The Unfathomable Arms Modernisation', and E. Krippendorff and M. Lucas, 'One Day We Americans Will Have To Consider The Destruction of Europe', in *Germany Debates Defence* (London: Sharpe/Committee for a Nuclear-Free Europe, 1983) pp. 16–43.
37. Carl von Clausewitz, *On War* (ed. and translated by M. Howard and P. Paret) (Princeton UP, 1976) pp. 91–2.
38. See, for example, D.K. Simes, 'Deterrence and Coercion in Soviet Policy', *International Security*, vol. 5, no. 3 (1980–1), especially pp. 86 and 88; D. Holloway, *The Soviet Union and the Arms Race* (Yale UP, 1983) pp. 29–64; and R. Arnett, 'Soviet Attitudes Towards Nuclear War: Do They Really Think They Can Win?', *Journal of Strategic Studies*, vol. 2, no. 2 (1979) pp. 172–9.
39. A. Horne, *To Lose A Battle: France 1940* (London: Penguin, 1979 edition) pp. 647–9.
40. Quoted in 'Defence Planning Committee Final Communiqué, 18 May 1977', *NATO Review*, July 1977, p. 26.
41. R.M. Nixon, *US Foreign Policy For The 1970s: A New Strategy For Peace* (Washington: USGPO, 1970) p. 6.
42. See D. Gates, 'Light Divisions in Europe', *Occasional Paper, 39* (Institute for European Defence and Strategic Studies, 1989).
43. Record, *Revising US Strategy*, p. 43.
44. See, for example, *The Guardian*, 8 May 1990, pp. 1 and 8; B.F. Schemmer, 'Army Volunteers 5-Division Cut By 1994' and 'Air Force, Navy

Offer Fighter Wings, Carriers in Budget pruning Exercise', *Armed Forces Journal International* (January 1990) pp. 14–15.
45. *Strengthening Conventional Deterrence in Europe: Proposals For The 1980s. Report of the European Security Study, ESECS* (London: Macmillan, 1983) pp. 251–2. On pp. 50–1, The Union of Concerned Scientists' report *No First Use* (1983) made six major recommendations which broadly overlap with those of the ESECS. Implementing the 'most urgent' was estimated to cost $100 000 million.
46. S.P. Huntington, Conventional Deterrence and Conventional Retaliation in Europe', in *Military Strategy in Transition: Defence and Deterrence in the 1980s* K.A. Dunn and W.O. Staudenmaier (eds) (Boulder and London: Westview, 1984) p. 18.
47. See J.H. Mearsheimer, *Conventional Deterrence* (Cornell UP, 1983) pp. 19–20.
48. *Strengthening Conventional Deterrence*, p. 8.
49. Huntington, 'Conventional Deterrence', p. 25.
50. Ibid., pp. 26–7.
51. Ibid., pp. 35–6.
52. Ibid., pp. 30–1.
53. Ibid., p. 30.
54. See J.J. Mearsheimer, 'The Military Reform Movement', *Orbis*, vol. 27, no. 2 (1983).
55. *Military Strategy in Transition*, p. 46.
56. Huntington, 'Conventional Deterrence', p. 32.
57. See *Military Strategy in Transition*, p. 211, footnote 21.
58. See Congressional Budget Office, *Rapid Deployment Forces: Policy and Budgetary Implications* (Washington: CBO, 1983) p. 25.
59. *Military Strategy in Transition*, pp. 202–3.
60. See, for example, H. Harvey, 'Defence Without Aggression', *Bulletin of the Atomic Scientists*, vol. 44, no. 7 (September 1988) pp. 12–13.
61. See, for instance, US Presidential Commission on Integrated Long-Term Strategy, *Discriminate Deterrence* (Washington: USGPO, 1988).

2 Supporters and Models of 'Non-Offensive Defence'

1. See, for example, D. Gates, 'Non-Offensive Defence: A Strategic Contradiction?', *Occasional Paper*, no. 29 (London: Institute for European Defence and Strategic Studies, 1987) pp. 20–8 re Denmark; The Alternative Defence Commission, *Defence Without The Bomb* (New York: Taylor and Francis, 1983); F. Barnaby and S. Windass, *What Is Just Defence?* (Oxford: Just Defence, 1983); A. Karkoszka, 'Merits of the Jaruzelski Plan', *Bulletin of the Atomic Scientists*, vol. 44, no. 7 (September 1988) pp. 32–4; A Kokoshin, 'Restructure Forces and Enhance Security', ibid., pp. 35–8; and S. Shenfield, *Minimum Nuclear Deterrence: The Debate Among Soviet Civilian Analysts* (Center for Foreign Policy Development, Brown University, Providence, 1989).
2. See Von Bonin's essay in *Opposition gegen Adenauers Sicherheitspolitik: Eine Dokumentation*, H. Brill (ed.) (Hamburg: Verlag Neue Politik, 1976).

3. See, for instance, H. Afheldt, *Defensive Verteidigung* (Reinbeck: Rowohlt, 1983); E. Afheldt, *Verteidigung ohne Selbstmord: Vorschlag für den Einsatz einer leichten Infanterie*; A. von Bülow, 'Strategie vertrauensschaffender Sicherheitsstrukturen in Europa: Wege zur Sicherheitspartnerschaft', *Blätter für deutsche und internationale Politik*, no. 10 (1985); SAS, 'Landstreitkräfte zur Verteidigung der Bundesrepublik Deutschland', *Strukturwandel der Verteidigung* (Cologne-Opladen: Westdeutscher Verlag, 1984), and *Vertrauensbildende Verteidigung* (Gerlingen: Bleicher, 1989); A. von Müller, *The Integrated Forward Defence* (Starnberg: Manus, 1985); N. Hannig, *Abschreckung durch konventionelle Waffen: Das David-Goliath-Prinzip* (Berlin: Arno Spitz, 1984); J. Löser, *Weder rot noch tot: Überleben ohne Atomkrieg: Eine sicherheitspolitische Alternative* (Munich: Olzog, 1981); and A. von Bülow, A. von Müller and H. Funk, *Sicherheit für Europa* (Koblenz: Bernard and Graefe Verlag, 1988).
4. *Germany Debates Defence*, p. 152.
5. Ibid., p. 143.
6. See, for instance, J. Dean, 'Alternative Defense: Answer To NATO's Central Front Problems?', *International Affairs* (Winter 1987–8) pp. 61–82; and S. Flanagan, 'Nonprovocative and Civilian-based Defenses', in *Fateful Visions: Avoiding Nuclear Catastrophe*, J.S. Nye et al. (ed.) (Cambridge: Ballinger Mass., 1988).
7. G. Brossolet, *Essai sur la Non Bataille* (Paris: Belin, 1975); 'Das Ende der Schlacht: Versuch über die Nicht-Schlacht', in *Verteidigung ohne Schlacht* (Munich: Carl Hanser, 1979).
8. See Chapter 4, Part 1.
9. See, for example, H.W. Hoffman, R.K. Hüber and K. Steiger, *On Reactive Defence Options* (Munich: Bericht No. S–8403, Institut für angewandte Systemforschung und Operations Research, Hochschule der Bundeswehr, 1984).
10. General H. von Sandrart, 'Forward Defence: Mobility And The Use Of Barriers', *NATO's Sixteen Nations, Special*, vol. 30 (January 1985) pp. 37–43.
11. See, for example, Gates, 'Non-Offensive Defence', pp. 20–8; and *The Guardian*, 12 May 1988.
12. Quoted in J. Steele, 'The New Weapon in the Soviet Defence Vocabulary', *The Guardian*, 5 August 1987.
13. *Pravda*, 17 February 1987.
14. See, for instance, S. Shenfield, *The Nuclear Predicament: Explorations in Soviet Ideology* (London: Routledge/RIIA, 1987).
15. See, for example, R. Forsberg, 'Toward A Nonaggressive World', *Bulletin of the Atomic Scientists*, vol. 44, no. 7 (September 1988) pp. 49–54.

3 War, Peace and Collective Security

1. R. Forsberg, 'The Case for a Nonintervention Regime', *Defense and Disarmament News*, vol. 3, no. 1 (1987) pp. 1, 4.

2. Ibid., pp. 4–5.
3. Ibid.
4. See, for instance, M. Howard, *War and the Liberal Conscience* (OUP paperback edition, 1981) pp. 13–18.
5. I. Kant, *Zum ewigen Frieden* (Stuttgart: Reclam, 1984 edition) pp. 10–15.
6. Howard, *War and the Liberal Conscience*, p. 30.
7. See T.C.W. Blanning, *The Origins of the French Revolutionary Wars* (London: Longman, 1986) p. 113.
8. See P. Brock, *Pacifism In Europe* (Princeton UP, 1972) p. 339; and A.C.F. Beales, *The History Of Peace* (London, 1931) pp. 46–53.
9. See J. Dymond, 'War: Its Causes, Consequences, etc.', in *Essays on the Principles of Morality, and on the Private and Political Rights and Obligations of Mankind* (London, 1829).
10. See Howard, *War and the Liberal Conscience*, pp. 45–6.
11. G. Ritter, *Staatskunst und Kriegshandwerk: Das Problem des Militärismus in Deutschland* (Munich, 1954) vol. I, p. 329.
12. Howard, *War and the Liberal Conscience*, p. 53.
13. See R. Stadelmann, *Moltke und der Staat* (Krefeld, 1950) p. 206; and J. Colin, *The Transformation of War* (London, 1912) p. 343.
14. See Bartlett, *Global Conflict*, pp. 7–8.
15. See, for example, G. Mann, *The History of Germany Since 1789* (London: Pelican, 1974) p. 434.
16. Quoted in Mann, ibid.
17. Quoted in Bartlett, *Global Conflict*, p. 9.
18. See also R. von Caemmerer, *The Development of Strategical Sciences During The Nineteenth Century* (London, 1905) p. 95.
19. See A. Horne, *To Lose A Battle*, pp. 77, 217–221.
20. Quoted in E. Friedrich, *War Against War* (London: Journeyman, 1987 edition) p. 13.
21. Ibid., pp. 21–8.
22. See Howard, *War and the Liberal Conscience*, pp. 70–1, 79 and 95.
23. *War and the Human Race*, M.N. Walsh (ed.) (London and New York: Elsevier 1971), especially pp. 6, 9 and 77.
24. Important psychological studies include: E.F.M. Durbin and J. Bowlby, *Personal Aggressiveness and War* (London, 1939); W. Brown, *War and the Psychological Condition of Peace* (London, 1942); and J.D. Frank, *Sanity and Survival: Psychological Aspects of War and Peace* (London, 1968).
25. Blanning, *The Origins of the French Revolutionary Wars*, p. 4.
26. R. Dawkins, *The Selfish Gene* (OUP, 1976). Other important ethological works include: R. Ardrey, *The Territorial Imperative* (London, 1967); D. Morris, *The Naked Ape* (London, 1967); and K. Lorenz, *On Aggression* (London, 1966).
27. See, for example, B. Malinowski, 'An Anthropological Analysis of War', *American Journal of Sociology*, vol. 46 (1941); K.F. Otterbein, 'The Anthropology of War', *Handbook of Social and Cultural Anthropology*, J.J. Honigmann (ed.) (Chicago, 1973); and A. Montagu, *The*

Nature of Human Aggression (New York, 1976).
28. See, for example, Blanning, *The Origins of the French Revolutionary Wars*, p. 14.
29. G. Blayney, *The Causes of War* (Melbourne, 1977) p. 150.
30. Clausewitz, *On War*, pp. 75–7.
31. Ibid., p. 87.
32. See, for instance, L. Morton, 'Japan's Decision for War', in *Command Decisions*, K.R. Greenfield (ed.) (Washington: USGPO, 1960) p. 124.
33. M. Howard, *The Causes of Wars* (London, 1983) p. 22.
34. Clausewitz, *On War*, pp. 89, 606.
35. R. Forsberg, 'The Case for a Nonintervention Regime', p. 1.
36. H. Afheldt, 'A Comment on General Rogers' Paper', presented to the conference of the International Institute for Strategic Studies, Berlin, 1985.
37. P.A.G. Sabin, 'Shadow or Substance?' *Adelphi Paper*, no. 22 (London: IISS, 1987) p. 59.
38. See, for example, W. Millis, *Arms and the State* (New York, 1958), p. 325.
39. See, for instance, Bartlett, *Global Conflict*, pp. 172–3, 199–200.
40. See Horne, *To Lose a Battle*, pp. 176–89.
41. Ibid., p. 177.
42. See Bartlett, *Global Conflict*, pp. 182–3, 196–202.
43. For a Norwegian perspective, for example, see *Soviet 'Reasonable Sufficiency' And Norwegian Security*, R. Tamnes (ed.) (Oslo: Institut for Forsvarsstudier, 1990).
44. *London Declaration On A Transformed North Atlantic Alliance* (NATO Press Service Communique S-1 (90) 36, 6 July 1990).
45. Quoted in A. Horne, *To Lose a Battle*, p. 103.
46. I. Kant, *Zum ewigen Frieden*, pp. 10, 56.
47. R. Forsberg, 'The Case for a Nonintervention Regime', p. 5.
48. M. Howard, *Liberal Conscience*, p. 135.

4 Dimensions of 'Defensive Defence'

1. Clausewitz, *On War*, p. 84.
2. Ibid.
3. Ibid., p. 357.
4. Ibid., pp. 379–80.
5. Ibid., pp. 390–2.
6. Ibid., pp. 357–70.
7. Napoleon I of France, *The Military Maxims of Napoleon* (London: Greenhill, 1987 edition) p. 62.
8. Clausewitz, *On War*, p. 380.
9. Ibid., p. 173.
10. Y. Molostov and A. Novikov, 'High-Precision Weapons Against Tanks', *Soviet Military Review*, no. 1 (1988) p. 13.
11. See, for example, P. Bracken, 'Urban Sprawl and NATO Defence', *Survival* (November–December 1976) pp. 254–60; *FM 90–10: Military Operations in Urbanised Terrain* (Washington: Army Department,

1979) pp. 1–3; D. Gates, 'Area Defence Concepts: The West German Debate', *Survival* (July–August 1987) pp. 302–3.

12. See D. Gates, *The British Light Infantry Arm* (London: Batsford, 1987) passim.

13. See J. Erickson, L. Hensen and W. Schneider, *Soviet Ground Forces: An Operational Assessment* (London: Croom Helm, 1986) p. 43.

14. See, for examples, *Voyenno-istoricheskiy zhurnal*: no. 9 (September 1980) pp. 12–21; no. 1 (January 1987) pp. 30–6; no. 2 (February 1982) pp. 33–40; no. 11 (November 1984) pp. 59–67; and no. 4 (April 1986) pp. 52–7. Also see *Soviet Military Power* (Washington DC: USGPO, 1988) pp. 74–5.

15. See G. Sharp, *The Politics of Nonviolent Action* (Boston: Porter Sargent, 1973); and A. Roberts, *Nations in Arms*, pp. 261–7.

16. R. Aron, *Paix et Guerre entre les Nations* (Paris: Calmann-Lévy, 1966) p. 617.

17. See V. Mastny, *The Czechs Under Nazi Rule: The Failure of National Resistance, 1939–42* (Columbia UP, 1971).

18. See B. Tuchman, *August 1914* (London: Macmillan, 1987 edition) pp. 247–9, 307–14.

19. See Roberts, *Nations in Arms*, pp. 78–9.

20. Ibid., p. 235. Also see D. Gates, *'The Spanish Ulcer': A History of the Peninsular War* (London and New York, 1986); and D.W. Alexander, *Rod Of Iron: French Counterinsurgency Policy in Aragon During the Peninsular War* (Delaware: Scholarly Resources, 1985).

21. See, for example, H. Afheldt, *Verteidigung und Frieden: Politik mit militärischen Mitteln* (Vienna and Munich: 1976) p. 287 et seq..

22. Clausewitz, *On War*, p. 480.

23. See Roberts, *Nations in Arms*, p. 287.

24. A. Boserup, 'Two Papers On Maritime Defence', *Working Paper*, no. 1 (Centre of Peace and Conflict Research, Copenhagen University, 1987).

25. The Allied conventional bombing attacks on German cities in the Second World War, for example, led to the destruction of twenty per cent of the housing stock, 300 000 civilians killed, 780 000 wounded and 7 500 000 homeless. See *US Strategic Bombing Survey* (New York: Garland, 1976). Modern munitions would prove even more devastating.

26. J. Grin and L. Unterseher, 'The Spiderweb Defence', *Bulletin of the Atomic Scientists*, vol. 44, no. 7 (September 1988) p. 30.

27. H.A. Kissinger, *The Troubled Partnership* (New York: McGraw Hill, 1965) p. 162.

28. Afheldt, 'Friedenspolitik mit militärischen Mitteln in den neunzigern Jahren', in *Sicherheitspolitik*, K.D. Schwarz (ed.) (Bad Honner-Erpel, 1978) p. 647.

29. Afheldt, 'New Policies', p. 27.

30. Afheldt, 'Friedenspolitik mit militärischen Mitteln', p. 265 et seq..

31. See also H. Afheldt, 'Kriegsverhütung setzt voraus, dass man in einer Krise warten kann: die Optionen einer defensiven Verteidigung', in *Krieg oder was sonst? NATO: Strategie der Unsicherheit*, D. Schröder (ed.) (Manburg, 1984).

32. See Afheldt, 'New Policies', pp. 26–7; and *Defensive Verteidigung* (Reinbek: Rowohlt Verlag, 1983) p. 107.
33. See, for instance, J. de Ruiter, *Reinforcement of the Conventional Defence and 'Emerging Technologies'* (Government of the Netherlands Memorandum, June 1985) paragraph 26.
34. G. Bernhardt, 'The Military Helicopter', *RUSI Journal Special Supplement* (Winter 1989) p. 15.
35. J. Galvin, 'A Strategy For The Future', *RUSI Journal*, vol. 134, no. 3 (Autumn 1989) p. 18.
36. See D. Gates, *British Light Infantry*, p. 140.
37. W.W. Kaufmann, 'Nonnuclear Deterrence' in *Alliance Security and the No-First-Use Question*, J.D. Steinbruner and L.V. Sigal (eds) (Washington: Brookings, 1983) p. 73.
38. 'Ogarkov Interview With Krasnaya Zvezda', 9 May 1984, reproduced in *Survival*, vol. 26, no. 4 (July–August 1984) p. 186.
39. Also see Clausewitz, *On War*, pp. 184–6.
40. E.A. Shils and M. Janowitz, 'Cohesion and Disintegration in the Wehrmacht in World War II', *Public Opinion Quarterly* (Summer 1948) pp. 280–315.
41. See D. Irvine, 'The French Discovery of Clausewitz and Napoleon', *Journal of the American Military Institute*, no. 4 (1940) p. 143; and R.H. Sinnreich, 'Strategic Implications of Doctrinal Change: A Case Analysis', in *Military Strategy in Transition*, pp. 42–57.
42. Shils and Janowitz, 'Cohesion and Disintegration', p. 284.
43. Ibid., pp. 280–4.
44. Ibid., pp. 288–92, 305.
45. Horne, *To Lose a Battle*, pp. 63–4.
46. Shils and Janowitz, 'Cohesion and Disintegration', p. 289.
47. See Gates, *British Light Infantry*, p. 91.
48. Shils and Janowitz, 'Cohesion and Disintegration', p. 290.
49. Ibid., p. 289.
50. Ibid.
51. See D. Gates, 'Area Defence Concepts', *Survival*, vol. 29, no. 4 (July–August 1987) pp. 312–13.
52. C. Conetta and C. Knight, 'How Low Can NATO Go?', *Defense and Disarmament Alternatives*, vol. 3, no. 2 (February 1990) p. 3.
53. See Roberts, *Nations in Arms*, p. 237.
54. Ibid., p. 279.
55. See, for example, The British Maritime League, *World Trade, Military Logistics and Merchant Shipping Demand and Supply* (London, June 1989); and The General Council of British Shipping, *Supply and Demand For Merchant Shipping in Crisis and War* (London, 1989).
56. Conetta and Knight, 'How Low Can NATO Go?', p. 3.
57. Quoted in J. Mendelsohn, 'Gorbachev's Preemptive Concession', *Arms Control Today*, vol. 19, no. 2 (March 1989) p. 12. Also see A. Akhromeyev, 'Doktrina predotvrashcheniya voyny zashchity mira i sotsializma', *Problemy mira i sotsializma*, no. 12 (1987).
58. See Footnote 14 above and *Evolyutsiya voennogo iskusstva: etaphy, tendentsii, prinstipy*, F. Gayvoronskogo (ed.) (Moscow: Voenizdat,

1987); S. Covington, *The Role of the Defence in Soviet Military Thinking* (Soviet Studies Research Centre, RMA Sandhurst, 1987); E. Warner, 'New Thinking and Old Realities in Soviet Defence Policy', *Survival*, vol. 31, no. 1 (1989); P. Kunitskiy, 'Esli oborona prorvana', *Voenno-istoricheskiy zhurnal*, no. 12 (1988); A. Maryshev, 'Nekotorye voprosy strategicheskoy oborony v Velikoy Otechestvennoy voyne', *Voenno-istorichekoy zhurnal*, no. 6 (1986).

59. Akhromeyev, 'Doktrina predotvrashcheniya . . .', pp. 26–7. Also see G. Ionin, 'Osnovy sovremennogo oboronitel'nogo boya', *Voenny Vestnik*, no. 3 (1988) pp. 19–20; and V. Kulikov, *Doktrina zashchity mira i sotsializma* (Moscow: Voenizdat, 1988) pp. 77–9.

60. A. Kokoshin and V. Larionov, 'Kurskaya bitva v svete sovremennoy oboronitel'noy doktriny', *MEMO*, no. 8 (1987); Protivostoyanie sil obshchego naznacheniya v kontekste obespecheniya strategicheskoy stabil'nosti', *MEMO*, no. 6 (1988).

61. See, for instance, Akhromeyev, 'Doktrina predotvrashcheniya . . .'; M. Gareev, 'Soviet Military Doctrine: Current and Future Developments', *RUSI Journal*, vol. 133, no. 4 (1988).

62. Napoleon, *Maxims*, p. 64.

63. H. Afheldt, *Verteidigung und Frieden: Politik mit militärischen Mitteln* (Munich: DTV, 1976) p. 238.

64. First Duke of Wellington, *Dispatches of Field Marshall The Duke of Wellington*, Col. Gurwood (ed.) (London, 1834–9) vol. VI, pp. 493–4.

65. See Horne, *To Lose a Battle*, pp. 622–7.

66. See, for example, G. Herolf, 'New Technology Favours Defense', *Bulletin of the Atomic Scientists*, vol. 44, no. 7 (September 1988) pp. 42–4.

67. See, for instance, Gates, *British Light Infantry*.

68. See, for example I. Vorobyev, 'Novoye oruzhiye i printsipy taktiki', *Sovetskoy Voennoye obozreniye*, no. 2 (February 1987), 18.

69. *The Guardian*, 16 February 1990.

70. *The Croker Papers*, L.J. Jennings (ed.) (London, 1884) vol. III, p. 276.

71. See, for instance, Vorobyev, 'Novoye oruzhiye i printsipy taktiki', p. 18.

72. See F. Barnaby, *The Automated Battlefield* (London: Sidgwick and Jackson, 1986) especially pp. 41–4, 155, 163.

73. See S.J. Flanagan, *NATO's Conventional Defences* (London: Macmillan/IISS, 1988) pp. 72–3.

74. See ibid., pp. 71–2; ESECS, *Strengthening Conventional Deterrence*, pp. 230–3.

75. Y. Kardashevskiy, *Voyenniy Vestnik*, no. 7 (July 1988) p. 64.

76. A. Cockburn, *The Threat: Inside The Soviet Military Machine* (New York: Random House, 1983) p. 109.

77. L. Martin, 'Theatre Nuclear Weapons and Europe', *Survival*, vol. 14, no. 4 (November–December 1974) p. 272.

78. See Barnaby, *The Automated Battlefield*, pp. 7, 41.

79. See, for example, L. Spector, *The Undeclared Bomb* (London: Ballinger/Carnegie Endowment For International Peace, 1988); and F. Barnaby, *The Nuclear Arms Race In The Middle East* (London: Tauris, 1989).

80. See, for example, Horne, *To Lose a Battle*, pp. 113–16.
81. See J. Connell, *The New Maginot Line* (London: Secker and Warburg, 1986).
82. Barnaby, *Automated Battlefield*, p. 166.
83. Ibid., pp. 162–9.
84. See *The Conventional Defense Of Europe: New Technologies and New Strategies*, A.J. Pierre (ed.) (New York: Council On Foreign Relations, 1986) p. 162.
85. See Horne, *To Lose a Battle*, pp. 60–2.
86. See B. Tuchman, *August 1914*, pp. 163–7, 189–91; Horne, *To Lose a Battle*, pp. 255–9.
87. Clausewitz, *On War*, pp. 119–21.
88. See, for instance, T. Nash, 'Guns And Missiles For Air Defence', *Armed Forces*, vol. 6, no. 12 (1987) p. 556.
89. See G.W. Goodman, 'New Army IR-Guided Missile', *Armed Forces Journal International* (May 1989) p. 74.
90. For constrasting opinions on the usefulness of high-technology see: British Atlantic Committee, *Diminishing The Nuclear Threat: NATO's Defence And New Technology* (London, 1984); J.A. Burgess, 'Emerging Technologies And The Security Of Western Europe', in *Securing Europe's Future: Changing Elements Of European Security*, S.J. Flanagan and F.O. Hampson (eds) (London: Croom Helm, 1986); S.L. Canby, 'The Operational Limits Of Emerging Technology', *International Defense Review*, vol. 8, no. 6 (1985) pp. 875–80; C.J. Dick, 'Soviet Responses To Emerging Technology Weapons And New Defensive Concepts', in *Emerging Technologies And Military Doctrine*, F. Barnaby and M. ter Borg (eds) (London: Macmillan, 1986); and J. Connell, *The New Maginot Line*.
91. F. Barnaby, *Automated Battlefield*, p. 74.
92. V.G. Reznichenko, *Taktika* (Moscow: Voyenizdat, 1987) p. 206.
93. D.T. Yazov, 'Soviet Military Doctrine', in *RUSI And Brassey's Defence Yearbook* (London: Brassey's, 1990) pp. 28–32.
94. Ibid.
95. P.G. Lushev, 'Soviet And Warsaw Pact Goals And Developments', *RUSI Journal*, vol. 134, no. 3 (Autumn 1989) p. 5.
96. See D. Gates, 'Non-Offensive Defence: A Strategic Contradiction?', *Occasional Paper* No 29 (London: Institute for European Defence and Strategic Studies, 1987) pp. 46–7.
97. See D. Gates, 'The US Army's Light Divisions: Power Projection and Strategic Mobility', *Occasional Paper*, vol. 3, no. 1 (Georgia: Institute for the Study of Geopolitics, Valdosta State University, 1990).
98. See K. Hunt, 'The Alliance And Europe: Part II: Defence With Fewer Men', *Adelphi Paper* No. 98 (London: IISS, 1973) p. 37.
99. See, for example, *The Guardian*, 1 August 1989, p. 32.
100. See, for instance, C. Chapman and J. Speight, 'Problems Of Monitored Storage', *Bulletin Of The Council For Arms Control*, no. 47 (December 1989) pp. 5–6.
101. For a range of views see: W. Sombart, *Krieg und Kapitalismus* (Munich, 1913); J. Nef, *War And Human Progress* (London, 1950); H. de

Haan, 'Military Expenditure And Economic Growth', in *The Economics Of Military Expenditure: Military Expenditures, Economic Growth And Fluctuations*, C. Schmidt (ed.) (London: Macmillan, 1987); G. Adams and D.A. Gold, 'The Economics Of Military Spending: Is The Military Dollar Really Different?', in *Peace, Defense and Economic Analysis*, . Schmidt and F. Blackaby (eds) (London: Macmillan, 1987); C. Trebilcock, 'British Armaments And European Industrialisation, 1890–1914', *Economic History Review*, vol. 26 (1973); K. Hartley et al., 'The Economics Of UK Defence Policy In The 1990s', *RUSI Journal*, vol. 135, no. 2 (Summer 1990) pp. 49–54; and M. Chalmers, *Paying For Defence: Military Spending And British Decline* (London: Pluto, 1985).

102. See, for example, A. Aganbegyan, 'The Economics Of Perestroika', *International Affairs*, vol. 64, no. 2 (Spring 1988) p. 117.
103. See Ibid., p. 178; and R. Bova, 'The Soviet Military And Economic Reform', *Journal Of Soviet Studies*, vol. 40, no. 3 (July 1988) pp. 388–9.
104. Tass Press Release, New York, 15 January 1986.
105. See D. Herspring, 'On Perestroika: Gorbachev, Yazov And The Military', *Problems Of Communism* (July–August 1987).
106. Also see J. Eyal and I. Anthony, *Warsaw Pact Military Expenditure* (London: RUSI/Jane's, 1988).
107. See 'The Soviet Economy', *The Economist*, 9 April 1988, p. 13.
108. See 'Delikate Fragen', *Der Spiegel*, vol. 32 (1990) pp. 34–6.
109. See, for example, A. Roberts, *Nation In Arms*, p. 109; and J. Bjorklund, 'The JAS 39 Project And Swedish Defence', in *RUSI And Brassey's Defence Yearbook 1990*, pp. 199–216.
110. See, for example, ACOST, *Defence R & D: A National Resource* (London: Cabinet Office, 1989), which highlights the British experience in this regard.
111. See J. Fagerberg, 'International Competitiveness', *Economic Journal*, vol. 98 (June 1988) pp. 355–74.

Index